Shree Vakratunda Mahakaya Suryakoti Samaprabha|
Nirvighnam Kuru Me Deva Sarva-Kaaryeshu Sarvada||

Salutations to Ganesha, the Lord with a majestic body and a curved trunk, whose splendour is of a million suns. Please bless all my endeavours, so that they can always be accomplished without any obstacles.

NEVER OUT *of* PRINT

NEVER OUT *of* PRINT

The Rupa Story

The Journey of an Independent Indian Publisher

RAJEN MEHRA

Published by
Rupa Publications India Pvt. Ltd 2024
7/16, Ansari Road, Daryaganj
New Delhi 110 002

Sales centres
Bengaluru Chennai
Hyderabad Jaipur Kathmandu
Kolkata Mumbai Prayagraj

Endpaper image courtesy 123rf
Front cover image iStock

Design by PealiDezine

Illustrations by Mohit Suneja
Photographs: Author's archive

P-ISBN: 978-93-5520-419-6
E-ISBN: 978-93-5520-424-0

First impression 2024

10 9 8 7 6 5 4 3 2 1

Printed in India

To my parents, my family and my colleagues
who have been part of this journey

What matters in life is not what happens to you
but what you remember and how you remember it.

—Gabriel García Márquez

∽

CONTENTS

THE MEHRA FAMILY

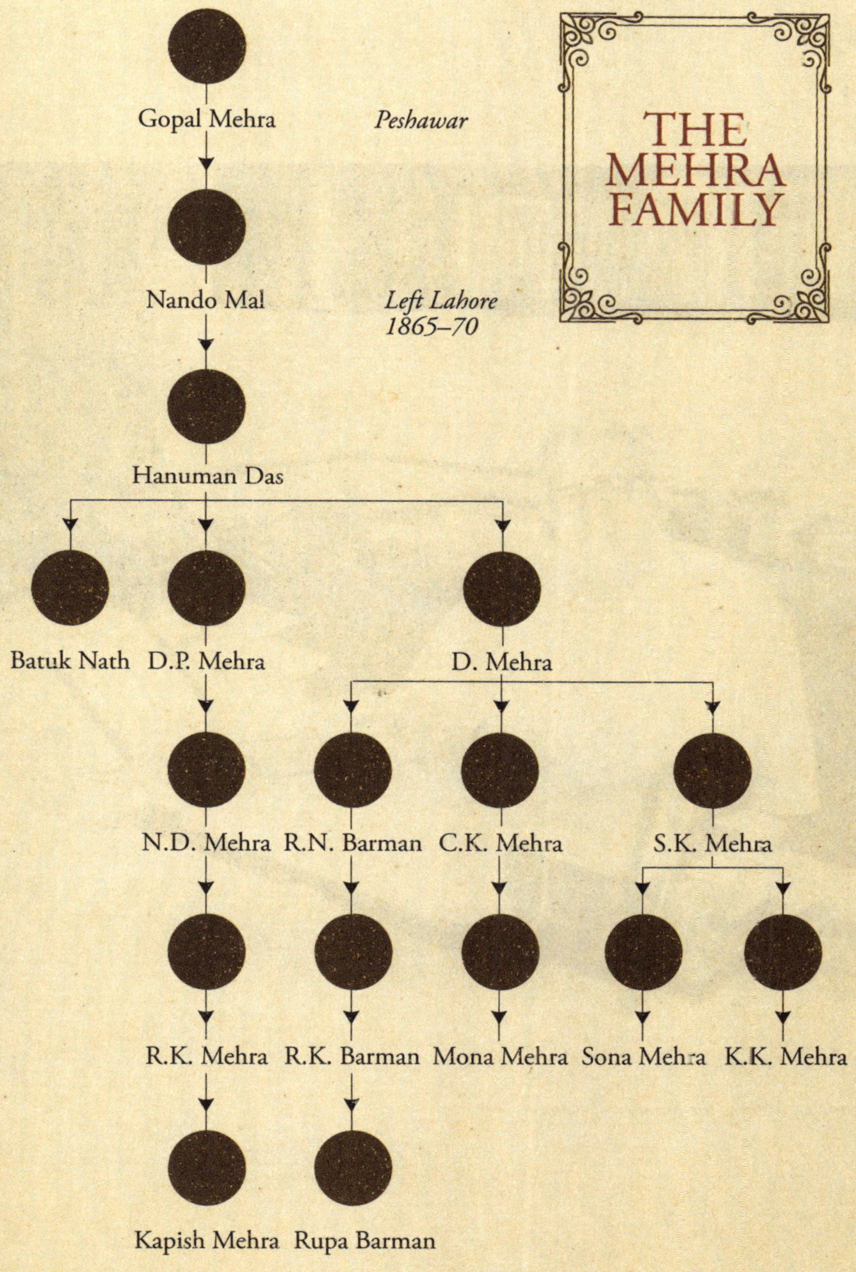

Gopal Mehra — *Peshawar*

Nando Mal — *Left Lahore 1865–70*

Hanuman Das

Batuk Nath

D.P. Mehra

D. Mehra

N.D. Mehra

R.N. Barman

C.K. Mehra

S.K. Mehra

R.K. Mehra

R.K. Barman

Mona Mehra

Sona Mehra

K.K. Mehra

Kapish Mehra

Rupa Barman

Daudayal Mehra, the founder of Rupa

PROLOGUE

Summer of 1936: a young man dressed in a dhoti and kurta stood on the banks of the Hooghly watching the river swirl below his feet. If he had read Shakespeare's *Henry IV,* he would've known the idiom 'sink or swim', because that was precisely what he was intending to do. Undressing himself, the man jumped into the water. The waters of the great river closed over him, as he didn't know how to swim. Rising to the surface, he desperately began to flail his arms about and clumsily made his way to the shore, half-drowned but triumphant. The young man had come to the river to test his survival instinct. He would either survive the experience or drown. He survived and it was that same spirit of daring, confidence and talent for survival that would lead the youth, whose name was Daudayal Mehra, to leave the family hosiery business and strike out on his own into a profession he knew nothing about—publishing. Today, 87 years later, Rupa, the company he founded, is still going strong.

It is my greatest regret that I could never persuade my granduncle to write a memoir that would tell the story of the founding of Rupa. In *Never Out of Print,* I have tried to chronicle the journey of the publishing house that he set up, in addition to the larger story of being a publisher in India.

I am not a writer but D. Mehra was not a swimmer either, before he plunged into the Hooghly!

In many ways,
this book is an homage
to D. Mehra, a great
visionary and publisher,
and a man who still
inspires me as a custodian
of the Rupa legacy.

·PART ONE·

THE RUPA JOURNEY

This is the place where D. Mehra started selling books. Though the contours have changed, the feel of the place remains the same because, even now, hawkers sell their wares here in full swing. At the corner of the lane lies 18-B Shyama Charan De Street, where Rupa's office was once located. It now houses Sarat Book House.

• Chapter 1 •

THE ORIGINS OF RUPA

Daudayal Mehra, my granduncle, belonged to a Punjabi Khatri* business family, which migrated in the nineteenth century from Peshawar to Amritsar via Lahore and then moved to Banaras (now Varanasi). From Banaras, the patriarch of the family, Gorakhnath Khatri, respectfully called 'Baba', moved to Calcutta (now Kolkata) along with his two brothers, Durga Prasad Khatri (my grandfather) and Daudayal Mehra†. Gorakhnath Khatri worked hard to establish the family hosiery business (as representatives of Anderson Wright & Co.). While Gorakhnath Khatri's voice boomed inside our household and he decided the affairs of the family, the middle brother, Durga Prasad, was a mild-mannered individual with few ambitions of his own. He retired early from the family business and lived a content life, detached from the daily cares of the family business. Soaking in the sun, yoga and a massage every day would bring him great satisfaction. He ate one meal a day, gorged on all things sweet and loved his 555 cigarettes‡—a simple life, albeit lived regally. The youngest of the three brothers was D. Mehra, who was fond of my father, N.D. Mehra. My father had just passed his matriculation exam and the lack of zeal that he saw in his own father made him gravitate towards his more enterprising uncle, D. Mehra. He aimed to make a mark in life.

The New Market area in Calcutta is a municipal market that defies Rudyard Kipling's 'East is East and West is West, and never the twain shall meet', for here European architecture fuses effortlessly with the desi landscape.

*The Khatris or Kshatriyas are a North Indian community, originating in Punjab.

†He first used the surname 'Mehra' in the family.

‡State Express 555, popularly known as 555, was a common brand of cigarettes back then.

*Anderson Wright & Co. printed these logos depicting Lord Rama's durbar to boost their sales since 1936**

Inaugurated on New Year's Day in 1874, the Gothic building was designed by Roskell Bayne, an architect who worked for the East India Railway Company. Dotted with hundreds of shops and kiosks of various sizes and styles, the market initially catered to the sahibs, alienating the local Bengali and making it an elitist space. When the Union Jack came down from state buildings on 15 August 1947, New Market, owing to its association with the rulers, suffered a nationalist backlash even though the traders were all Indians! Gradually, these lines blurred and the locals made New Market their own. Boasting of selling everything and anything under the sun, this maze of bustling commercial activity was one of D. Mehra's beats. One rain-soaked day, when he was selling hosiery, he attracted the attention of a Scottish book sales representative, K. Jackson Marshall, who was in New

*From the family archives

Market selling books. Marshall watched D. Mehra at work and was impressed by this young lad's sales technique—how he was able to sell hosiery in an aggressive yet persuasive and courteous way. Marshall walked up to him and posed a question that would change the fortunes of the Mehra clan forever.

'Would you be interested in selling English books?' Marshall asked, getting straight to the point. But D. Mehra knew his limitations. He had dropped out of school because the family had been unable to pay for his education. He was a dhoti-kurta-clad hosiery seller who didn't speak English. Despite his restless energy and determination to experiment, Marshall's offer seemed like something that would be too much for him to pull off. His market—the *bhadralok* (gentlefolk) and babus of Calcutta, newly Westernized and English-speaking—tended to look down on other Indians, especially those who weren't fluent in English. D. Mehra was aware of the challenge of being taken seriously as a seller of English books. But Marshall was a shrewd judge of people and wasn't about to give up so easily. He continued to badger D. Mehra to try his hand at selling books. The latter continued to refuse. After days of persuasion, the young hosiery seller relented. Marshall was overjoyed. 'Come and visit me at the Grand Hotel tomorrow,' Marshall said.

K. Jackson Marshall, the Scottish book sales representative who first spotted D. Mehra's selling talent and asked him if he would sell books. The rest is history.

A decade before Independence, the Grand Hotel was a glittering symbol of colonial supremacy.* D. Mehra knew beforehand that he would be denied entry to the hotel if he turned up dressed in his dhoti. Nevertheless, he showed up for his appointment as scheduled. As he'd expected, at the entrance of the lavish

*Now owned by an Indian family and known as The Oberoi Grand

K. Jackson Marshall handing D. Mehra three books to sell—The Collins English Gem Dictionary, Chambers Dictionary *and* Pears Encyclopedia—*with The Grand Hotel in the background*

hotel, the Indian doorman refused to let this fellow Indian enter. Undeterred, D. Mehra began remonstrating with the man, saying he was expected by one of the guests at the hotel. Hearing the commotion in the hotel lobby and seeing that his potential recruit was at the centre of it, Marshall came hurrying down and apologized to D. Mehra for the hostile reception. They went on to discuss the terms of the business, and the young, would-be entrepreneur agreed to try his hand at selling English books.

To his surprise, D. Mehra found that his family was supportive of his decision to sell books rather than hosiery. His eldest brother gave him the go-ahead and his mother gave him an unorthodox piece of advice to succeed. She told the budding young bookseller that if his first customer was a Muslim, his business was bound to succeed. This could be dismissed as superstition, but, to me, it is representative of a time pre-Partition, when the two communities, Hindus and Muslims, lived in amity and their trade, profits and losses were dependent on each other.

On 17 August 1936, K. Marshall gave D. Mehra three books to sell—*The Collins English Gem Dictionary*, *Chambers Dictionary* and *Pears Encyclopedia*—it was a momentous day. He would need to pay for them the following day. His business turf would now be the bustling book market of College Street where his salesmanship would be tested. Humbly, he placed an old bedsheet on the pavement opposite Presidency College, just under the staircase of 18-B Shyama Charan De Street, and displayed his books. He did not have the money to even pay for a rudimentary stall to stock his books, nothing to protect his wares or himself from inclement weather. The only thing that kept him going was a steely desire to succeed in this venture. Soon enough, a dapper, pipe-smoking gentleman, who was passing by, stopped and picked up *The Collins English Gem Dictionary*. He was not carrying money and offered to pay by cheque. D. Mehra could not trust this monetary instrument called a cheque, which he knew nothing about. So, he asked to be paid in cash, much to the amusement of the pipe-smoking gentleman.

D. Mehra was an avid theatregoer who once watched a play and was mesmerized by its characters, Sona and Rupa. He later named his company Rupa.

'Okay, I will bring you the money and take the book. But don't sell it to anyone until I return,' the man told the young bookseller. Later that afternoon, the customer returned with cash and bought the book. He introduced himself as Professor Humayun Kabir, who went on to become the minister of education in the government of Jawaharlal Nehru and whose nephew, Altamas Kabir, became the Chief Justice of India. D. Mehra's mother's prophecy that he would find success if his first customer was a Muslim came true. Rupa's first customer in 1936 continued his association with the publishing house till his death in

1969. Once the young salesman sold his first book, there was no looking back. He would soon establish and christen his new company Rupa.

D. Mehra was an avid Calcutta theatregoer and a fan of Sisir Kumar Bhaduri, known as the father of modern Bengali theatre. One day, D. Mehra was watching a play in which there were two characters named Sona (which means gold) and Rupa (which means silver). He was so taken with this play that he decided to name his company after one of the characters. He opted for the humble Rupa, over her glittering cousin Sona. This was entirely in keeping with his character. My earliest memory of watching a play is at the Empire Theatre, a relic of the British Raj. As a child, I went to watch the towering Prithviraj Kapoor perform the lead role in play called *Paisa*, which talked about the moral degradation caused by greed for money.

Rupa's first customer, Professor Humayun Kabir (1906–1969)

My granduncle was a man of simple taste who led his life according to Gandhian principles. Yet, he had dreams. Within a year, he rented a single room in the same building outside of which he had started selling books. Rupa now had an address: 18-B Shyama Charan De Street. It started with three employees: D. Mehra, my granduncle and the founder, N.D. Mehra, and Jyoti Sengupta, the manager of the company. No salesperson was hired, and all three of them were selling, billing, keeping a check on inventory and managing accounts. As the cash register kept ringing, the team needed a full-time accountant. In walked Bhagwati Das Khatri, who was called BDK. He worked from two in the afternoon till dusk.

War clouds were hovering over the world once again and by 1939 we were forced to leave Calcutta and open an office in Allahabad (now Prayagraj), another educational and intellectual hub of that time.

A window to the publishing world—Rupa's first office in Calcutta

The freedom movement was at its peak throughout the country and Allahabad was at the centre of the nationalist ferment. It was the city of Motilal and Jawaharlal Nehru, of Purushottam Das Tandon and Madan Mohan Malaviya. The fervour of patriotism permeated the city's ecosystem and it was awash with anti-British sentiment. During this time, D. Mehra offered a service that he was proud of till the very end of his life. He supplied Rupa books to Panditji, as Pandit Nehru was respectfully called, and to other jailed freedom fighters. In one of his letters to his daughter Indira, Nehru wrote, 'A firm of booksellers in Calcutta—Rupa & Co.—with a branch in Allahabad, have sent me books from time to time. They have been good books as a rule and new English publications.'

One day, D. Mehra was caught while bringing books to the jailed freedom fighters. The local daroga, an Indian, came to our house with an arrest warrant for my granduncle. He was accused of supplying reading materials to freedom fighters in jail, which was deemed an anti-national activity. D. Mehra, while being an absolute patriot was also a sharp businessman who knew exactly how to walk out of danger.

Rupa's Allahabad office till 2010 at 135 South Malaka

and round about it for some days. It was not much but it interfered with my sleep and exercises. What annoyed me was that I should have had it at all for any bodily weakness or disability irritates me. I got over it by massage and fomentation and especially sunbaths. I have been completely free from it and have been indulging in my exercises as usual. The plague inoculation came in the way but that too is over with all its after effects.

I have received the books and a pamphlet which Jinarajadasa sent you —They are :

1 Sean O'Faolain : *The Great O'Neill*
2 H. Fortes Anderson : *Borderline Russia*
3 Jinarajadasa : *Economics and Theosophy*

The Human Situation, which you mentioned, was not in this lot.

I might mention that I have also received the two new books from Rupa & Co. who sometimes send me books. These are: Wavell's *Allenby in Egypt* and A. L. Rowse: *The English Spirit.*[614] Wavell's book was in a list of books required that I sent you last year. You can strike it off from it.

I have returned the following books to you:

1 Julian Huxley : *On Living in a Revolution*
2 Shaukat Ansari : *Pakistan*
3 Borodin : *Soviet & Tsarist Siberia*
4 Nym Wales : *New China*
5 Tikhov Semushkin : *Children of the Soviet Arctic*
6 *History of the Communist Party of the Soviet Union*
7 Alexei Tolstoy : *My Country*
8 Dean of Canterbury : *The Socialist Sixth of the World*
9 Do : *Soviet Strength*
10 *Correspondence with Mr. Gandhi* (Government publication)

Semushkin's *Children of the Soviet Arctic* I found rather fascinating reading. It is simply written, but the account of change creeping in, or rather sweeping in, into those remote areas is very interesting. Apart from this, the Arctic and wide stretches of snow and ice have always attracted me.

I have read in the newspapers that Rafi has been transferred to Naini Prison. Why he should have been transferred to a place where special medical attention is not easily available is difficult to understand, more especially at this time of the year with the summer looming ahead. I wonder if you could arrange to send him fresh fruit regularly. What

These two letters are extracts from Selected Works of Jawaharlal Nehru, Volume 13

SELECTED WORKS OF JAWAHARLAL NEHRU

a letter to me and the intricate and difficult question of whether the letter should be delivered to me or not had to be decided by competent authority. Did he come within the prescribed list of near relations who were authorised to write? I do not know and I doubt if anybody else knows exactly. Anyway I have not received the letter and I want you to inform Kishan *chacha* of this. During the past two years two brief letters from Birju *chacha* were delivered to me. He and Kishan *chacha* stand exactly in the same relationship to me—first cousins. And yet it appears that first cousins belong to a doubtful category, though brothers-in-law are allowed to write. It is all very odd and peculiar.

A firm of booksellers in Calcutta—Rupa & Co.—with a branch in Allahabad, have sent me books from time to time. They have been good books as a rule and new English publications. Yesterday I received from them Bernard Shaw's new book—*Everybody's Political What's What.*[386] I mention this so that you might not send this book.

Do not trouble yourself about Tolstoy's *Anna Karenina*—I have plenty of reading material. I have just received two large bundles of foreign periodicals, presumably sent by you.

I have noted what you say about giving the money to Feroze for relief work. He can keep this sum apart for emergencies if he likes.

It is desirable that Feroze should engage himself in some regular work —what this work should be, it is for him to decide. I hope what he has chosen suits him.

I am glad Rajiva is putting on weight and is otherwise well.

Love

Your loving
Papu

This is letter No. 93.

The name Rupa existed much before other similar sounding brand names came into being—a fact validated through Pandit Nehru's letter to his daughter Indira Gandhi in 1944

He told the police inspector that the books he supplied came from England. His arrest would mean that the local police considered material published in Britain as anti-national. He cautioned the inspector that any action taken against him would insult the King's language and the Crown. The hapless daroga now found himself in a quandary; unable to figure out a response that would match the way D. Mehra had turned the tables on him, he had to leave without making an arrest.

Interestingly one of the books, *The Wisdom of China and India,* by a Chinese scholar Lin Yutang was published in 1942 during the Quit India Movement. Pandit Nehru's *Glimpses of World History*, the first non-Eurocentric history of the world was published for the first time in 1934 by an Allahabad-based publisher, Kitabistan. The book, a collection of 196 letters written between 1930 and 1933, during Pandit Nehru's incarceration in various jails, was written in an informal manner and was meant as an introduction to world history for his daughter. It was magisterial in its breadth and approach to world history. *The New York Times* later described it as 'one of the most remarkable books ever written'.* Allen & Unwin, a British publisher, bought the global rights for this book and later approached Rupa to sell it in the Indian market. The book begins with Pandit Nehru's first letter to Indira, in which he wrote, 'On your birthday you have been in the habit of receiving presents and good wishes. Good wishes you will still have in full measure, but what present can I send you from Naini Prison? My presents cannot be very material or solid.'† This lamentation of a father for not being able to send a birthday gift to his daughter was a poignant moment. But Pandit Nehru surely was a gift for us. Rupa sold so many copies of the book that we built our Allahabad house using profits made off it, at a princely sum of a few hundred rupees at that time!

---

*Muller, Herbert J., 'The Pandit and the Past; Nehru on World History. Condensed by Saul K. Padover from "Glimpses of World History." By Jawaharlal Nehru. 304 pp. New York: The John Day Company. $5.', *The New York Times*, 5 June 1960, https://tinyurl.com/3ev9uatz. Accessed on 24 July 2023.
†Nehru, Jawaharlal, *Glimpses of World History*, Asia Publishing House, 1964.

The adda *to end all addas—the Indian Coffee House, a cafe frequented by the city's intellectuals for decades*

After the end of the Second World War, we returned to Calcutta, to pick up where we had left off. The war clouds had disappeared, leaving behind a battered and bruised world. It was time to heal and reset our lives. The silver lining for us though was that Rupa now had an address in Allahabad too.

We had to look for a new, preferably bigger office in Calcutta while retaining our old office at 18-B Shyama Charan De Street (which was used as a warehouse until the 1990s). We finally settled on 15 Bankim Chandra Street, which housed the Indian Coffee House*, easily one of the most bohemian and intellectual addresses of its time. Ideas and ideologies brewed over multiple cups of coffee; poetries and stories were penned here in unmitigated spirits. Two floors above this creative mayhem, the Rupa office was set up, the atmosphere of the place adding to the charm of the books. Business was going steady and soon K. Jackson Marshall came

*Established in 1876 and earlier known as Albert Hall after Queen Victoria's husband, Prince Albert

into the picture again. This time, he had six new paperback titles from Penguin, and he gave their Indian distribution rights to Rupa. Paperbacks were rare those days and all the titles were an instant hit. Our accountant BDK was busier than ever!

After setting up shop in Calcutta in 1936 and in Allahabad in 1939, it was time for us to expand further. In 1954, Rupa's Bombay (now Mumbai) office was inaugurated. Our footprints were now in western India as well. I was six years old then and I remember staying with my parents in a flat in Sion, with one room allotted to us and another to our Bombay manager Mr Bhuvan Bhai Patel, who was also living there with his family. We were there for two months. Since I was not able to attend school, a good Samaritan neighbour, a Gujarati lady and her daughter gave me tuitions during our time there.

By 1960, Rupa became an established name in the game. D. Mehra's philosophy of keeping consumption to a minimum and living a modest lifestyle became the company's guiding light. Stationery was strictly rationed and a pen was only replaced when it was no longer worthy of being called one. All employees had to clean the floors and bookshelves, and everyone was expected to be punctual. D. Mehra was a self-taught man. He was a smart negotiator but knew that an early entry in the business had deprived him of the luxury of immersing himself in books. So, he read and read. He read everything, from all the authors that mattered—like John Updike, Thomas Mann, George Bernard Shaw and George Orwell—to dictionaries and encyclopedias. A team player, he had a group of advisers who would assemble in his office in the evening, where new manuscripts were read out loud and discussed. Debates and dissenting voices were encouraged. He diligently read editorials from *The Statesman, Amrita Bazar Patrika* and *Hindustan Standard,* attended lectures and seminars and numerous reading sessions. He matched his commercial skills with his

The Penguins come to the Indian shore

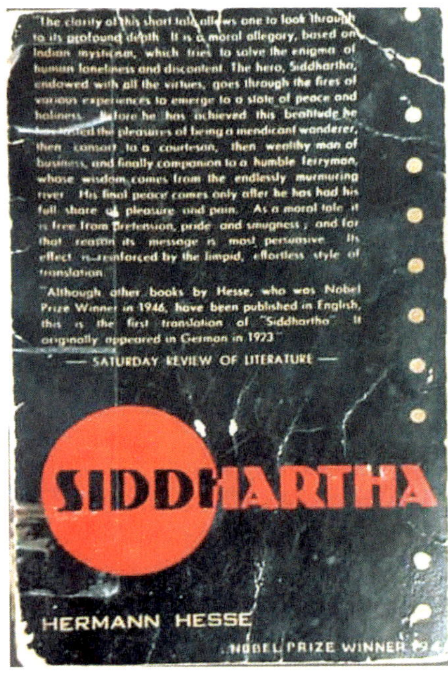

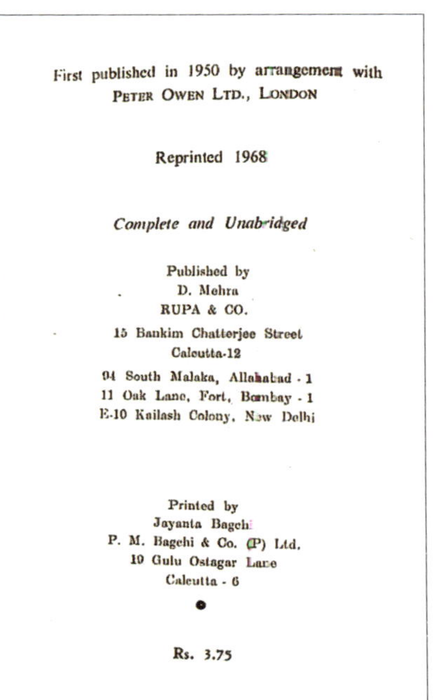

First published in 1950 by arrangement with
PETER OWEN LTD., LONDON

Reprinted 1968

Complete and Unabridged

Published by
D. Mehra
RUPA & CO.
15 Bankim Chatterjee Street
Calcutta-12
94 South Malaka, Allahabad - 1
11 Oak Lane, Fort, Bombay - 1
E-10 Kailash Colony, New Delhi

Printed by
Jayanta Bagchi
P. M. Bagchi & Co. (P) Ltd.
10 Gulu Ostagar Lane
Calcutta - 6

Rs. 3.75

First edition of Hermann Hesse's Siddhartha *published by Rupa & Co. in India*

intellectual curiosity.

In 1960, James Laughlin, the chairman of New Directions Publishing company in New York, visited Calcutta. The scion of American steel giant, Jones & Laughlin Steel Company, Laughlin ventured out of his family steel business and found his calling in poetry, prose and stories. Being a prolific writer and poet, he founded New Directions while he was still an undergraduate at Harvard University. He looked out for new writers and underdogs. He instantly liked D. Mehra when they met, and it was natural that he persuaded the latter. He convinced him to publish Herman Hesse's *Siddhartha*. And with *Siddhartha* began Rupa's journey into publishing.

'Despite the lack of money, I had an enjoyable childhood. Calcutta offered myriad enchantments even to those without the ability to splurge.'

• Chapter 2 •

MY BOYHOOD

मेरा जूता है जापानी
ये पतलून इंगलिस्तानी
सर पे लाल टोपी रूसी
फिर भी दिल है हिन्दुस्तानी

Mera juta hai Japani
Ye patloon Englishtani
Sar pe laal topi Roosi
Phir bhi dil hai Hindustan

My shoes are from Japan
My trousers are from England
The hat I am wearing is Russian
But at heart I am still an Indian

My mother, Sarla Mehra

These words still echo in my ears. My mother used to sing this song while tying my shoelaces and preparing me for school in the mid-1950s. The simplicity of the lyrics ensures that nothing is lost in translation. This song from Raj Kapoor's classic movie *Shree 420* perhaps defined the Nehruvian age of my boyhood and youth in which India had a cosmopolitan exterior but remained Indian at heart. The same sentiment governed our home. Since my birth in 1947, I always saw my family as one of modest means. But as the first child of the new generation of our extended family, it was decided that I should go to the best school in our neighbourhood. Accordingly, in the fourth grade, I was enrolled in the Shri Daulatram Nopany Vidyalaya in Jorasanko, Calcutta—a neighbourhood made famous by Thakurbari, the famed ancestral residence of Rabindranath Tagore. As our family was in the business of selling books, reading everything one could lay one's hands on was encouraged. My granduncle ensured we received a regular supply of Indian magazines—*Kalyan*, *Navneet*, *Chandamama*, *Parag*, *Desh*, *Dharmayug* and *The Illustrated Weekly of India*. In addition, he stipulated that it was essential for me to read an English newspaper every day. He understood the importance of the English language without undermining desi values. The Hindi and Bengali magazines firmly rooted in me Indian cultural values while the English language newspapers offered me a global outlook and cultivated liberal values. Thus, I grew up with a *Hindustani dil* and an *Englishtani patloon* (albeit without deep pockets).

I only owned one school uniform—a set of shirt and pants. Every day, when I returned from school, it was washed and 'ironed' with a heavy metal pot. It was then placed under my mattress to crease the folds. While I slept through the night, it would be pressed under my mattress. The frugal habits inculcated in me during my childhood would stand me in good stead throughout my life. Even after the family business grew in size and profitability, I was never attracted to flashy cars or other expensive material possessions. My upbringing taught me that one's aspirations should be big but not imprudent, especially in financial and material terms.

Despite the lack of money, I had an enjoyable childhood. Calcutta offered myriad enchantments even to those without the ability to splurge. One of them being the Kabuliwallahs immortalized by Rabindranath Tagore in his short story of the same name and later by Balraj Sahni on celluloid. These Afghan traders and moneylenders were star attractions for children in Calcutta back then. They were immensely popular, the large pockets in their Pathan suits full of chocolates and cashews. I remember one of them would come to our neighbourhood early in the morning and stand outside our gate. He knew that I was an early riser, so he would turn up to bribe me with his Morton chocolates and extract information about the whereabouts of our neighbour, who owed him money. I liked the Kabuliwallah a lot. One day, when I got lost around the Esplanade area of Calcutta, he noticed me and brought me back home. Over time, he became like family to us and was always greeted with a warm hug by my grandfather. It is heartbreaking to see the plight of Afghans in their home country today. It reminds me of a book *Thrown to the Wolves* by Pyarelal, published in 1966 by Eastlight Book House. It is a moving biography of Khan Abdul Ghaffar Khan, better known as Badshah Khan or Frontier Gandhi, lamenting the ordeal of Pathans after Partition in 1947. Even today, I remember the Kabuliwallah with great affection and wonder what might have become of his family.

The other migrant community I remember from my Calcutta days is the Chinese community. They had lived in the city for generations and ran all manner of businesses—restaurants, laundries, shoe shops, and the like. They were an integral part of the city and, as a child, I was intrigued by them.

Then, in 1962, the Sino-Indian War broke out. I was in my teens and was deeply disillusioned by our country's leaders at the time, especially Prime Minister (PM) Nehru. I was also saddened by the attacks on the Chinese community in Calcutta. The war took over our lives, and I wanted to do my bit to help during this national crisis. Then, an organization called the

The Chinese were a vibrant migrant community who ran many businesses in China Town

Jan Sangh came to my attention. They ran youth camps and were building a territorial army to help with the defense of the nation should that become necessary. They also helped with the collection of funds and basic necessities contributed by businessmen to help the war effort. I was very interested in their *shakhas*, where they conducted physical drills and exercises. I felt I could do my bit for the nation by attending them. I asked my father to give me 20 paise, which was the one-time fee needed to pay to join the Jan Sangh. It was a small amount and my father didn't ask me what it was for nor did I volunteer the information. I started attending the shakhas and participating in martial activities, exercises and games. One day, I came home in the evening with a little wooden stick from the shakha only to be slapped by my granduncle, D. Mehra. I couldn't understand why I was being treated that way but didn't have the courage to remonstrate with him. It was only later that I discovered that my granduncle, being a staunch Gandhian and admirer of Pandit Nehru, could not abide his grandnephew participating in the activities of a Right-wing organization. In retrospect, though, I believe this phase of my life helped me as a publisher. It taught me to have a balanced approach to the writers and politicians we published from both sides of the aisle.

During my teenage years, I disliked Pandit Nehru for losing the war to the Chinese, but I greatly admired his command over the English language and his ability as a public speaker. Although our family sold English language books, we spoke Hindi at home. So, I was extremely keen to improve my English language skills. I had started reading newspapers, but how was I going to learn to speak the language well? The answer came from my school principal who once told me that if I wanted to improve my English, I needed to listen to people who spoke flawless English. I started listening to the news on All India Radio. At 8.00 p.m., the legendary Devki Nandan Pandey would read the news in Hindi on air; at 9.00 p.m., the immaculate English of Melville de Mellow or Suraji Sen or V.M. Chakrapani would resonate throughout the Mehra household. Their perfect English pronunciation and intonation would make me their Eklavya for the next half an hour. I also learnt of a place in Calcutta University called Burdwan Hall where eminent personalities, such as Dr Sarvepalli Radhakrishnan, Ashok Mehta, Humayun Kabir, Dr Shailesh Bandopadhyay and others, would deliver lectures every week or once in two weeks. I made sure I didn't miss a single one. On the day of the lecture, I would make my way to Burdwan Hall and take a seat in the front row, so I did not miss a word. Often, in the last row of the hall, my granduncle would also be present, listening to the speaker and quietly commending his grandnephew's zeal to learn the ropes of the English language.

Besides my attempts to familiarize myself with the mysteries of the English language, I also prevailed upon my father to use some of our family's meagre resources to pay for a private tutor who would ensure that I did my homework. Although I prevailed upon my father to hire a private tutor for me, which was an exception in those days, today I see that it has become a norm, a practice that disheartens me. If one goes to school or college to receive quality education, why does one need private tutors at all?

I remember with great gratitude some of the outstanding teachers who taught me. Subhas Roy taught mathematics and music—a magical combination to my impressionable young mind. Knowing my modest background, he looked after me like an older brother. Another teacher who had a lasting impact on me was B.S. Zakhmi, a tall, well-built, handsome Sardar—our physical-training teacher. A disciplinarian with a magnetic personality, he was a tough taskmaster and brought out the best in us. He was my hero in school and I fancied becoming a disciplinarian and an administrator like him. However, one day, Zakhmi Sir stopped coming to school. We were told that he had joined the army during the 1962 war. My hero became a legend for me that day. I didn't see him again for the next three decades, until one day in the mid-1990s.

My wife and I were at the Roshanara Club, in New Delhi, for a social event. As we were about to leave, I saw a noticeboard with the words 'Administrative Officer Major B.S. Zakhmi, Retd'. *Could this be him?* I thought. I left my

With then Union Minister of Human Resource Development, Arjun Singh. Major Zakhmi's enthusiasm for matters of education was unmatchable.

visiting card at his office reception with a message, 'Sir, if you are the same Mr Zakhmi, who taught at Shri Daulatram Nopany Vidyalaya in Calcutta, please call me.' Days passed and nothing happened. Then, one day, my receptionist buzzed me and said, 'Sir, a gentleman by the name of Major Zakhmi is on the other line.' We had a very warm and cordial conversation. Major Zakhmi said he remembered me and was immediately able to put a face to the name on the visiting card. He wanted to see his student's workplace and made his way over through the narrow, bustling streets of Daryaganj to the Rupa office in Delhi. When his arrival was announced, I went down to the reception to receive him. To see this legend in the flesh after more than 30 years was overwhelming for me. I bowed down to touch his feet. He embraced me in return. In the course of our meeting, Major Zakhmi said he was tired of the monotony of an administrative officer's job in a club and wanted to do something more meaningful with his life. He shared that he had been asked

Major B.S. Zakhmi with Shakti Sinha who was secretary to then Prime Minister Atal Bihari Vajpayee

to run a gurdwara, which he was considering. As he spoke, an idea formed in my mind. With great trepidation, I broached the topic with him, 'Sir, why don't you join us? I wouldn't presume to pay you a salary but we could give you an honorarium for your services. Be our administrative officer.' He had been my teacher and could never be an employee, but this seemed like an alternative worth proposing. He smiled and the meeting ended a short while later. After I had seen him off, I wondered if I had overstepped any boundaries. But I needn't have worried.

A few days later, Major Zakhmi joined us as Rupa's administrative officer. He brought administrative order to our otherwise chaotic office. He created records of staff members and suppliers, documented bills, made templates for company circulars, and even streamlined the number of people who would sit on each floor and the number of telephone lines required. We follow Zakhmi Sir's systems to this day. A few months later, the publisher in me thought we could use Major Zakhmi's expertise in physical education and training to publish some books on the subject. I talked to him about this and he was keen. In due course, we published a series of books by Major Zakhmi. *First, teacher, then our administrative officer, and now my author,* I would think to myself with a warm glow of satisfaction every time I signed a royalty cheque made out to Major Zakhmi. Last year, on 8 November, which is observed as Guru Purab, my 94-year-old teacher called and blessed me. Major Zakhmi will always be one of the main reasons I continue to cherish my schooldays.

Besides having inspiring teachers like these, a lot of my schoolmates were also extraordinary and went on to become highly successful. I remember one such classmate whose palms would always be sweaty. Little did we know that he would go on to become one of the world's greatest steel magnates, Lakshmi Mittal.

My boyhood was full of so much more than just school. I have vivid and exciting memories of walks along the maidan, visits to the zoo, street theatre, pujas, Baul songs, and more. By 1965, though, my boyhood and schooldays were coming to an end. It was time to start preparing for college and perhaps, most importantly, start learning the family business.

A city within a train—Toofan Mail

• Chapter 3 •

THE UP CONNECTION

'*Garmi ki chhutti*', a common term for summer vacation in northern India, was when the family would make its annual excursion to the plains of Uttar Pradesh (UP). While most of my school friends would share stories of their vacations in Darjeeling, Mount Abu, Shimla, Kullu or Manali, I would narrate tales of Banaras, Allahabad and Kanpur. The family couldn't afford expensive holidays in hotels and resorts. So, we would take a break in the cities of my aunts, uncles, nana and nani. Visits to the Ganga and its ghats, and the taste of kachoris, jalebis and lassi make these glorious places live on in my memory.

Every year, we would spend our summer vacation in these UP towns and cities. And every year, it was the same train, the Toofan Mail, which took us to these destinations. This was a train that defied its name when it came to speed—it did not move at the speed of a storm or cyclone but chugged along at sedate pace. Our modest budget ensured that the family could not take a premium train like the Kalka–Howrah Mail, in which seats had to be reserved in advance. On the Toofan Mail, the reservation of your seat depended on how athletic your coolie was and how fast he could run and throw your luggage onto a seat. The Toofan Mail was a truly socialist, inclusive train. It would not differentiate between a big and a small station when it came to halting; it would stop at every station on the route. It would also stop in between stations because passengers were constantly pulling the emergency chain, so they could get down at their villages or farms; the fact that the emergency chain was meant only for emergencies was cheerfully ignored. This was a train that anyone could enter and sit wherever they wanted to. Someone would get on and ask to be seated alongside you. In a few hours, despite being ticketless, the new passenger would occupy more than half of your seat. If he saw the train ticket examiner (TTE) approaching, he would go to answer nature's call in the free-for-all toilet of the train. If the toilet was already occupied by another ticketless passenger, he would smile innocently at the TTE when asked to show the ticket. Eventually, he would be ordered to get off at the next station only to enter through another door.

The Toofan Mail truly was a big-hearted train, as it did not differentiate between the ticketed and the ticketless travellers. As it entered Bihar, it became even more egalitarian and hospitable. More passengers than the train could comfortably accommodate would clamber aboard and anarchy would follow.

As the train entered Dhanbad (part of Bihar until 2000), the rule of law would deteriorate further. In fact, it would disappear. Back then, the coal mafiosi were active in the region, which was a coal mining hub. In the1960s, coal was in great demand as the country's primary source of energy. As a child, gazing out of the train window, I would often see dacoits stopping trains ferrying coal and emptying a couple of their wagons. It was done with a casual ease and almost unapologetically. On other occasions, the fish plates of railway tracks would be removed, sometimes railway sleepers would be dug out—the outcome was the same, the train transporting the coal would stop, be looted of its cargo, and move on; it was almost like a ritual.

Our first stop in UP would be Banaras where my bua lived. *Kashyam marnam muktih* means one is liberated if one dies in Kashi (another name for Banaras). But for us kids, that concept was too much to understand, and our liberation ended up being jalebi, stuffed kachori, banarasi lassi and tiranga barfi. Ah, the tiranga barfi! If by picking up salt at Dandi, Gandhiji declared open rebellion against the British, the *halwais* of Banaras had crusaded against the goras with sugar.

The British government had been discouraging local manufacturing of jaggery, traditionally used in Indian sweets, to encourage the production of sugar in mills promoted by the British government. When the halwais criticized this decision, the British government banned jaggery in Banaras to ruin the

The iconic tiranga barfi (left) that unleashed a revolution, albeit a sweet one; Shri Ram Bhandar of Madan Gopal Gupta (right)

businesses of the local halwais. However, they were undeterred and continued to make sweets using jaggery and *misri* (sugar candy). The tiranga barfi, created by Madan Gopal Gupta (the owner of Shri Ram Bhandar at Thaheri Bazaar in Banaras), became the most famous symbol of the confectioners' rebellion.

Legend has it, the Maharaja of Kashi once hosted an English officer for dinner. At the end of the lavish dinner with the Maharaja, the English officer was served dessert in the hues of the Indian National Congress's tricolour flag. Saffron was used to provide a saffron tint, almonds were used for white and pistachios gave it a green colour. This barfi became a unifier in our struggle for freedom and had a strong patriotic message. Upon seeing this sweet symbol of rebellion, the fuming English officer demanded, 'And what is that in the middle?'

Madan Gopal Gupta, who was also present at the Maharaja's dinner, responded in a unique, Banarasi manner, '*Janab*, this is misri to tell you that we Indians are as sweet as this.'

This was too much for the *firang* to handle. He ordered the immediate arrest of Madan Gopal Gupta. With his small but powerful act of rebellion, he had started a different kind of revolution. During Mahatma Gandhi's Quit India Movement, the tiranga barfi was supplied in huge quantities to the revolutionaries. Soon,

The timeless ghats of a timeless city—Kashi

Jawahar laddoo, Gandhi Gaurav, Moti Paak, Vallabh *Sandesh* and Nehru barfi became part of the Indian dessert revolution. In our Calcutta home, there was a huge picture of Madan Gopal Gupta who fought the British in a rather 'sweet' manner. The third and fourth generations of his family helm the shop now.

~

चलती चक्की देख के, दिया कबीरा रोये ।
दो पाटन के बीच में, साबुत बचा न कोए ।।

Chalti chakki dekh kar, diya Kabira roye
Dui patan ke beech mein, sabut bacha na koye

Kabir looks at the mill and laments
that nothing stays intact between the millstones.

This couplet by Kabir, frequently seen on the walls of the ghats and houses of Banaras, defines the finality of our existence. Death is inevitable and it lives amidst the cheer and chaos of life. Along the ghats of Banaras, dotted with burning funeral pyres, this philosophy has played out day and night, through the ages. As a child, this timeless merging of death and life did not leave much of an impression, although it never failed to move me as an adult during my frequent visits to the city. Each ghat has its own cultural life and idiosyncratic evolution, which attracts travellers and locals alike.

During my summer vacations, I would look forward to going to the ghats and plunging deep into the holy waters of Ganga. After a thorough bathing ritual, a plate of stuffed kachori and lassi awaited us. I would gulp these down lest my eager cousins get hold of my plate after finishing theirs. Another culinary hotspot in the holy city was Shiv Bhandar—having hot, syrupy jalebis there was pure bliss. The taste and memories of my childhood visits to Banaras have never left me.

Akbar Fort and the confluence of Ganga, Jamuna and the mythical Saraswati at Sangam, Allahabad (now Prayagraj)

After Banaras, our next stop would be Allahabad, our second home and the city where Rupa's second sales centre, after the one in Calcutta, was opened in 1939. If Banaras lived in its ghats and narrow lanes, Allahabad could be found in its colonial bungalows, educational institutions and centres of arts and music. I have many indelible memories of the city. The mohalla where our house was located had a huge park out front. Every year, an enormous pandal would be set up in the park to celebrate Durga Puja, which would always be a rather riotous affair. Another holiday pastime on long summer was trying to stop the trains passing by our house, which was about half a kilometre away from the railway line. We had memorized the timings of various trains and my cousins and I would rush towards the track waving a red cloth, hoping to fool the driver and stop the train. The train never stopped and neither did our game.

Allahabad had its own delicacies to tempt our tastebuds—dahi jalebi, pedas and the ubiquitous Allahabad samosa from Hari Namkeen. The shop still stands where it had been set up—amidst the narrow lanes of the old city of Allahabad. It doesn't have any big signs or neon lights but continues to do a roaring business—its namkeens and samosas have never lost their fan following at home and abroad.

The statue of Chandrashekhar Azad in Alfred Park (now named Azad Park), in Prayagraj. He was engaged in a fierce gun fight with the British in this park and shot himself in the head rather than surrendering to the British forces on 27 February 1931.

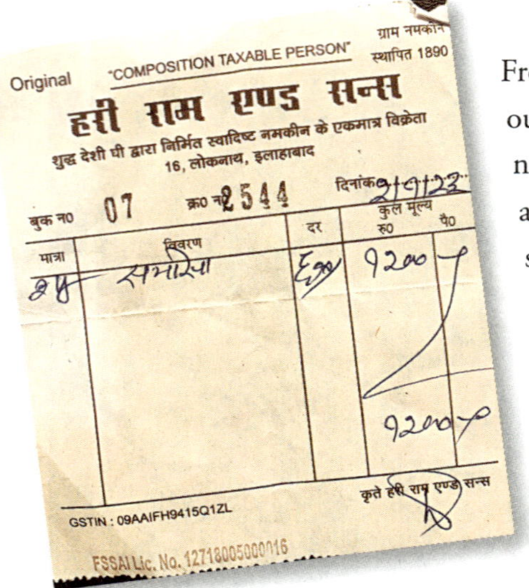

Original "COMPOSITION TAXABLE PERSON"
स्थापित 1890
हरी राम एण्ड सन्स
शुद्ध देशी घी द्वारा निर्मित स्वादिष्ट नमकीन के एकमात्र विक्रेता
16, लोकनाथ, इलाहाबाद
बुक न० 07 क्र० नं० 2544 दिनांक
मात्रा | विवरण | दर | कुल मूल्य रु० पै०
समोसा
कृते हरी राम एण्ड सन्स
GSTIN : 09AAIFH9415Q1ZL
FSSAI Lic. No. 12718005000016

The cash memo of Hari Namkeen still doesn't bear their phone number

From Allahabad, we would move on to our final destination, Kanpur, where my nana and nani lived in a grand mansion along with my maternal uncles. Every summer, around the scorching months of May and June, this mansion would become a melting pot of celebrations, laughter and bonhomie. My nana–nani had three sons (my mamas) and five daughters (my mausis) and during the summer break, their house used to be full. My mausis, who were married by then, would come to visit nana and nani, and would return with packets of sweets, namkeens and snacks of all kinds. This was a traditional way of elders expressing their love; daughters should not leave empty-handed from their parents' home—sweets to gloss over the pain of separation, perhaps. My three mamas stayed with my nana and assisted in the family business. The three of them could not have been more different from each other. My eldest mama, G.N. Khanna, was a lawyer but he never practised law. The time he saved by not going to the courtroom, he utilized in his family business. A curious personality with a sharp fiscal mind, he managed the finances of my nana's business. He had two eccentricities: one, the currency notes in his pocket would always be new and crisp (a habit I have picked up from him) and second, while travelling, he never carried clothes he had worn previously in his suitcase. A garment donned while on a tour would only find a place back in his suitcase when it was cleaned, ironed and fresh as before! M.N. Khanna was my second mama and was brilliant at marketing and public relations. He was a man of sober personality who liked good things in life, and he was also a book lover. Naturally, this brought me closer to him. I always sent books to him, a practice I followed till his last days; and he always paid for these books, a practice he followed till his last breath. My youngest mama

My three maternal uncles: G.N. Khanna (left), M.N. Khanna (middle) and K.N. Khanna (right)

was K.N. Khanna, an able administrator who had a commanding presence in the family business. He spent his evenings socializing with business associates and had friends across different segments of society.

Compared to my father's side of the family, my nana was a fairly successful businessman. Though he had started with a very small venture, making sweet khatai, the business grew rapidly. Brand Annapurna came to be associated with biscuits and snacks and became a household name in the region. Given the prosperity of her family, I sometimes wondered how my mother was content and happy with the less wealthy family she married into. When I grew older, I had my answer. Even though my maternal grandparents were financially in a better position than my father's family, they never made us feel inferior. This is why my mother could easily fit into our small house in Calcutta.

Form X.

LETTER OF APPOINTMENT

[Prescribed under Rule 53 of the West Bengal Shops and Establishments Rules, 1964]

Name of the Shop/~~Establishment~~ Rupa & Co

Address 15. BANKIM CHATTERJEE STREET, CALCUTTA-12.

Name of the ~~Shop-keeper~~/Employer Narayan Dass Mehra/Daudayal Mehra.

Registration No. Cal/Amh/P-1/942

Shri/~~Shrimati~~ Rajendra Kumar Mehra is appointed as (describe here the nature of appointment Asstt. Secretary in this shop/~~establishment~~ with effect from. 1st September 1968

2. His/~~Her~~ appointment is on probationary basis for Six months. (insert ~~the period)/temporary/casual basis for (insert the period)~~ ~~(permanent basis.~~

3. His/~~Her scale of pay~~/rate increment in wages per x (insert the period) shall be

4. He/~~She~~ will draw a total wages of Rs 350/- per ~~day/week~~/month composed of the following, namely,—

   (i) Basic pay of Rs 350/-

   (ii) Dearness allowance Included in Salary.

   (iii) Other allowances x

For Rupa & Co.

Partner

Signature of shop-keeper/employer.

My first appointment letter at Rupa; I drew a salary of ₹350 per month

• Chapter 4 •

MY INDUCTION INTO RUPA

Calcutta has been called many things. 'God's excreta' was Günter Grass's description. Dominique Lapierre called it the 'City of Joy'. Rudyard Kipling thought it was a 'dreadful city'. But for me, it was a rainbow city—a city as diverse at heart as the seven colours of the rainbow. The Calcutta I remember was home to Bengali bhadralok; Marwari 'businesswallahs'; the Chinese with their eateries and shoe shops; Anglo-Indian sahibs and memsahibs; Oriya plumbers, cooks and gardeners; paanwallahs from UP; and Bihari school teachers, rickshawallahs and labourers. In addition to its varied populace, there were other things that made Calcutta unforgettable. It was the only city in the world where some of the streets—Bara Bazaar and Strand Road—were washed at 4.00 a.m.—with the holy water of the Ganga. It was the only city in India where books and learning were worshipped to a greater degree than the rest of the country. Calcutta was also the only major city in the country where some revolution was always around the corner. This revolutionary zeal had a marked impact on my future.

Günter Grass (left) with Raju Barman at the Rupa stall in Calcutta

Soon after I joined college, in August 1965, the Naxalite movement—an armed peasant revolution led by Charu Mazumdar, Kanu Sanyal and others, that had been brewing for some years in the hinterland of Bengal—began spilling onto the streets of Calcutta. I had joined the Goenka College of Commerce, as I wanted to pursue management studies and consider a career in teaching thereafter. Contrary to the popular perception of business families in India, there was no pressure on me to join the family business. But these plans were thwarted as the violence unleashed by the Naxalite movement disrupted the city. College and university campuses were especially hard hit. Classes would be postponed or cancelled altogether because teachers would be gheraoed or attacked by unruly students. '*Mukti chayi* (we want freedom)!', was a common battle cry for these Charminar-cigarette or bidi-smoking revolutionaries. I would often go and read in the library. However, even that stopped being a safe haven soon. The librarian would often come up to us in the reading room, huffing and puffing, and say: '*Ladka log aa raha hain, fasad ho gaya* (the boys are on their way, it seems some disturbance is going to happen).' Eventually, we would have no option but to leave the college premises and head for home.

Out on the street, violence would greet us. We would frequently see blood-stained streets, broken trams and burnt down buildings in many areas of the city, including neighbourhoods close to our home. Caught up in this spiral of death and destruction, the lives of the city's inhabitants grew uncertain. This was especially true of the student population as the violence swamped college campuses. I was extremely frustrated

The Calcutta of the 1970s, where protests were a common sight

'We in Bengal are in the midst of darkness'. This poster tells the story of the state during the 1970s.

and unsure of what I could do in the prevailing situation, but my granduncle soon had the situation under control. On days when I couldn't attend college, he asked me to come and sit in his office and get a sense of the book business. As the Rupa office on Bankim Chandra Street was just a kilometre away from my college, this was a very convenient way of dealing with the frequent shutdowns.

Although it was a family business, my granduncle wanted to be very professional about how I became part of it. Accordingly, I was made the assistant to my granduncle's secretary at a monthly salary of ₹350. The message was clear—I had to learn everything from scratch and then work my way up. My first tutors were two office boys, Madhu and Rishi, who were responsible for sweeping and wiping the floor, and dusting the books. On my first day at office, I was given a broom and a dusting cloth by these two men and was told to get to work. 'Babu, please sweep the floor and once you are done, begin dusting the books,' one of them told me. That was my initiation into the family business. No lecture on company policy, no orientation into the company's culture and no fancy office. D. Mehra's company policy was simple: it didn't matter who you were or where you came from, everyone would be treated equitably and respectfully, and compensated fairly. In return, employees would be expected to do their job thoroughly. My workstation comprised a small steel table and chair near the entrance. I learnt to arrange books in alphabetical order and to segregate them based on their authors and genres. The learning curve was fairly steep, but I had good mentors. Soon enough, I had a good grasp of the processes to be able to pull my weight. Peter Drucker, the sales and management guru, famously commented that 'a well-kept stock is half sold'. It's something I learnt early in my career as a distributor and seller of books, and later as a publisher. A customer who is allowed to browse through a well-chosen inventory of books in a clean, well-ordered, well-lit bookshop is more likely to make a purchase, and that lies at the heart of the business.

Father Paul Joris, principal of St Xavier's College

As months rolled by, my responsibilities at Rupa grew. I began making inventories for the company. I was also expected to be familiar with the salient points of every book we had in stock—title, author's name, book description, and so on. Every morning began with a new book or two on my table. And every afternoon, I had a familiar visitor, Father Paul Joris, principal of the prestigious St Xavier's College.

A tall man of Belgian descent, Father Joris was a bibliophile who would regularly browse through the books in our office, seeking titles he could order for both the college library as well as his own. However, Father Joris was much more than a customer. I was a student back then, full of doubts about all manner of things, especially life's big questions, and he was more than willing to patiently answer all my queries, personal and otherwise. Ours became a guru–chela relationship. Father Joris had one notable eccentricity, which all his students (Vijay Mallya being one of them) were aware of—he would never allow anyone, whether students or booksellers, to carry his books. He would get quite voluble, even aggressive, if anyone dared to try and help him with his precious burden. For some reason, he broke this rule with me. I probably became the first man in Calcutta to carry

Father Joris's books for him. Pleased with myself for being granted this honour, I would be all smiles as I carried books to his house or his office in the college, basking in the envious glances of the students of St Xavier's College. The time I spent with Father Joris remains one of my most cherished memories.

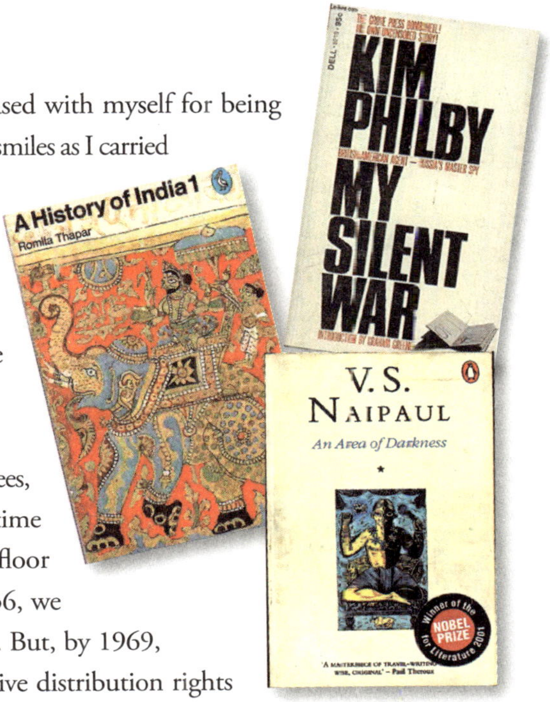

Rupa had started with four employees, in 1936, in a single room. By the time I joined, in 1969, it was a two-floor office with 20 employees. In 1936, we had been distributing three titles. But, by 1969, we had exclusive and non-exclusive distribution rights of 24 British publishers. Our bestseller list at the time included *Asian Drama* by Gunnar Myrdal, *An Area of Darkness* by V.S. Naipaul, *Ambassador's Journal* by J.K. Galbraith, *A History of India* by Romila Thapar, *The Wonder That Was India* by A.L. Basham and S.A.A. Rizvi, *My Life* by Golda Meir and *The Far Pavilions* and *Shadow of the Moon* by M.M. Kay. Percival Spear, Gore Vidal, Agatha Christie, George Mikes, P.G. Wodehouse, Eric Newby, Henry Cecil and Alistair MacLean were some of our bestselling authors. This was the period of the Cold War and just the right time for spy and espionage stories. Kim Philby, the double agent of MI6 who spied for Soviet Union during the Second World War, came up with his spy fiction *My Silent War* in 1967. It was a masterpiece in espionage writing and paved the way for many such authors in the genre. Kim Philby had fictionalized his life and written this book from Moscow, but it shook the world. By distributing it in India, Rupa shook the book world too. Retired and serving intelligence officers and government agencies wanted a copy of their own to read about the murky and dangerous world of espionage.

• Chapter 5 •

CALCUTTA DAYS AND NIGHTS

Even as my career slowly began to take shape within the company founded by my granduncle, I ensured that I did not miss out on the varied delights that Calcutta had to offer. One of the things I enjoyed the most was watching movies, especially big budget epics from Bollywood and Hollywood like *Mughal-e-Azam* (1960), *Ben-Hur* (1959) and *The Ten Commandments* (1956). I was also a fan of apna Bangali cinema with strong story-led films like *Balika Badhu* (1967) and *Goopy Gyne Bagha Byne* (1969). My la-la land was the Bina Cinema on Cornwallis Street. Since I couldn't stay away from office for too long, I developed an innovative way to watch movies—every ticket I bought was shared between me and my partner-in-crime for that day. Each of us would watch half the movie on same ticket and the next day, we would narrate half the movie to each other. Watching movies in this unique way made the experience quite memorable for me.

Besides movies, the fact that Calcutta was an incredibly rich melting pot of history, religion and culture, made it a great place to explore. You could say all of Calcutta was my *adda*, whether I was wandering through the Zoological Garden with friends or witnessing the spectacle and glitter of its mammoth religious festivals, such as Durga Puja, Diwali, Holi, Christmas and Eid.

Durga Puja was a time to visit each *pandal* for the *darshan* of the immortal goddess and to admire mortal Bengali beauties. In the pandals, the spiritual met the temporal.

The city had its paradoxes. Vivekananda Road and Kalibari coexisted amicably, although Vivekananda had opposed idol worship! It had its distinctive attributes.

There was a plethora of coaching centres on Mirza Ismail Road. St Jude was the place that churned out some of the best secretaries in the city. It was a city of people who followed gurus, like Ramakrishna Paramahansa, and their shishyas, like Swami Vivekananda, in this case. Belur Math, the headquarters of the Ramakrishna Math and Mission, founded by Swami Vivekananda, the chief disciple of Ramakrishna Paramahansa, was located on the west bank of the Hooghly. The architecture of the *math* fuses Hindu, Christian and Islamic motifs as a symbol of the unity of all religions. To me, that was the essence of my Calcutta. It embraced everyone irrespective of their religion or status in life. Everywhere you looked, its syncretism was on display. For example, the Kalighat metro station, near the famous Kalighat temple, contains a large mosaic of Mother Teresa. The Albanian Catholic nun came to the city in 1929, where she obtained Indian citizenship and devoted her life to helping the poor and diseased people of the city. She died in 1997 and was buried in her adopted city.

There wasn't a nook of the city that didn't beckon me. The colonial architecture of the city, embodying Victorian, baroque, oriental, gothic and Rococo styles, transformed it into a city of palaces. One of my favourite haunts was the Victoria Memorial, completed in 1821. The beautiful white marble structure reminded me of the Taj Mahal. As a child, I was fascinated by the grandeur of

The majestic Victoria Memorial

its architecture and the richness of its museum exhibits devoted to the history of the British in India. Victoria Memorial was not just an attraction for lovers of colonial architecture and history, though. Dotted among the trees surrounding the monument and the enormous maidan out front would be innumerable couples who would be much more drawn to each other than the magnificent setting in which they were courting. Fort William, built during the early years of British in India, was another one of my favourite spots. Even through the monument had been taken over by the Indian Army, a special permit was required to enter the place. One day, when I was loitering in the maidan outside Fort William, I saw an army officer riding a stallion. Just as the rider was about to pass, summoning up all my courage, I asked whether he could take me in to look around. Smiling, he reined his mount in and pulled me up behind him. To my great astonishment and delight, we then began slowly trotting towards Fort William. Once my short tour was over, as I was dismounting, I asked the great man his name.

Within the embrace of Nirmal Hriday, everyone is loved and valued

'Sam. They call me Sam Manekshaw, young man.'*

*Sam Manekshaw's wife used to visit Rupa's Calcutta office every Saturday, and his brother used to visited our Bombay office on Oak Lane Road every Thursday.

Besides the Victoria Memorial and Fort William, another Calcutta landmark imprinted in my memory is St Paul's Cathedral, with its beautiful mosaics, murals and frescoes, and paintings of biblical scenes. Over 60-metre high, it is an imposing landmark. As with the Victoria Memorial and numerous other parks and gardens, the area around St Paul's also used to be full of young lovers.

Calcutta's most important street, Jawaharlal Nehru Road, formerly known as Chowringhee Avenue, was another adda of mine. One of its attractions was the country's largest library—the National Library of India. It was founded in 1836, and became the hub of a vibrant cultural community; it was one of the places that fostered my interest in arts as well as politics.

Calcutta is unimaginable without its clubs. One such club was the Tollygunge Club, which had, within its august environs, a golf course, horse riding facilities and residential accommodations. Only members and their guests were allowed in. Although neither my parents nor I were members, I managed to smuggle myself into the club on more than one occasion through the good offices of friends to sample its various attractions.

Another of my haunts was the Calcutta Race Course. My friends and I would pool our money and bet the 'princely' sum on a jockey or a horse we liked the look of. We used to be quite ignorant of the horse's lineage or the jockey's track record, though. Consequently, I would lose my bets more often than not, and when my friends would mock me, I would say, 'But I will be lucky in love.' They would find this very funny but I had the last laugh in this case, as we shall see in the next chapter.

The Hooghly always captured my imagination, not just because of my granduncle's exploit with which I began this book. Not only did the great river mesmerize me but its ghats also provided an endless carnival of delights. I would spend hours on Outram Ghat just watching the ceaseless bustle of activity: boatmen plying their trade, hawkers selling fast food, couples murmuring

Indian Coffee House, situated at 15 Bankim Chandra Street and an abode for the city's intellectuals for decades

sweet nothings to each other, commuters hastening to and fro, the *bisarjan* of idols after the puja ceremonies, and of course, addas—an activity Calcutta natives are most famous for.

And then there was the food. Bengalis are obsessed with food. They are either eating or planning a future meal. A trip to the ghat was never complete without the joys of mouth-watering roadside food. All along the ghat, hawkers sold delicious fast food—phuchka, gol gappa or pani puri and jhal muri. How can one forget the mouth-watering aloo-dum and ghugni? As a result of my total immersion in the delights of Calcutta as a boy, Bengali remains my favourite cuisine to this day. If I were to choose one dish I relish above all, it would be sandesh or more properly *shôndesh*.

The story of my life is incomplete without College Street—the street in central Calcutta, where D. Mehra made his first foray into bookselling. It stretches from Ganesh Chandra Avenue Crossing in the Bowbazar area to Mahatma Gandhi Road crossing. The road north of M.G. Road continues as Bidhan Sarani

(Cornwallis Street). College Street houses many centres of intellectual activity in the city. Well-known academic institutions such as Presidency University, Sanskrit College, the Medical College and Hospital, Kolkata, the Indian Institute of Social Welfare and Business Management, Hare School, Hindu School and the University of Calcutta are situated on the street. And then there was *amaar adda*—the Indian Coffee House, a cafe frequented by the city's intellectuals for decades. Numerous bookstores dotted the area around the coffee house. It must have been a matter of great prestige for Indian Coffee House to host the brightest minds of the time, like Satyajit Ray, Manna Dey, Ashok Mitra, Taraknath Sen and other intellectuals and cultural icons, such as Amartya Sen, Mrinal Sen, Sukumar Choudhury and Aparna Sen. Other distinguished scholars, editors, artists, writers and cultural celebrities who formed its clientele included Ritwik Ghatak, Narayan Gangopadhyay, Sunil Gangopadhyay, Sanjib Chattopadhyay, Samaresh Majumdar, Subhas Mukhopadhyay, Shakti Chattopadhyay, Pritish Nandy, M.J. Akbar and Hiranmay Karlekar. In the late 1960s, the coffee house became one of the city's centres of intellectual ferment when the founders of the Naxalite movement began frequenting it. Although the iconic poets Malay Roy Choudhury and Samir Roychoudhury, who were among the founders of the movement, were arrested and prosecuted, the movement they spearheaded ushered in new post-colonial thinking in academia and literature.

But the coffee house was not the domain of intellectuals and peaceful revolution aries alone. Among its patrons were stalwarts of the Naxalite movement, such as Kanu Sanyal and Charu Mazumdar.

During the tenure of Congress Chief Minister (CM) Siddhartha Shankar Ray, the Calcutta police went after the Naxalites with a vengeance and the streets of the city were stained with blood. A whole lot of Naxalite leaders were killed. It's an open secret that the then ruling Congress Party planted spies inside the unguarded Naxalite organization to gather information about its secret bases and arrest its supporters. Government intelligence personnel and police disguised as Naxalite sympathizers could easily infiltrate the party's inner organization.

Many of its leaders were arrested, including Charu Mazumdar. The police had information about Mazumdar's movements after he went underground in 1970, and he was finally arrested in Calcutta in July 1972. He died in jail days after his arrest, probably on the night of 27 or 28 July. It is not known how he died, although the government reported that he died of a heart attack.

The cigarette shop of Ismail from where I fetched innumerable cigarettes for revolutionaries like Kanu Sanyal. The shop is now run by his next generation.

After the Naxalite movement was brutally put down, Jyoti Basu emerged as the state's top leader and ushered in an era of peace that lasted for decades. I will not go into the politics of Bengal in any great detail, nor will I delve into the reasons why the Naxalite movement failed. However, one of my treasured memories as a youth is that of being in the presence of charismatic revolutionaries like Kanu Sanyal at the Indian Coffee House. From time to time, he would summon me and say: '*Ki rey, ekta packet cigarette niye aach* (Hey, there, fetch me a packet of cigarettes).' I would do his bidding, heedless of his politics or what he was plotting. Such was the atmosphere of the Indian Coffee House in my youth.

There were other spots that I didn't get to go to frequently but was intensely aware of—night clubs and restaurants like Trincas, Blue Fox and Moulin Rouge. Alas, neither had I any money to indulge myself in the epicurean pursuits offered by these night clubs nor would the puritan Mehra household have approved of such escapades. No evocation of the Calcutta of the late 1960s would be complete without a mention of its football clubs (FCs), especially the epic rivalry between East Bengal and Mohan Bagan clubs. *Boro match* (big match), as the clash between the two clubs was called, was a game of football not only on the ground but clash between two cultures on either side of the river Padma. The rivalry between Mohan Bagan and East Bengal is the oldest football rivalry in Asia and probably the fiercest too.

Mohan Bagan, established in 1889, mainly consisted of players from affluent, bhadralok Bengalis, those living on the west of the river Padma. Being from Calcutta, they were considered natives and called Ghotis. East Bengal (now the independent nation of Bangladesh) had players from the east of the river Padma and were called Bangals. In 1911, the barefoot footballers of Mohan Bagan defeated the English side, East Yorkshire Regiment, and the club became immortal. Then, in 1920, something happened. Mohan Bagan was all set to play against Jorabagan, another club, in the Cooch Behar trophy. Jorabagan dropped one of its star player Sailesh Bose and all hell broke loose. It was said that Sailesh came from the 'other side', implying that he was from East Bengal. Suresh Chandra Chaudhuri, an industrialist and vice president of Jorabagan, was deeply hurt by this decision. Sailesh Bose, too, felt wronged. Battered and bruised, the two, along with Manmatha Nath Chaudhuri (Raja of Santosh after whom the Santosh Trophy was named), Ramesh Chandra (Nasha) Sen and Aurobindo Ghosh started

East Bengal FC with their 1949 IFA Shield

a new club and called it East Bengal. Football in Bengal changed forever. Mohan Bagan represented the establishment while East Bengal became the challengers. David and Goliath in football jerseys—they spoke different dialects of Bengali, had different sartorial habits and even their fish was different—chingri was lucky for Mohan Bagan while illish swam for East Bengal.

Even at the Rupa office, Saturday afternoons were reserved to experience this gladiatorial event. We would shut shop at 2.00 p.m. and all our staff would assemble at our home, gathering in front of the only TV set, united by their passion for the game and divided by their allegiance to their respective teams. D. Mehra's decorum ensured no broken jaws or torn shirts when either of the teams lost, but this was home. Witnessing the match on the ground was an event of a different magnitude. Amidst jhal muri, chana and chai, one could learn the choicest abuses at these matches. Exchanging blows while watching the game was a rite of passage. If you dared to stand in front of anyone, you would be whacked and your response, inevitably, would be, '*Aeey baap re, aami to apnar jonney hi score korchilam* (I was cheering and scoring for your team)!' No one can come between a Bengali and his football.

~

Calcutta's many charms soon took a back seat to the heady world of books as I was given greater responsibilities at the family firm. Although, I was keen to get a management degree from Indian Institute of Management (IIM), the unending series of student bandhs and strikes and violence on campus meant that I had to wait. This proved to be very frustrating. Noticing this, my granduncle came up with a tempting offer: 'Why don't you travel throughout India to witness the country's various cities and our partners there? See how publishing works.'

This was an enticing offer and one that changed my life. Within days, R.N. Barman, D. Mehra's foster son and a senior executive with Rupa, and I set off on our yatra. Besides my childhood excursions to Banaras and Allahabad, this was the first time I was stepping out of Calcutta. We covered Banaras, Allahabad, Kanpur, Lucknow, Amritsar, Ludhiana, Delhi, Chandigarh, Hyderabad, Bangalore (now Bengaluru), Madras (now Chennai), Coimbatore and Ernakulam in over a month's time. The trip proved to be both educational and overwhelming for me. I experienced the unique culture of each city and how they conducted business and trade. Gone were my frustrations and disillusionment with the education system, and my inability to attend a management institute. Instead, I was swept away by the prospects and challenges that a career in publishing and bookselling held out. It was 1969, I was 22 years old, and I knew without a shadow of a doubt what I wanted to do for the rest of my life. Over the five decades since this decision, I have never once doubted my wholehearted plunge into publishing.

The year after the tour of India, another event whetted my appetite for publishing—the annual Indian Science Congress. In 1970, it took place in Kharagpur, 150 kilometres away from Calcutta, and it was decided that I would attend the event as the firm's representative. Rupa was the distributor of an Israeli scientific publisher called Israel Programme for Scientific Translation (IPST). It was an important publisher, which published a range of scientific and technical books in physics, chemistry, biology and medicine. The Indian Science Congress was the perfect venue to showcase our scientific books. I was accompanied by my colleague from Bombay, G.A. Shenoy. A cold Kharagpur awaited us in January. The organizers had promised us beds and mattresses but, unfortunately, they did not keep their promise—we were given two steel benches and a table to set up our stall. During the day, the benches served as our office and as night fell, they turned into our beds. We didn't have a mattress; all we had brought with us was a bedsheet and we had to decide whether to lie on top of it or to cover ourselves with it. The cold made that decision for us, and we shivered under the bedsheet all night. There were no catering arrangements made by the organizers. For the first two days, we survived on bread and tea in the morning, tea and some biscuits in the afternoon followed by another round of tea and some bread. Somehow, my father got to know about our travails, and it was decided that food would

G.A. Shenoy, an old Rupa hand, seen here with Indira Gandhi. Mrs Gandhi, an avid and curious reader, was a regular at Rupa book stalls.

be sent to us from Calcutta, almost 150 kilometres away from the venue. One of the local Gujarati booksellers, commonly known as Thakkar, came to our rescue. He started bringing us home-cooked khichdi every day! This indigenous concoction of rice and pulses tempered with desi ghee and dollops of love made things immeasurably better for us, and I finally began to focus on the job at hand rather than worry about the hardships we had been facing.

One day, PM Indira Gandhi visited our stall and even purchased a book on the issues confronting the Third World Order. The book seemed to resonate with her, given the challenges she had been facing at that time. Among other things, her Congress Party had just split, refugees from East Pakistan were streaming across the border and there were myriad other problems. Although she was not at the peak of her power, she definitely looked every inch the leader she had always been as she browsed through the books. A year later, when India went to war with Pakistan, she proved her mettle by humiliatingly defeating our neighbour. Years later, in one of her other visits to our stall, I remember giving her *Deschooling Society* by Ivan Illich. Soon she came back to our stall

(From left to right) R.N. Barman, N.N. Sinha, D. Mehra, André Deutsch, N.D. Mehra, K.L. Barman and Jyoti Sengupta at the Rupa office

looking for me and returned the book, saying she already had a copy with her. Soon after my successful expedition to the Indian Science Congress, I was given another opportunity to prove my worth to my granduncle and the family. A delegation of publishers from the UK, consisting of Oxford, Macmillan, Longman, Hamlyn, William Heinemann, André Deutsch and several others, was visiting India in search of new distribution partners. Calcutta was first on their itinerary. The team was led by the legendary John Attenborough of Hodder & Stoughton (now Hachette) and Calcutta's publishing fraternity was planning to throw a lavish party with Scotch whisky and European food on the menu to impress the visiting Brits. There was nothing wrong with that plan except that it was an idea that had been done to death; it also didn't align with D. Mehra's philosophy of unpretentious living. Why did we always have to impress the goras with food and frolic? Why couldn't we show them something different, something that would show our prowess in fields that they can relate to? An idea then struck me. We felt we should welcome the delegates through a message published in the city's largest-circulated English daily, *The Statesman*. The idea soon became a reality, and a message from Rupa welcoming the visiting delegates was printed in the newspaper. The advertisement created a buzz and André Deutsch insisted on meeting us. Rupa was represented by D. Mehra, N.D. Mehra, R.N. Barman, K.L. Barman and myself. It was an exclusive meeting with André Deutsch and we would meet him in one of the storied restaurants of Mocambo. Poor D. Mehra! His idea of socializing was meeting with friends at a tea stall near the office over tea and *shingaras*. However, there was no escaping this meeting. So, he dragged himself over to the restaurant where he was further discomfited by being at the receiving end of a diatribe delivered by the legendary founder of the eponymous firm that was scathing about the competence of Indian book distributors. He felt they were lazy and lacked enterprise, and questioned Rupa for its lack of presence in Delhi. By this time, we were distributing a large number of titles published by André Deutsch, including John Updike's *Couples,* a bestseller hailed as 'artful, seductive, savagely graphic portrait of love, marriage and adultery in America'.* Our association with André Deutsch, thus, was commercially successful but his fulmination at us was surprising. Was he getting greedy and wanted more of the pie? His criticism hurt and humiliated my granduncle. This humiliation set in motion a chain of events that helped the company grow even bigger. The very next morning, D. Mehra called me for morning tea and, to my immense excitement, tasked me with establishing a Rupa office in Delhi.†

A few days later, I remember crooning a song while crossing the streets around Maidan one evening. It was from Raj Kapoor's film *Jagte Raho*, '*Zindagi khwaab hai, khwaab mei sach hai kya, aur bhala jhooth hai kya* (Life is but a dream, and in a dream what is true, what is untrue).' The song spoke about the fleeting pleasures of life and why it was important to follow the dictates of one's heart. I was certainly following the dictates of mine by going to Delhi to establish the firm's office. I would soon discover yet another aspect of my heart's desire in Delhi.

---

*Updike, John, *Couples*, Penguin Books, 1968.

†A decade after establishing our Delhi operations, I was on a visit to London and was staying at Hotel Imperial near André's office. To my surprise, I got a call from him, and we started doing business again!

17 May 1970: A date and year to be remembered. Rupa marks its footprints in Delhi.

T.B. Mehra (left), my father-in-law, is seen here talking to my father along with Mini Kapoor, our distributor then and Mr B.D. Gupta of the Metropolitan Book Company on the opening of Rupa's Delhi office. My mother-in-law (extreme right), Vimla Mehra, was a pillar of strength for me.

• Chapter 6 •

DELHI IS NOT DISTANT

मुझे इश्तिहार सी लगती हैं
ये मोहब्बतों की कहानियाँ
जो कहा नहीं वो सुना करो
जो सुना नहीं वो कहा करो

Mujhe ishtihar si lagti hain
Ye mohabbaton ki kahaniyan
Jo kaha nahi, wo suna karo
Jo suna nahi, wo kaha karo

Stories of love look
but like displays to me.
Listen to what has not been said.
Say what has not been heard.

—*Bashir Badr, Urdu poet*

A Calcutta boy meets a Delhi girl, and love blossoms. Sixty years have passed since I first encountered Kaminee, my wife, and I can say unequivocally that in my journey as a publisher, my wife has been my most beautiful story, a definite bestseller, if you will pardon the mixing of metaphors. Our story began one Christmas evening, in 1962, in Calcutta when Kaminee came over to our home to spend the Christmas holidays. Our parents were family friends. Kaminee's father was a prosperous businessman who had achieved his success through sheer grit and determination. He had a beautiful sense of colour and patterns, and he made good use of his talent by starting a block-printing business. The small shop he began eventually grew into a big business in Old Delhi's famous Sitaram Bazaar. He was a disciplinarian and a man of few words. Kaminee's mother and my future mother-in-law was a woman of great strength and resilience. Despite hailing from an affluent family, she had been unfazed by the prospect of marrying a businessman who was still setting up shop. Even as my father-in-law worked long hours to establish his business, she did not hesitate to take up a job as a teacher, so the household would have a stable income. She eventually became the principal of the school she had begun teaching in—she achieved this despite all the demands on her time that came with raising a family and supporting her husband in ways big and small. She was a woman I greatly admired.

Kaminee's and my parents had been long-time friends, and they would visit us from time to time. I first saw Kaminee on one such visit during Christmas in Calcutta, which used to be a big affair in that part of the world. Bengalis had been the first few people to adopt and adapt to the Crown's language and culture. Consequently, the Christmas tree and Santa Claus easily fused into Bengali festivities. I was all of 15 years and she was 13. I remember we spent time together, talking about our hobbies, sharing comics and toffees, and visiting zoos and museums. The short Christmas vacation came to an end, and Kaminee went back to her home in Delhi. I carried on with my life in Calcutta, waiting for the next Christmas break.

Christmas celebration at Park Steet, Calcutta

Muir Central College, which was founded in 1872 and which later merged into University of Allahabad

As I mentioned earlier, the Naxalite violence in Calcutta in the late 1960s disrupted my plans to get a management degree, and I was inducted into the family business by my granduncle. As my responsibilities grew, I would be dispatched to various cities to attend to sales and distribution matters. Whenever I found myself in Delhi, I would visit Kaminee's house, where her mother would introduce me to her circle as the son of a family friend. By then, Kaminee had passed out of school and been admitted to Muir College in Allahabad, where she was pursuing a bachelor's degree in botany. Allahabad was also one of the cities I visited frequently for business. Allahabad University was a thriving centre of education and I would visit the professors and teachers there in order to interest them in our books. On my visits to the city, I would also, without fail, visit Kaminee at the women's hostel. Our meetings would happen under the watchful supervision of the warden of the hostel or one of the attendants. On occasion, we would bump into each other on the university campus and spend a few minutes chatting with each other. Although we were growing close, our relationship was platonic, and there were no grand or fervent declarations of love and passion; it was simply not the way things were done at the time.

A couple of years later, I moved to Delhi and started the Rupa office in Daryaganj. Mir Taqi Mir, the great Urdu poet, famously wrote:

> दिल्ली जो एक शहर था आलम में इंतिख़ाब
> रहते थे मुंतख़ब ही जहाँ रोज़गार के
>
> *Dilli jo ek sheher tha aalam mein intekhaab*
> *Rehtey thay muntakhab hi jahan rozgaar ke*
>
> Delhi, which was a city unique in the world,
> Where lived only those chosen by time
>
> باختنا ںیم ملاع اھت رہش کیا وج یلد
> ےک راگزور ںاہج یہ بختنم ےھت ےتہر

Two hundred years after these lines were written, Delhi remained a sought-after city, attracting talent from every field including the world of business. By the late 1960s, it was a city infused with entrepreneurial energy, around the rewards and thrills of a free market economy. It suited my own restless longing to do something with my life.

Pataudi House Road, Old Daryaganj, became my new address. After D. Mehra decided to open an office in Delhi, the groundwork for my move to the city began. Before I actually relocated, between February and April 1970, I made several trips to the city. We had appointed P.N. Mago to be our representative in Delhi and hunt for an office space. Soon after moving to the capital, I spent a few days at Hotel Flora in Daryaganj but, within five to six days, I found the tariff too steep and moved out. A small room behind Pataudi House Road in Old Daryaganj became my temporary home. It had a rudimentary toilet—just a hole on a raised platform. Aiming right was key to a happy ablution. For the first few nights, I slept on the floor, battling nocturnal insects. After saving some money, I bought a charpoy.

Where knowledge finds its home: Rupa's showroom in Delhi

P.N. Mago (left) is seen here with a customer on the opening day of Rupa's office in Delhi

Finally, on 1 May 1970, we found an office space. On 17 May 1970, it officially became Rupa's office in Delhi at a monthly rent of ₹1,450, an amount which remain unchanged for decades, even when the entire geography of the area underwent a radical change! During the day, this was our office, and when the shutters came down in the evening, it served as my living quarters. The aroma of freshly cooked food would fill the space, and late at night, I would stretch out on a mattress. Luckily, it had a small kitchen and, guess what, a proper toilet!

The saddest songs come from forlorn hearts; they also come from empty stomachs craving home-cooked food! One of the low moments of leaving Calcutta was missing home-cooked food, the aroma of spices floating out from our kitchen and seducing our olfactory senses, heightening the anticipation of what lay ahead of us to satisfy our gastronomical desires. More than a century ago, when Nawab Wajid Ali Shah was ordered by the British to leave his favourite city of Lucknow and settle in Calcutta, he did so and brought with him his favourite khansamas who created the flavours of Oudh for the homesick Nawab. I was no Wajid Ali Shah, nor had I been banished from my home. But, my family did sense that I craved home food and very kindly sent me my own khansama—an old family housekeeper and cook named Kisto. Born in Orissa (now Odisha), he had been a presence in the Mehra household since before I was born and was naturally a trusted aide. He would look after me like his own child, cook baigun bhaja and aaloo poshto in the alleys of Old Delhi. Home-cooked food is less about the recipe and more about the hands that make it—mother's, grandmothers', aunts'.

My craving for Calcutta street food made the matters worse. Jhal muri, phuchka, kachalu and tikki became staples from a glorious but bygone culinary era from my life. During my college days, I had the freedom to walk up to our office where my granduncle, my father or R.N. Barman would always treat me to either a fish fry, cutlet or a shingara to be savoured with a hot brew from the coffee house. The sweet indulgence.

Rupa & Co.

PHONE : SHOWROOM : 34-4821
OFFICE : 34-6305
GRAMS : RUPANCO : CALCUTTA
PUBLISHERS, AGENTS AND WHOLESALE BOOKSELLERS

Post Box No. 7808 / 15 Bankim Chatterjee Street, Calcutta-12

Copy

16 May, 1970.

Agents for :—
Abelard-Schuman
Andre Deutsch
Anthony Blond
Artemis Press
A. Thomas
Calder & Boyars
Concrete
Darwen Finlayson
Dobson
Elliot Rightway Books
Foulsham
Foulsham-Sams
(Tech. Books)
Frank Cass
Grafton
[illegible] Program (IPST)
[illegible] Pub.
Lund Humphries
Merlin Press
Neville Spearman
Peter Owen
Phaidon
Reader's Digest
(School Books)
Sidgwick & Jackson
Souvenir Press
Thomas Yoseloff
Thorsons
Vision
W. H. Allen

•

Stockists for :—
Allen & Unwin
[illegible] & Faber
Methuen
Penguin
Pitman

•

Addison-Wesley
D. Van Nostrand
Harper & Row
McGraw-Hill
Prentice-Hall

•

Affiliated
East-West Press
Prentice-Hall (India)

My Dear Pattu,

For a wholesaling house to survive for 34 years, maintaining its name and dignity is a great feat. Any house wishing to become great must be reborn from time to time. Opening new outlet is the price of survival. Book wholesaling is a cultural part of the country.

On the occassion of opening ceremoney of Delhi office I wish to thank allconnected with Rupa in all offices and everywhere. It is the good will of our collegues and well-wishers that we prosper. You will be great one day. It is easy to become great but it is difficult to remain great. It requires a lot of self sacrifices in every walk of life. I can not explain it but you can well understand and you will realise in course of your commercial, social and family life.

I wish you success not only in business but in every walk of life. I do not want to build your character by taking away your initiative and independence. I should not help you permanently by doing more for you than you can do yourself. Have patience. Restrain yourself in anger and emotion. Do not be week. From weekness no good ever comes out. If you want to be happy, valuntarily be poor. Try to do what is right. The rest will take cure of itself. Be polite - civility costs nothing but buys everythisg.

With best wishes,

Yours affectionately,

DAUDAYAL MEHRA.

To
Sri R. K. Mehra,
C/o. T.B.Mehra,
F.1/11 Model Town,
Mani Deep, Delhi-9.

DM/RP.

ALLAHABAD - 24 SOUTH MALAKA
BOMBAY - 11 OAK LANE, FORT

D. Mehra's encouraging message for me when we opened Rupa's Delhi office

Rupa & Co

Phone : Showroom-34-4871
Office-34-6305

Grams : **Rupanco : Calcutta**

PUBLISHERS, AGENTS AND WHOLESALE BOOKSELLERS

Post Box No. 7808 : 15 Bankim Chatterjee Street, Calcutta-12

Agents for :—

ABELARD-SCHUMAN
ANDRE DEUTSCH
ANTHONY BLOND
ARTEMIS PRESS
A. THOMAS
CALDER & BOYARS
CHARLES SKILTON
CEMENT CONCRETE ASSOCIATION
DARWEN FINLAYSON
DOBSON
ELLIOT RIGHTWAY BOOKS
FOULSHAM
FOULSHAM-SAM (TECH. BOOKS)
FRANK CASS
GEORGE RONALD
GRAFTON
HEALTH SCIENCE PRESS (HOMOEOPATHIC BOOKS)
LEO COOPER (MILITARY BOOKS)
LORRIMER PUB.
LUND HUMPHRIES
MERLIN PRESS
NEVILLE SPEARMAN
OSWALD WOLFF
PETER OWEN
PHAIDON
READER'S DIGEST (SCHOOL BOOKS)
SIDGWICK & JACKSON
SOUVENIR PRESS
THOMAS YOSELOFF
THORSONS
VALLENTINE MITCHELL
VISION
W. H. ALLEN

Stockists for :—

ALLEN & UNWIN
COLLINS
FABER & FABER
McGRAW-HILL (LONDON)
METHUEN
PENGUIN
PITMAN

ADDISON-WESLEY
HARPER & ROW

JAPAN PUBLICATIONS
JOHN WEATHERHILL
KOGAKUSHA

AFFILIATED EAST-WEST PRESS
PRENTICE-HALL (INDIA)

30 May, 1970

I am glad to inform you that we have opened a new branch in Delhi at 3831 Pataudi House Road, Daryaganj, Delhi-6. My Grandson R. K. Mehra is in-charge of its administration.

I crave for your help to serve you.

With kind regards.

Yours sincerely,

D. MEHRA,
Mg. Director.

DM/RP.

ALLAHABAD - 94 SOUTH MALAKA ▪ BOMBAY - 11 OAK LANE, FORT

164 THE INDIAN PUBLISHER & BOOKSELLER

A formal announcement of our Delhi office opening

INTER-OFFICE MEMO

FROM CALCUTTA

Date

To

(5)

Success is sure if you can win the hearts of your soldiers (staff).

(6)

A person, successful at one post, may not be successful at another post. Serious consideration is required when you transfer work of a staff.

Rupa . Co

Such memos to me came regularly from D. Mehra. They were a source of motivation.

The Nolen Chandra Das's delicious and timeless roshogullas and Girish Dey and Nakul Nandy's sandesh would complete one's pursuit of 'sweet' happiness.

But I was in Delhi now, and all this was in the realm of memory. However, my parents knew what I was missing. Mother used to send namkeens and Father discovered a person who happened to be our vendor and worked for one of our customers, A.H. Wheeler. He was a frequent traveller from Howrah to Delhi, and this good Samaritan carried Bengali sweets laced with parental love for me.

Across from Pataudi House Road was Ansari Road, the mecca of publishers in Delhi. Acquiring an office space on Ansari Road was beyond my means. So, I settled for a more humble address. Nonetheless, I wasn't too far from the action. Some of my neighbours were celebrities, including the veteran film actor Om Prakash, Board of Control for Cricket in India (BCCI) President R.P. Mehra and Vishnu Prabhakar, an important name in Hindi literary circles. Daryaganj, where Pataudi House Road and Ansari Road were located, was home to some of the country's greatest publishers at that time. At Kashmere Gate was Hind Pocket Books, owned by Dinanath Malhotra, and Rajpal & Sons, owned by his brother Vishwanath Malhotra, both of whom had migrated from Pakistan. These firms dominated trade publishing in English and Hindi. Their lists included literary giants like Suryakant Tripathi 'Nirala', Firaq Gorakhpuri, Harivansh Rai Bachchan, Mahadevi Verma, Sumitra Nandan Pant and Premchand to name a few. Rajkamal Prakashan was already doing great work in the Hindi market and R.P. Puri's Atma Ram & Sons in Kashmere Gate was another publishing house that had made an impact on the textbook market. Another major player at that time was S. Chand of Shyamlal Gupta, a doyen in the field of Indian textbooks. Vikas Publishing House owned by C.M. Chawla was a dynamic publishing company at the time as was the Sri Lankan Peter Jaisingha's Asia Publishing House in Bombay. Oxford University Press had also set up shop in Daryaganj under Charles Lewis and Macmillan had entered the school textbooks market.

These were the players Rupa had to contend with, and I needed to quickly find my feet and start carving out a niche for the company.

My mandate was to increase our distribution in Delhi, eventually expanding throughout North India. From 1971 to 1976, the focus was on acquiring rights of foreign books for the Indian market and strengthening the distribution system. By 1976, we also started to reprint these foreign titles depending on market demand. I also took upon myself a task for which Rupa is known to this day—getting to know our customers and improving customer satisfaction, that is to say, ensuring that the booksellers and distributors who sold our books were carefully listened to and were happy with our books, supply chain and other operating procedures. I ensured that I met as many of our booksellers and distributors as frequently as possible. I would take a four anna *phat-phat sewa* (a cross between a minibus and autorickshaw) and personally deliver books to booksellers in Connaught Place—Galgotia Book Shop, Ramakrishna, New Book Depot, etc. This also gave me an opportunity to hear about which books were selling where, see how booksellers kept and displayed their stocks and which areas we could expand to while commissioning new titles. The tangible benefits of personally delivering stocks in the morning were that it allowed me to smooth out any wrinkles in the supply chain and ensured that there was always enough stock for customers. Becoming the face of Rupa to the book trade in Delhi was one of the things I was pleased with after moving to the capital. It laid the foundation for the growth of our business.

Many a book were delivered sitting on these unique phat-phat sewa

Although my days were hectic, I kept in touch with Kaminee's family. They were the only family friends I had in Delhi and I would often visit them for the simple pleasures of a home-cooked meal and their warm and gracious company. There was another reason I was a frequent visitor—Kaminee would write letters to me and mail them to her parents' address. 'Your letter has arrived,' my future mother-in-law would say with a cheeky smile. During vacations, when Kaminee returned to her house in Delhi, we would often go out for dinner or a movie, but these excursions were always chaperoned by her parents; it was out of the question for two young people to go out on a date on their own.

However, romance was not the only thing on my mind at the time, as establishing Rupa's presence in Delhi required a lot of hard work. Delhi was certainly a city that offered enterprising publishers and book distributors far more opportunities than cities like Calcutta or Allahabad. Back then, the city had three big universities—Delhi University, Jawaharlal Nehru University and Jamia Millia Islamia—and their students and faculty represented an enormous market. The city was also experiencing a boom in trade. Allied Publishers, UBS Publishers & Distributors, India Book House, India Book Distributors, S. Chand & Company, Hind Pocket Books, Orient Longman, Macmillan and Oxford University Press were the few prominent and established players in publishing and distribution at the time in Delhi. Each firm occupied its own market space. Rupa had to break through this ceiling, and acquiring and reprinting foreign titles became our driving force. Soon, Rupa's imported titles were populating the leading bookstores, prompting a petty remark from a leading publisher that Rupa was a reprint publisher. But didn't Sir Allen Lane start Penguin as a low-cost reprint publisher? History has all the answers.

Besides visiting prospective and existing customers in the national capital, I also travelled extensively to various cities on business, living out of my suitcase and staying in the waiting rooms of railway stations. I would arrive in a city by train, deposit my bags in the waiting room and set off on my rounds, meeting clients and prospective customers. In the evening, I would be back at the railway station, waiting for my train to the next city. I would shuffle between train compartments and waiting rooms for days on end. If the business was going to succeed, there was no extra cash in hand to waste on fancy hotel rooms. So, during the early years of Rupa's Delhi office, this was my routine. Looking back, I realize those early years taught me a lot—the virtues of austerity, dealing with hardships, working on customer relationships, and much more. I have never regretted those years of trying to establish a toehold in Delhi's tough, competitive market.

Even as I worked hard, I kept a nervous eye on Kaminee's prospective suitors. Being the daughter of a prosperous business family, many thought she would make a suitable match for their eligible sons. It was something of a tradition for successful business people to forge matrimonial alliances with high-profile bureaucrats. So, I fully expected her to be married off to an up-and-coming bureaucrat. This was not unusual, for I always say Delhi comprises two cities—*ek lalaji ki Dilli aur doosri afsarshahi ki Dilli* (one is the Delhi of traders and the other is the Delhi of bureaucrats). Kaminee's suitors weren't the only worry, though.

I was 24 by this time, and as with parents in those times, my own parents were anxious about my bachelor status. I was living on my own, in a new city, and with complete independence—this was more than enough to worry them. My father said to me on more than one occasion: 'What if you are up to something? What if you marry someone without our consent?' To these questions would be added a dose of emotional blackmail: 'Shouldn't you be marrying a suitable girl without delay so that your grandfather, who is getting old, can bless the daughter-in-law of the family?' One day, as one of these dramatic interrogations was taking place, I blurted out: 'Kaminee. If I am going to marry anyone, it's going to be her.' A startled silence followed. I was probably the first one in the Mehra clan to openly declare my love for

A life of companionship, conversations and camaraderie with wife Kaminee

someone. Fortunately, after that first shock, my parents were quick to come around. Even more fortunately for me, Kaminee had refused all the proposals that had come her way. Shortly after, both families agreed to the marriage. We got married in 1972. Kaminee was 23 and I was 25. It would be no exaggeration to say I was overjoyed to be finally united with the woman I had loved for so many years. I now had someone to go home to every evening, and not just unsigned vouchers to be attended to or unfinished manuscripts to be reviewed.

The years that followed our marriage were hectic ones, as the business was growing rapidly. I spent a great deal of time at work and Kaminee was very understanding about this. Then, to my great delight, a few years into our marriage, she decided to learn everything she could about book distribution and publishing operations and became an integral part of the

Rupa management team. Authors respected her, our clients and distributors trusted her and debtors feared her. She was involved in the business for over 40 years and only stepped away a decade ago, when our grandson, Akshaj, was born.

Over the years, we never tried to change each other. There was just one thing Kaminee insisted on soon after our marriage. When I was single, I would routinely write in my diary at night before going to sleep. It was my way of expressing my feelings, recording my observations on the life around me, pondering life's uncertainties and opportunities. Two weeks into our marriage, Kaminee put all the diaries aside and said, 'You need not commit your thoughts to a diary anymore.'

I now had a partner to talk to, who would not only listen to me but also, unlike the inanimate pages of the diary, respond to things I wanted to talk about. In 2022, we completed 50 years of our married life—a life of companionship, conversations and camaraderie.

College Street with book kiosks and shops

• Chapter 7 •

STEPPING INTO PUBLISHING

The very first book that Rupa ever published, as stated earlier, was the Indian edition of Hermann Hesse's *Siddhartha*. D. Mehra did this at the urging of James Laughlin, the founder of New Directions Publishing, when he had visited Calcutta. After that initial foray into publishing, there wasn't any concerted effort to publish, and the focus continued to be on growing our business of representing publishers from around the world and selling their books.

However, D. Mehra never totally ruled out the idea of publishing books. The first sustained foray into publishing was for Bengali books. This was not surprising because, within the Mehra household in Calcutta, Bengali was the language we worshipped; English was the language of commerce—we conducted our business in that language; Hindi was our mother tongue—the language we fought, spoke and worshipped in. D. Mehra was keen that every member of our family should know the language of our *karmabhoomi,* Calcutta. A tutor was appointed who drilled Bangla (Bengali language) into us every evening, until we had mastered our 'o's—*'Nawmoshkaar', 'Onugraho', 'Ami ki bhabhey korbo?', 'Tumi ki korcho?', 'Dhonnobad!' 'Shundor!'* Every successive generation bettered its Bangla genes. D. Mehra could speak Bangla, my father could speak and understand a little, while I could read, write, speak and curse in Bangla!

D. Mehra's obsession with Bangla was not rooted in sentiment alone—there was also a sharp business mind at work. Calcutta was the only city in India that lived for books, the art of storytelling and literature—all in the Bengali

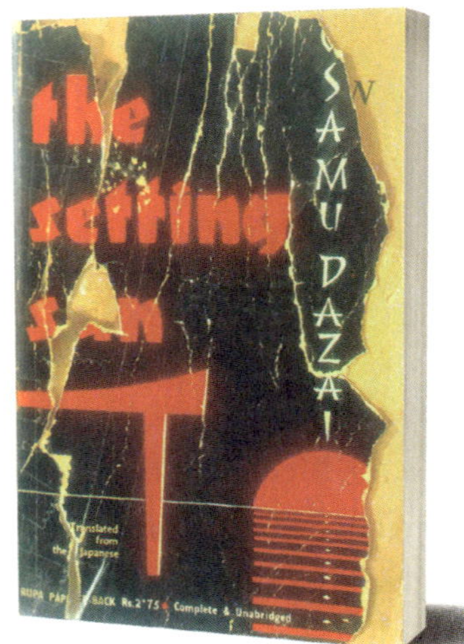

One of the first six paperbacks of Rupa 1960, The Setting Sun

language. The Bengali publishing ecosystem was dominated by storied publishing firms such as Ananda Publishers, Dey's Publishing and Mitra & Ghosh. But D. Mehra saw no reason why Rupa shouldn't get a piece of the publishing action. We started publishing original books in Bengali as well as Bengali translations of books written in other languages in the early 1960s. As he wasn't well versed with the language, my granduncle appointed two consulting editors, Chittaranjan Maiti and N.N. Sinha, along with seven other Bengali intellectuals and editors to take charge of Rupa's fledgling publishing programme. Called Rupa's Bengali Navratnas, these bhadralok editors would meet every evening at our Bankim Chandra Street office. A Bengali adda would begin. Proposals and manuscripts in Bengali would be read out aloud to D. Mehra, who would consult everyone and take a decision on whether to publish them. At the time, the government was keen to popularize Japanese culture in India to overcome the antipathy against Japan due to its role in the Second World War. They funded translations of Japanese books into English and various other languages. Consequently, we published our first translated Japanese title *The Setting Sun* (1947) written by the maverick, Left-leaning Osamu Dazai. The power of the novel was such that the phrase 'people of the setting sun' began to be applied in 'the land of the rising sun' to all the common people of Japan who were impoverished and affected by the Second World War.

After this, we started publishing some Japanese titles in Bangla, especially Japanese Nobel Prize winner Yasunari Kawabata's works, like *The Dancing Girl of Izu* (1927), *Snow Country* (1937), *The Lake* (1954), *The House of the Sleeping Beauties* (1961) and *The Old Capital* (1962) to name a few. They proved to be popular and so we began to branch out into other subject areas. A translation of *The Arabian Nights* into Bengali, in 24 volumes, was one of the most ambitious projects we undertook, and it was a hit. Soon, Thomas Mann, D.H. Lawrence, W. Somerset Maugham, William Makepeace Thackeray, Charles Dickens, Guy de Maupassant and O. Henry found Bangla readers.

Our first foray into books on contemporary subjects rose out of a day of deep sorrow. On 27 May 1964, India lost its first PM Jawaharlal Nehru. A pall of gloom descended on the Mehra household, as D. Mehra was a devout Nehruvian. This was such a personal tragedy for him that he couldn't eat for three days. Like the majority of his contemporaries, he couldn't comprehend a world without his beloved leader. Out of his grief, an idea emerged. He felt he should honour his hero. He asked his editor Chittaranjan Maiti to create a 32-page book of couplets (jointly written by him and Maiti) dedicated to Pandit Nehru. Within 10 days, the book titled *Amar Johar* went to press. D. Mehra himself designed the cover, a simple pink and blue affair with a red rose placed tangentially across the type. The book was priced at a rupee per copy but was distributed in packs of 20 copies. Despite the emotional reasons that had led to the publication of the book, D. Mehra's commercial instincts shone—a hundred thousand copies of *Amar Johar* were sold. He followed this successful template when Lal Bahadur Shastri died (on 11 January 1966), publishing *Mateer Manush Lal Bahadur*, which sold around 60,000 copies.

Pandit Nehru's death was a personal tragedy for the Mehra household

With these successes, Rupa began to establish itself as a publisher in Bengali. Books that made their mark included the memoir of Sarala Devi Chaudhurani, the feisty lady from the house of the Thakurs of Jorasanko, and Rabindranath Tagore's niece. *Jiboner Jhora Pata* or *The Scattered Leaves of My Life* was first serialized in the Bengali magazine *Desh*. But we felt that the life of Sarala Devi, the freedom fighter who spoke on issues of gender during the first half of the twentieth century, should be documented in book form. Sarala Devi led an extraordinary life. She fought the prejudices and biases of her time, especially those that were grounded in the patriarchal mindset of Indian society and emerged triumphant. She studied physics when it wasn't so common for girls to study science; she left the family home and went to Mysore (now Mysuru) to earn her livelihood, when she could have taken an easier path and led a life of luxury. She was born into a wealthy family and was married into an equally wealthy one. She started the first feminist organization in India called the Bharat Stree Mahamandal in Allahabad in 1910. The pages of her memoir narrate the steely resolve of a woman who was much ahead of her times. *Jiboner Jhora Pata* is still considered a classic in Bengali writing.

Jiboner Jhora Pata *is still considered a Bengali classic*

Another such success was based on the life of another remarkable woman, the American dancer, Isadora Duncan, known as the 'mother of modern dance'. Besides her prowess in dance, she was also an adventurer with a free spirit. She challenged the hidebound world of ballet dancing and created modern dance. A cultural icon during the early twentieth century, she died just as dramatically as she had lived. During a visit to the French city of Nice, she befriended a sports car driver and asked to be driven in his Bugatti sports car. Apparently, the last words she ever spoke were: '*Adieu, mes amis, je vais à la gloire* (Goodbye my friends, I go to glory)!' Moments later, her flowing scarf became entangled in one of the rear wheels of the car, breaking her neck instantly. A couple of months later, her unfinished autobiography, *My Life,* was published and created a huge stir in the United

States (US) and Europe. *My Life* became a bible for the bohemians of society in countries around the world. When we published a Bengali translation of her memoir called *Amaar Jiban,* Isadora Duncan became a household name in Calcutta, where she was affectionately known as *aye bidesi nortoki* or that foreign dancer.

From the 1960s to mid-1980s, we published more than 300 titles in Bangla, including the magisterial work of Suniti Kumar Chatterji, *The Origin and Development of the Bengali Language.* Considered a seminal work on the history of the Bengali language, the book was first published in 1926 by Calcutta University. We later bought the rights and published it in three volumes in 1985. It's a measure of the book's brilliance that, although it was written in the first half of the nineteenth century, it continues to be in print today. Our Bengali list also included the works of luminaries like Rabindranath Tagore, Swami Vivekananda and Ashapoorna Devi.

Unfortunately, our business in Calcutta suffered a downturn in the 1980s and we had to shut down our Bengali publishing wing. The company would begin publishing again—largely in English—and I will narrate that story later in the book.

A magisterial work on the history of Bengali language that we first published in 1985

No account of Rupa's early days as a publisher in Calcutta would be complete without a mention of the booksellers who kept us going. The city is powered by the Bengalis' passion for books and the bookshops of the city are cultural hubs in their own right. Before I moved to Delhi, much of my working life was spent hanging out in the city's bookshops and interacting with their legendary proprietors and managers. D. Mehra once assigned me the task of selling paperbacks to

Oxford Books and Stationers. He arranged the meeting with the store owner, and I was supposed to close the deal. I didn't disappoint him and that evening, following the traditional Indian way of celebrating victories, D. Mehra ordered sweets for the entire office. I experienced another such adrenaline rush when I walked up to a small, nondescript kiosk selling magazines in one of Calcutta's busy thoroughfares and said to the shopkeeper, '*Dada kemon aachen* (How are you brother)? Would you like to order some books?' And lo and behold, he placed an order for 1,200 copies of Joan Robinson's book *The Cultural Revolution in China*.

This book, written by a hardcore economist, sold like hot cakes back then

Experiences like these in Calcutta made me much more than a businessman and entrepreneur.

The passion for books that these Calcutta booksellers instilled in me ensured that I would never stray from the book industry. There were two bookshops, one opposite New Empire Cinema Hall and the other in front of Lighthouse Cinema, that were a sounding board for us. If they felt a book would sell, it was likely to do well. One of these was Modern Book Depot, manned by Deewan Chandra, and Mohan's Bookshop and Magazine, started by Mohan Tiwari. These men weren't great readers and didn't know a whole lot about the books they stocked but they instinctively knew which books would work, and they were usually right. Mohan Tiwari had migrated to Calcutta from Ballia in UP at a very young age, in search of a good city and a better life. He hawked newspapers and sold books on the roadside till he opened his bookshop, which soon became another literary hotspot of the city. Frequented by Satyajit Ray and other celebrities, like Soumitra Chatterjee and Aparna Sen, Mohan Tiwari's bookshop was testament

New Market in Calcutta had wonderful bookstores

to city's affinity to the written word. Sarat Book House, located behind Rupa's Calcutta office, was another great bookseller. Mritunjay Dey, the owner of the bookstore, took me on as a disciple and guided me at every step. I used to sit with him, learning the tricks of the trade—the literary scene in Calcutta, how to approach authors, how to sell and, most importantly, what to sell. Mr Dey knew his books, cover to cover.

In New Market, there were wonderful bookstores, such as Dey Book Store, Shukla Book Depot, etc., which were frequented by the city's rich and famous. Book lovers could not miss a modest but ideal bookshop called the Family Book Shop located just below the Asiatic Society, very close to the Oxford Books and Stationers. Set up by Ashok Barman and his family members Jagdeesh and Pramod, the shop was tastefully done, with unique and popular titles. Contrary to its name, the owners of the Family Book Shop, the Barman brothers, Ashok and Pramod, never had a family of their own and remained bachelors!

Contrary to the popular portrayed perception, Calcutta had a huge market for Hindi books too. The Marwaris who migrated from Rajasthan to set up their businesses in the enterprising state of British Bengal contributed in the dissemination of Hindi in Calcutta. They needed their language to assert their identity and to be on an equal cultural footing with their Bengali brethren. Hindi publishers and distributors stocked the latest Hindi titles, matching their English counterparts. Those were the days when bookshops were spaces for cultural expression of identity and existence. It pains me to see them gradually withering away.

I would be failing my duty as a publisher and as a former bhadralok of Calcutta if I do not mention its *boi mela*, the Calcutta Book Fair. In 1972, the National Book Trust of India, with the joint efforts of Federation of Publishers, and Booksellers Association and All India Hindi Publishers as well as educational publishers organized a book fair at the back of The Janpath Hotel in Delhi.

Visitors at the Calcutta Book Fair

My father N.D. Mehra took a delegation to Dr Jatin Chakravarty, the then PWD minister and patron of Calcutta Book Fair to get his approval. The minister took no time in getting convinced.

And thus was born New Delhi World Book Fair. Taking inspiration from Delhi publishers, the ever so enthusiastic book lovers of Calcutta followed suit. Soon, a group of publishers formed the Publishers & Booksellers Guild, Calcutta, and within a couple of years, in March 1976, organized a massive book fair at the Brigade Parade ground opposite Victoria Memorial. The group included Bimal Dhar (academic publishers), Debajyoti Dutta (Shishu Sahitya Samsad), Ashok Kumar Sircar (Anand Publishers), N.D. Mehra (Rupa), Janki Babu (Scientific Books Company), Neil O'Brien (Oxford), K.P. Churamani (Orient Longman), Dey Book Store and several other book traders and intellectuals. Bengalis' legendary craze for books can be gauged by the fact that there were almost 2,000 Bangla publishers in Bengal, some publishing just one book a year but able to sell a thousand copies of the same! The market was just ripe for this madness to be given a form and what better way than to have a congregation of traders and readers? Fortunately, Dr Ashok Mitra, the finance minister of West Bengal in Jyoti Basu's Cabinet was our author. When N.D. Mehra approached him for permission to host the book fair, it was just a matter of formality. The minister agreed to accept ₹1 as a token fee for the ground on which first event was to be organized. Dr Jatin Chakravarty, who never saw eye to eye with Dr Mitra, was the public works department (PWD) minister and his approval was also mandatory. But when it comes to books, Bengalis are willing to turn over a new leaf. He cleared the file even before the publishers' delegation could visit him formally. The first boi mela was thus organized on the ground opposite Academy of Fine Arts, next to Victoria Memorial with an entry fee of 50 paise. Dr Chakravarty remained a patron of the book fair while he was the PWD minister. With each year, the number of participating publishers kept increasing. In 1983, a milestone was achieved when the secretary general of International Publishers Association (IPA), Geneva, attended the inauguration ceremony and gave the Calcutta

Dr Ashok Mitra, the then finance minister of West Bengal, took a fee of one rupee for the ground where Calcutta's first book fair was held

A common sight at Rupa stall in Calcutta Book Fair

Book Fair its international accreditation. It is now Asia's largest book fair. In March 2022, during its forty-fifth edition, it recorded the highest sales since it was started in 1976—over ₹23 crore.

Former Union Minister Priya Ranjan Dasmunsi, who passed away in 2017, once complained to me that it was difficult for him to enter Rupa's stall at the book fair, as the queue was too long. Not all customer complaints make your day, but this one did.

The '70s and '80s of Calcutta were prone to agitation, labour unrest, demonstrations and protests, sometimes even without any real cause

• Chapter 8 •

TRAUMA OF THE 1980s

*In retrospect, it is now clear that the years following Independence in fact marked the death of colonial Calcutta—the city of managing agencies, jute mills and the export trade, of the colonial civil service and nationalist revolutionaries, of parvenu wealth and easy living, of genteel prose and lyrical poetry, of starvation deaths and communal riots. In its place, a new city was born, and the decade of the 1960s showed all the signs of painful adolescence.**

Political scientist Partha Chatterjee thus remembered Calcutta while describing the political culture of the city over the years. The painful adolescence of the '60s, which he wrote about, fused into a confused middle age of the city by the '80s, prone to agitation but without any real cause. Demonstrations and protests would happen more as a celebration of celebrating a collective past than to make any real change in the present. It was a city still hung up on trade unionism, bandhs, gheraos and lockouts. It was only a matter of time before our Calcutta office too was engulfed in such labour unrest.

Around the beginning of April 1980, as Delhi was warming up for summer, my phone rang. It was a call from D. Mehra. 'Can you come over to Calcutta? Sooner the better.' His words sounded more like an appeal than an order. Cancelling all my appointments, I reached Calcutta the very next day and immediately dashed off to our office, only to find a worried and vulnerable D. Mehra, looking like a pale shadow of his robust self. The usual warmth in the office was missing; something was simmering, and I needed to know what it was. The events leading

*Chatterjee, Partha, 'The Political Culture of Calcutta', *Calcutta: The Living City, Volume II, The Present and Future*, Sukanta Chaudhuri (ed.), Oxford University Press, Delhi, 1990, pp. 32–3.

up to that day were finally revealed to me. One day, D. Mehra had rung a bell in his office to call his peon. He had wanted a glass of water—nothing unusual about that. However, that day, his peon hadn't answered. He had rung again. Still no response. He had rung the third, fourth and fifth time, and still the peon hadn't turned up. Finally, the peon had arrived, his rebellion camouflaged as reluctance, and had refused to give him the glass of water. This had been unusual, something that D. Mehra had never witnessed before. He had reprimanded the peon for his callous behaviour and all hell had broken loose. A union leader had emerged out of nowhere, threatening D. Mehra of dire consequences. The founder of Rupa could not believe that this was happening in his office. At that time, our wages were higher than the industry standards, our increments were good, and our bonuses were timely and well received. Rupa worked as a family (it still does), we knew what was happening in each other's lives, cheered loudly after every tiny success and introspected together after every defeat—we received our bouquets and brickbats together, as a team. But now, it all seemed to be the distant past; a chasm of mistrust grew between management and the workers. Suspicion, misgivings, doubt and uncertainty surrounded our corridors. A new phenomenon, unknown in Rupa until then, crept in every crevice and corner of our office—indiscipline. Workers stopped marking their attendance in the register, lunch breaks extended for hours, not reporting to work became common, cashiers left cash counters unattended while customers waited endlessly for their bills to be raised. Our Calcutta office became a microcosm of everything that plagued the City of Joy at that time—degrading work culture and stagnancy.

Jyoti Sengupta, our long-time manager, stopped coming to office. A die-hard Marxist who lived a bachelor's life in a small room on Suryasen Street, he felt betrayed by the workers. If they had truly been dissatisfied with the management, they could have gone to their Jyoti babu knowing full well that he would have stood up for them. Instead, the long-time workers of Rupa had trusted trade unionists, and this hurt Jyoti Sengupta. Being loyal to the company and his ideology, he withdrew in his world, never to come back to Calcutta office again. My professional life had started at Rupa's Calcutta office; it was both my womb

The dharnas and demonstrations can never be conducive for any harmonious growth, neither of the employee nor the employer.

and my umbilical cord. I was close to the staff and knew everything that was happening in their lives—good or bad. But this time, there was silence. The staff didn't know what was happening or maybe they did not want to talk, which was even worse. Aloofness was breeding more resentment.

Calcutta was still Rupa's headquarters, and our business started getting affected. I had to frequently visit Calcutta while running the Delhi office. With each trip, the situation seemed to have deteriorated further. At one point, violent threats were issued against D. Mehra, me and our family, not by our rebel workers but by outside forces—the self-declared trade union leaders. Advised by family and well-wishers, D. Mehra stopped going to office. All of us were living in a constant fear of any unknown attack, a feeling inimical to any entrepreneurial zeal. My own transport to office was changed daily to evade any possible attackers. In office, I was accompanied by my childhood friends Subodh and twin brothers Swapan and Tapan. One of the twins was a professional boxer while the other worked with us. And then there was Kamal, a close family member, who stood by me like a shadow. Their presence made me feel safe and their presence made me anxious too.

Something needed to be done and fast. We had asked for police protection but a politically volatile city plagued with protests and processions kept the city police forever on their toes; expecting them to guard us all the time would mean testing our luck too far. However, R.N. Barman had a contact—Mr Handa, a deputy commissioner in Calcutta Police, who assured us that he would be assigning another cop, Anil Chatterjee, an assistant commissioner of police, for our protection. As luck would have it, Barman had a good rapport with Chatterjee, who was a much-respected figure in Calcutta Police and known for his unconventional ways, the taste of which we were soon going to get.

One day, Mr Chatterjee called us to his police station, the AC Watson Street thana. A modest office awaited us with our saviour sitting royally in his lowly wooden chair, conducting his durbar and daily affairs of crime and criminals. There was a lock-up on one side, with some pickpockets and small-time offenders being the State's guests. On the other side was a small room full of rifles, cartridges and lathis. Suddenly, some commotion broke out and more than a dozen ladies in various states of undress (depends on your tolerance meter!) were presented before Mr Chatterjee. Reeking of alcohol, these ladies were talkative, being loud, bantering and even flirting with the policemen. A recent raid against sex workers had brought them here and they were in no mood to give in to the law. Mr Barman and myself kept staring at this drama unfolding inside a police station—an odd sight for us but clearly a ritual at the thana. After depositing the leading ladies of the drama in the lock-up, Mr Chatterjee shouted further orders in staccato to his subordinates, 'Get your rifles and pistols, load them. Take out the jeep.' Pointing at us he said, 'Load these two gentlemen in the jeep too.' Mr Barman and I looked at each other, our eyes asking, 'What the hell is happening here?' In no time, we were sitting inside the old police jeep and speeding towards an unknown location, the indecipherable wireless messages on Mr Chatterjee's walkie-talkie making this journey more suspenseful.

Kumartuli or potter's quarter is an old area of Calcutta, located north of the city. In this celestial colony—where divinity is created—clay artists work their alchemy and produce Durga idols, along with the idols of other gods and goddesses. Narrow lanes diffuse into narrower bylanes, with 10-handed goddess emerging from clay in one corner while her lion and four children—Ganesh, Laxmi, Kartikeya and Saraswati—emerging from the other, each artist producing his own divinity. The demon Mahishasur, created to be killed, was also seen. The maverick Mr Chatterjee's jeep was soon seen intruding into this abode, which existed between the divine and the mundane. He spoke with some people, threatened some, whispered to one, laughed at another, and he knew where to find his man. The jeep turned towards Dom Para, the colony inhabited by the keepers of cremation ground. This trip was surely getting interesting. Soon, a huge man with a menacing look approached Mr Chatterjee, albeit charmingly.

Devi rising from the clay! One of the creations of Calcutta's famous Kumartuli.

Pleasantries were exchanged, the man looked at us, nodded and the meeting was over. 'If I may ask Mr Chatterjee, who was he and what did you say to him?' I asked, curiosity overpowering my patience. 'His name is Jeevan Babu. I have asked him to keep an eye on you. He will protect you,' Mr Chatterjee replied. Jeevan Babu, we discovered, was the lionheart of Dom Para who commanded respect and awe of the needy and the downtrodden. Living near the cremation ground, surrounded by death and breathing in ashen air did not deter his entrepreneurial spirit. Being the master craftsman that he was, he had started making Puja pandals from the unused wooden sticks from the cremation ground and went on to become a much-respected artisan, who took his art to the foreign shores of the US, England and France. His fame took him places, but his heart stayed among his people. The infamous Sonagachi, the red-light area of the city near Dom Para, had many destitute souls—children who had fallen on hard times, orphaned or displaced. Jeevan Babu looked after them, trained them and converted these luckless and unfortunate youngsters into skilled craftsmen who went on to earn their livelihoods making pandals. Be it the bamboo sticks or the hapless children, Jeevan Babu was a true godfather of all that was left unattended, unwanted, unloved. We later made use of his mastery to make Rupa stalls at the Calcutta Book Fair, which won us several awards and accolades.

While our personal safety was ensured, the company was suffering. All forms of mediation and reconciliation with a provoked bunch of few workers seemed to be failing. In an unfortunate turn of events, we were left with no option but to announce a lockout of our office. On 29 August 1980, the gates of our Calcutta office were closed for everyone. An hour after the lockout was announced, angry protesters were seen marching towards our house. Slogans were raised and death threats issued. The administration immediately imposed Section 144 in the area. We became captive in our

Dr Ashok Mitra, who was finance minister of West Bengal during our lockout

Balancing economic welfare and trade unionism has been communism's dilemma

own house.

After 44 years of smooth sailing, suddenly we were amidst choppy waters. The bustling office assumed a deathly silence. Books on the showroom shelves lost their lovers and became lonely. Manuscripts lay abandoned, ideas had no takers. Ominous stillness greeted us in the mornings, afternoons and evenings. Nights became more unforgiving, thinking about another vacant day.

It so happened that *The Statesman* carried the news of our lockout announcement on its front page as a box item. Then Finance Minister Ashok Mitra, a Marxist managing the State's money, called up D. Mehra. Perturbed and sad by the turn of events, he asked D. Mehra to visit him immediately. Mitra wondered why a cultural and fair institution like Rupa had to resort to a lockout! We told him that we had approached the labour commissioner's office several times but to no avail—classic bureaucratic one-upmanship. Since the Finance Minister was himself taking interest, we soon received a call from the labour commissioner's office to visit us, sit with the disgruntled party and work out a solution. What

C.K. Mehra, on behalf of the company, signed the agreement with the then labour commissioner

happened next was straight out of a Bollywood potboiler.

The self-assumed and self-declared leader of our workers started dodging these reconciliatory meetings. I had to travel from Delhi for the appointed hour and every time his absenteeism awaited us at the deputy labour commissioner's office, his delaying tactics making the matter worse. One fine day, he arrived in all his hubris. We all sat before the deputy labour commissioner and I asked him if I could have a glass of water. 'Of course, Rajen babu, why not,' and he immediately asked his peon to get me water. I then politely asked the commissioner that I didn't need water but only wanted to know what if his peon had refused him water! Silence pervaded in the room; nodding heads acquiescing with my argument. I had conveyed my point without raising my voice. Our conversation was heading towards a solution when the lord of the workers tried to derail the talks. I was in my early thirties back then—a young man getting angrier by the minute. In what could have been a scene in one of Amitabh Bachchan's many angry-young-man movies, I grabbed the leader by his collar, pulled him towards the window and, almost as a natural next step, threatened to throw him out. Pandemonium ensued. The labour commissioner and other workers ran towards me, trying to dislodge him from me, pleading with me, shouting at him. Once the gladiator inside me returned to my publisher's avatar, it was time for the judgement. The leader washed his hands off the workers and vanished; the workers realized they were being misled into a mutiny of someone else's making and returned to the fold; the labour commissioner was more than relieved to see our backs and gulped that glass of water. I started to plan my journey back to Delhi.

However, before leaving the city, one more ritual had to be done—that of homecoming. I took all the rebel workers to meet D. Mehra at our home. Touching his feet, workers had tears in their eyes while D. Mehra had forgiveness in his heart. Promises were made of never breaking each other's trust. Smiles were back on the angry and sulking faces.

I left for Delhi only to be greeted with a surprise a month later, albeit a happy one. Some members of the Calcutta staff came to our Delhi office, with garlands and gratitude; they wanted to thank me for what had been done. With the lifting of the lockout, the Calcutta business had been restored and the office went back to its old avatar, with one absence.

D. Mehra was a man of different generation. The incident left him scarred for life, and he never returned to the Rupa office again. He surely missed his literary adda but his broken trust could not be regained.

Within days of a book becoming a bestseller, the pirates would print a cheap edition and sell it for half the price or even less in the grey market

• Chapter 9 •

THE WAR AGAINST PIRACY

Rupa gradually began to develop its English language publishing programme, and over a period of a few decades, the company moved from being primarily an importer and distributor of books published by overseas publishers and a publisher of Bengali books to a publisher of English language titles as well as some Hindi books.

One of our first big successes was publishing the autobiography of the legendary Indian cricketer, Sunil Gavaskar. *Sunny Days* was first published in 1976 and we signed off on its latest reprint in 2023! It has been over 40 years since it was first published and the book has never gone out of print. Publishing the most promising cricketer of his generation while he was still at his peak was nothing short of a coup. I was really thrilled that I'd been able to make my presence felt in Delhi. At the Rupa headquarters in Calcutta, D. Mehra was watching this with silent appreciation, a typical Mehra trait.

The success of *Sunny Days* and some other bestsellers alerted us of a problem that was bedevilling the publishing industry—book piracy! It was not a new phenomena, but it was a scourge of the book trade, and I soon found myself at war with the pirates. I started combating the menace in 1972–73 when Sir William Collins, head of Collins, was on his annual trip to India along with Lady Collins, his wife. When they arrived in Delhi, I took them around the city's bookshops. Sir William was almost 6 feet 7 inches, and I almost sprained my neck as I craned it to talk to him. Passing by the United Coffee House in Connaught Place, we were amazed to see a pile of pirated books stacked on the pavement. Unauthorized, shoddily produced editions of Agatha Christie,

Alistair MacLean and Robert Ludlum and many more well-known authors were being blatantly sold by these street vendors. Sir William was appalled at the scale and in-your-face actions of the criminals who were supplying the hawkers. In Calcutta, I had never seen anything like this.

After seeing how pirates operated with impunity in Delhi, I set out to investigate their modus operandi. We hired a detective agency run by one Wing Commander (Rtd) Hingorani to help us unlock the dirty maze of these looters of words. Within days of a book becoming a bestseller, the pirates would print a cheap edition and sell it for half the price or even less in the grey market. The booksellers of Delhi were very conscious of this hazard; all good bookstores were members of the Delhi State Booksellers & Publishers Association and would not indulge in such malpractices. However, the street hawkers had their own network and by the mid-1970s, the book pirates had figured out viable distribution and sales outlets—fly-by-night 'booksellers' and street vendors on Janpath and Parliament Street in New Delhi and the Fort area in Bombay stocked and sold pirated books.

I was keen to figure out how to end the menace of book piracy and spoke with Zamir Ansari, the representative of Penguin in India. Not too many books published by Penguin were being pirated in India at the time but Zamir gave me some valuable insights into both piracy and yet another problem that book importers and publishers in the country had to contend with—copyright infringement, wherein unscrupulous distributors would import editions that violated or infringed the copyright of the publisher or importer who legally owned the rights to publish or sell the books in question in India.

A very prominent bookseller pointed out to me that the American editions of various titles were being widely distributed in India, even though the British publishers owned the

(From left) With Mike Hogben, then export director of Penguin, UK, Zamir Ansari and Molly Kaye, the author of The Far Pavilions. *Both Mike and Zamir were instrumental in our fight against piracy.*

exclusive rights to publish and sell these books in India and other Commonwealth countries. Penguin decided to file a lawsuit against the distributors who were infringing their copyright. The case dragged on for a while and was eventually settled out of court.

On my part, I began discussing with Sir William how we might control piracy. Back then, due to licensing restrictions, more than a thousand copies of a book could not be imported from the UK. As a workaround, we decided to publish key titles in the Indian market by licensing their rights simultaneously with their publication in the UK. This ensured that the book pirates had little or no time to produce a facsimile because we could flood the market with a substantial number of copies. I was given a free hand to acquire rights and publish Indian editions. The royalty on these Indian editions was set at a maximum of 10 per cent of the MRP. In those days, one had to have the Reserve Bank of India's prior approval for the remittance of royalties in foreign exchange. Our head office in Calcutta was able to organize this and I was all set to begin a new chapter in my life as a publisher. Reprinting these imported titles would both neutralize the pirates as well as increase the sales of the books that we had been hitherto importing.

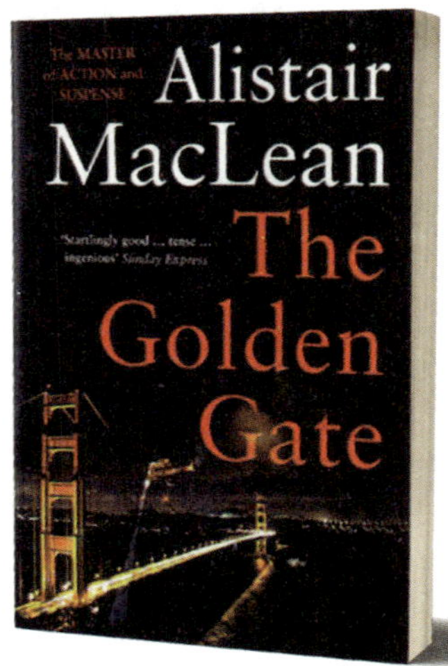

Soon, the plan Sir William and I had agreed on started showing results. One of our biggest successes was a book by Alistair MacLean, *The Golden Gate*. We decided to publish the book as a low-priced paperback original in India simultaneously with its publication as a hardback in the UK. I spoke to Rekha Printers and ordered a first print of 20,000 copies, an unheard-of print run in the early 1976. The price was fixed at ₹8 per copy, which the pirates would find difficult to undercut. The book was released on the same day all over India, without advance notice. Every aspect of its publication was conducted in complete secrecy, even Rupa's branch managers were not aware of its imminent arrival. The day after it was released, newspapers around the country carried advertisements announcing the novel's availability.

The book sold 10,000 copies on the very first day, which was a huge number. It sold over 50,000 copies in one month. This came as a huge surprise to Collins, who now began to gain a real understanding of the potential of the Indian market if the right strategy was followed to thwart the pirates and produce competitively priced editions.

A year and a half later, Rupa published another novel *Seawitch* by Alistair MacLean, and the same plan was executed, albeit with a twist. I cut down the size of the original book. I did this to fox the pirates. I knew the technology they used was primitive and inflexible—they would not be able to print the book if its dimensions were changed. This strategy worked to a large extent but as there were some pirated copies available, I started making surprise visits to bookshops to check their stock and ensure nobody stocked the pirated editions.

By making all these moves, I thought I had checkmated the pirates, but there were still some surprises in store. One day, I was in a bookshop in Delhi, checking on the stock of a recent Rupa publication. While browsing through the bookshelves, I overheard some people in the store discussing how they had produced a pirated edition. I began looking more closely at the copies of the book in the store and when I realized that there were pirated editions in stock, I bought around five copies and asked for a cash memo stamped by the bookstore. Realizing what was going on, the owner got very nervous and began making excuses for the presence of the counterfeit editions in his store. Even as he was doing this, one of the salesmen pulled down the shutters of the store. For a moment, I grew really alarmed—was I about to be assaulted by goondas whom I would have to fight off in Hindi movie style? Fortunately, this was not a Bollywood film set and there were no fisticuffs, real or imagined. The owner continued to apologize to me, but I figured that I would now need to take the matter to a higher authority to see if that would help.

Accordingly, the next day, I met then Additional Commissioner of Delhi Police P.S. Bawa and narrated the whole incident to him. His answer was straight and simple: piracy was not a cognizable offence under the Indian Penal Code (IPC). Rupa would need to approach the courts for any action to be taken. A couple of days later, I met a lawyer, Gurdial Singh, who specialized in copyright law

With P.S. Bawa, the then additional commissioner of Police in Delhi, who guided us in our fight against piracy, which at that time was not a cognizable offence under the IPC

and moved a petition in Tis Hazari Court for police raids to be conducted in Delhi to confiscate pirated books without specifying the shops. The Hon'ble Magistrate was very reluctant at the beginning, but the lawyer was able to make him understand that the complainant really needed the help of the court. It was clear to me that if the court ordered the Delhi Police to conduct raids and confiscate pirated books, word would spread quickly and the pirates would get a chance to avoid being caught. I therefore wanted the court to send an advance copy of the order to the police before it was formally declared. The court was not in agreement with this but they agreed to send a court messenger with me to the headquarters of the Delhi Police to pass on the message. When we got to police headquarters, I apprised Bawa of the court's decision. He, in turn, alerted Deputy Commissioner R.S. Sahay who asked his investigating officer, one Mr Dua (sadly all three are no more) to carry out the raids at the earliest.

There was a moment of humour during the discussion with the investigating officer. He thought we would be looking for illegal stashes of the adhesive Fevicol, as the lawyer fighting our case had previously represented the company that made Fevicol in a high-profile court action.

Once all the confusion was cleared up, preparations were made for the search and seizure of pirated books. Book pirates and bookshop owners who connived with them were in for a big surprise when the next day a massive search and raid was conducted in six to seven different places in Connaught Place and Janpath. A huge number of books were confiscated. Booksellers dealing in pirated editions were challaned ₹500. They got off lightly because there was no law under which they could be prosecuted. Besides this, I felt it was important for readers to become aware of the scourge of piracy. Accordingly, I made my way to newspaper offices on Bahadur Shah Zafar Marg and informed them about the raids that had taken place. When they published reports on these, not only was the general public informed about the counterfeit editions that were robbing writers and publishers of their due but they also led to raids in other places in the country. This resulted in the pirates and their accomplices incurring huge losses.

C.M. Chawla, the then president of Federation of Publishers and Distributors, speaking at the federation meeting

N.K. Anand (extreme right) of Anand & Anand Associates with Congress leader Inderjeet and Natwar Singh. While Anand provided his legal services, the two politicians stood behind the publisher's cause.

But I did not stop there. I sought the help of the Delhi State Booksellers & Publishers Association, of which C.M. Chawla was the president. A committee was formed to protect copyright and fight piracy. I persuaded C.M. Chawla to appoint Ravi Dayal of the Oxford University Press as the chairman of the committee. Other prominent representatives from the book trade, including Zamir Ansari, became members of the committee. Soon, a petition signed by authors and publishers was sent to PM Indira Gandhi to amend the copyright law to make piracy a cognizable offence. We sought the help of N.K. Anand and Praveen Anand's law firm, Anand & Anand Associates, to advise us on the intricacies of the law, and they obliged by rendering their service pro-bono. The media was flooded with various articles and stories on book piracy.

Srikant Verma, a prominent Member of Parliament (MP) (Rajya Sabha) frequently visited the Rupa showroom. I knew he was close to the PM and enlisted his support. I hoped he would be able to persuade the PM to expedite the anti-piracy legislation. A seminar was conducted on the problem at the India International Centre (IIC). Participants at the seminar included representatives of the Government of India, members of the book trade, authors and law enforcement agencies. The seminar was chaired by Khushwant Singh.
It soon became evident that public opinion was in favour of strong legislation and law enforcement to convey the message against piracy. We were told that Law Ministry, Education Ministry and Prime Minister's Office (PMO) were working together to come up with a strong, effective law to protect copyright and contain the scourge of piracy. On the last day of the monsoon session of parliament in 1984, Indira Gandhi's government placed the Copyright Amendment Bill before the house. It was passed without any objections. In fact, the leader of opposition Atal Bihari Vajpayee famously said to the PM, 'How can I oppose such a law?'

Om Mago of Om Book Shop, a down-to-earth man whom many would listen to

After the law was passed by Parliament, it was worrying that the president's office took its time over approving it—only after such presidential assent could the amended law be enforced. This delay led to worrying and unsettling days for us publishers. We had to run from pillar to post and witness the high handedness of the corridors of power to see the bill become a law. Eventually, presidential approval was obtained and the country had an effective piece of legislation with which piracy could be combatted.

However, the battle is far from over, and pirated editions continue to be available for sale to this day in India. My strategy to deal with the problem entails the following: a) ensure all titles are produced at competitive prices and are made widely available; b) titles should always be in stock, especially fast-moving ones, and c) readers need to be educated, so they don't buy pirated editions, and publishers need to be quick to alert the police about the existence of pirated copies, so they can be confiscated.

Pradeep Mago, nephew of Om Mago, pushed our anti-piracy agenda creating fear amongst the book pirates

Today, when I look back, I see our struggle to fight piracy and remember so many interesting people I met during our ordeal. One such remarkable personality was Om Mago of Om Book Shop. He had a unique, albeit intimidating way, of collecting his dues from the booksellers. Every evening, he used to go to every kiosk and seller to collect his money with his dog on a leash. If the seller refused or had some excuse, he would unleash his canine friend! But behind this rather unusual way of collecting money was a kind-hearted human being who, on so many occasions, took personal guarantee for pirates caught by us or by police. He made several book pirates turn into legal booksellers. Hats off to Mago Sahib!

By the time Rupa completed 50 years, it had made its mark throughout India

• Chapter 10 •

FIFTY YEARS OF RUPA

From 1936 to1960, Rupa depended on imports from Britain. The sun may have set on the British Empire, but their shadow loomed large over various dimensions of an Indian's life, and our business was no exception. However, in 1960, Rupa's identity was majorly transformed. D. Mehra met James Laughlin, the founder of New Directions Publishing, in New York. With Laughlin, came Buddha. Rupa's first published book was *Siddhartha* by Hermann Hesse. This was followed by six paperback titles with rock-bottom prices, which the price-sensitive Indian market welcomed with open arms. As he plunged into it, D. Mehra realized that there was a readymade market for local Bengali language publishing. A team of Bengali literati and intellectuals was formed and, thus, two Bengali classics—*Kadamabini* and *Bageshwari Shilpa Prabandhabali*—were published. Our Bengali publishing wing took off and by the time D. Mehra wrapped it up in the mid-1980s, Rupa had published more than 400 Bengali titles. By '80s, Rupa's publishing had become more Delhi-centric for originals and reprint titles in English.

In 1983, Kaminee and I also went to *vilayet* for the first time! Yes sir, we were off to England to meet our principal partners in Her Majesty's land. Rubbing shoulders with the legendary editor Sonny Mehta, the brown man who dominated an all-white publishing ecosystem, proved that our work at Rupa was on the right track; it was truly humbling. Meeting Salman Rushdie, Eric Newby and many other publishing and literary figures was an overwhelming experience. By the time Rupa turned gold in 1986, we had more than 400 titles under our belt—reprints, Bengali translations and original editions. What had started from a single room in 1936 had expanded into four direct offices by 1986—Calcutta, Allahabad, Bombay and Delhi—and six sales offices in Kathmandu, Jaipur, Chandigarh, Hyderabad, Bangalore and Madras, which later became our direct offices. By the time we celebrated our fiftieth anniversary, Rupa had established its footprint across India—in bookstores and on our readers' bookshelves.

The years following our landmark anniversary were a turbulent time for India. Prime ministers came and went in quick succession—Rajiv Gandhi, V.P. Singh, and Chandra Shekhar. This period also saw the tragic assassination of Rajiv Gandhi and the demolition of the Babri Masjid during the prime ministership of P.V. Narasimha Rao. A foreign exchange crisis also loomed. The turbulence finally began to subside in the mid-1990s.

Mirroring the uncertainty in the country, two events within Rupa changed the direction of the company's progress. The first, our association with Penguin came to an end, and the second, we embarked on a joint publishing venture with HarperCollins (both these developments are talked about in greater detail in succeeding chapters). During the '90s, there was a major restructuring of the company's priorities. During our first 50 years, we had been focussing on importing books from international publishers and reprinting select titles for the Indian market. Now, after the departure of Penguin, although we found new customers to keep the distribution business thriving, we felt we should ramp up our publishing wing—therein lay the company's future prosperity.

My mentor, Nirupam Chatterjee—a well-known name in Calcutta who taught at Presidency College and was senior editor at Oxford as well as Macmillan—and a young editor Rashmee Roshan Lall began to aggressively look for new authors. Our publishing strategy focussed on finding new authors, keeping costs under control, ensuring our books were competitively priced and well marketed. To kick off this initiative, a small 5 × 1 centimetre advertisement was placed in three English-language newspapers based out of Delhi, inviting manuscript submissions from first-time authors below the age of 40. Within

Nirupam Chatterjee (left) and Rashmee Roshan Lall (right) seen here with a foreign visitor. Both Nirupam da and Rashmee were instrumental in finding new authors for Rupa.

15 days, a pile of manuscripts arrived at our office. To evaluate this material, a team was set up. The first cut was done by two young editors. Once they had filtered out manuscripts they felt were unsuitable, Rashmee and Nirupam assessed the submissions that had landed on the longlist, so they could present me with a shortlist of manuscripts they felt Rupa should be publishing.

Finally, I was presented with a single manuscript encased in a green folder, wrapped in red ribbons. The manuscript was favourably reviewed by two people, including Nirupam who strongly recommended that we publish it. I did not open the folder for two weeks for a quirky reason—I didn't like the green and red colour combination. When Nirupam eventually asked me about the fate of that 'manuscript which came in a green folder with red ribbons', I had no option but to read it. I read it in one sitting and agreed with Nirupam and Rashmee that it was worth publishing. I then surprised them by saying we would price it very low—₹40. In the event, the strategy worked and *The Inscrutable Americans* by

Before Five Point Someone, *there was* The Inscrutable American! *The author is being felicitated here by Gulzar years after the book became a bestseller.*

Tabish Khair (middle), the new face in the emerging Rupa list, is seen here with Dileep Padgaonkar who released his book

Anurag Mathur became a bestseller, selling around 50,000 copies. It also marked Rupa's entry into the commercial space that would soon start seeing the emergence of authors like Chetan Bhagat. In a few years, Rupa's homegrown authors, like Ashok Banker, Upamanyu Chatterjee, Aniruddha Bahal, Tabish Khair, Makarand Paranjape, Sudeep Sen and Ranjit Hoskote, would share valuable shelf space with the likes of global bestselling authors of the time like Jackie Collins and Sidney Sheldon. Our books were widely reviewed and our marketing and distribution strategy was working. We were even able to make a success of poetry books that are notoriously difficult to market and sell. Poets like Tara Patel, Nissim Ezekiel and Keki N. Daruwalla published with us, and complimented Rupa's publishing programme.

The '90s saw the emergence of talented new authors. Aniruddha Bahal was one of them.

Apart from introducing new novelists and poets, we also diversified into various subjects such as self-help, women's health, fashion, cooking, city walks, and built a list that was holistic and catered to different segments of readers. The success of many of our books led to us being dubbed as 'The House of Bestsellers'. Rashmee even came up with a slick slogan for Rupa, 'Reach, Range and Reading Pleasure'.

Rupa wasn't the only company to have succeeded in local publishing in the 1980s. Penguin set up a local publishing venture, Penguin Books India, in 1985 in collaboration with Anandabazar Patrika (ABP). Peter Mayer was its CEO, Aveek Sarkar was the managing director , David Davidar was head of publishing and Zamir Ansari was in charge of sales and marketing, and Khushwant Singh was their consulting editor. Penguin India launched its first list in 1987 and went from strength to strength in the years to come.

The book that shook the Royal household

As mentioned before, Rupa soon made a name for itself as a publisher of bestselling authors, both Indian and foreign. Our international authors included the likes of Sidney Sheldon, Agatha Christie, P.G. Wodehouse, Alistair MacLean, Jackie Collins and Robert Ludlum. Besides bestselling commercial authors, I was keen to add literary and non-fiction authors to the Rupa list. So, I negotiated with publishers like Faber & Faber for Milan Kundera, Merlin Press for George Lucas and Allen & Unwin for Bertrand Russell to balance our commercial offerings with serious literature. As Rupa continued to forge ahead with its English language publishing programme, international publishers and authors began to pay attention to what we were doing. Authors like H.R.F. Keating, Eric Newby, Winston Graham, Philip Ziegler became regulars at my small apartment, where we would spend quality time discussing new titles and how and where to promote them. All this would happen over home-made Indian dinner. Soon, several international authors started requesting their originating publishers to license India rights to Rupa for the Indian market. One such author was Andrew Morton, whose wonderful book on Lady Diana sold more than 50,000 copies in six weeks.

One of the things that helped us in the early years of our local publishing venture was the devaluation of the Indian rupee. Imported books became very expensive and book buyers turned to our books. We were also able to use this development to persuade foreign publishers to license key titles to us so we could reprint

The many moods of Nirupam da, my editor, my mentor

(PERSONAL)

45D/7 Moore Avenue
Kolkata 700040
22 April '07
Phone: 2471 8127

Dear Rajen,

'Shubho Nababarsho'

I have taken a very long time to write to you. I don't know how to thank you sufficiently for all the condolence messages and your heart-felt letters. To be able to share one's personal loss and grief is indeed consoling. Death was all very sudden and quite unexpected. For us, at the beginning, there was a terrible sense of void and we could hardly enter the room where my husband stayed. Now, after three months, it seems that he is still around. Although physically absent, his mental presence is felt all the time. I write all this to you as a family member, for you will understand.

Since my husband did not believe in religious rituals, we held a small memorial meeting in his honour at which eminent scholars like Ashok Mitra, Amiya Deb, Sukanto Chaudhuri, among others, related their reminiscences of him. Someone even mentioned how little Bittoo used to enjoy playing with him. There were also short write-ups on him in two Bengali dailies: 'Ananda Bazar Patrika' and 'Ajkal'.

I am sending you three of his photographs which you might like to keep. They were taken by our son, Sambuddha, at our Model Town residence, and they are his last pictures.

I have been happy to find Kapish G. Mehra figuring as a successful publisher in 'Rupa Book News'.

With affection and best wishes for you, Kamini and Bittoobaba,

Yours sincerely,
Ruby Chatterji

Ruby Chatterji, Nirupam da's wife, sent me this letter along with his photo three months after he passed away. I still keep his photo and this letter in my briefcase.

them locally at competitive prices. But the rapidly changing economic scenario in India was challenging as well. In order to meet the guidelines set down by the World Trade Organization, the Indian market was opened up to foreign publishers. Now, they could set up joint ventures to publish in India, facilitating them to import their books from abroad and publish in India. We were able to obtain fewer and fewer licences to import overseas titles and that was one of the reasons we decided on a joint venture with HarperCollins. One of the things that I have been concerned about for the longest time is how little the Indian government has done to protect the interests of local publishers, unlike countries like France. Neither are we subsidized in any way nor are we supported in our attempt to compete with large multinational companies who have access to virtually unlimited resources from their parent organizations. If Indian publishing companies are to become self-reliant and thrive, the government needs to come up with constructive proposals to assist them. Contemporary bureaucrats and politicians should commit to this national cause. The government of the day, through our embassies and high commissions abroad, should promote Indian books that reflect and showcase our country's culture, thereby supporting national publishing and putting it on the global map.

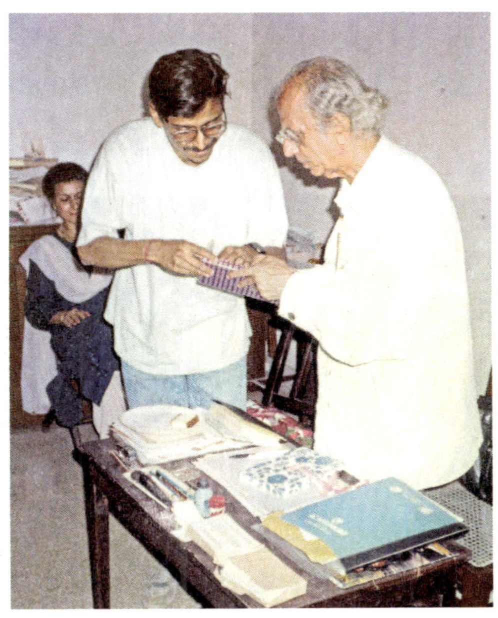

The young Makarand Paranjape's book was released by Nissim Ezekiel, a well-known poet.

RUPA EVENTS

Where books blossom and authors shine!

K.P. Sarthi, our assistant branch manager, Bombay, with Dr Karan Singh at the New Delhi World Book Fair, 1976

A young Rita Barman, daughter of R.N. Barman with Indira Gandhi

Saiyid Nurul Hasan, the Education Minister (1972–77) at the Rupa stall with N.D. Mehra

Mini Kapur, our distributor, showcasing our book to a possible customer in 1968, Delhi

Presenting a copy of Indira Gandhi's biography to Dev Kant Barooah (1975)

Rupa's Calcutta stall

R. Venkataraman signing his autobiography at the Rupa stall during World Book Fair

Veerappa Moily presenting his Shree Ramayana Mahanveshanam *to the then PM Dr Manmohan Singh*

Sitakant Mahaptra, well known Oriya poet and literary critic with R.N. Barman

Amitabh Bachchan has been kind enough to grace several Rupa book launches. Seen here with Richard M. Rothman, Trade Commissioner and Commercial Consul of the US, at the launch of Intelligent Endings.

T.N. Chaturvedi releasing Vikram Sampath's Splendours of Royal Mysore

(From left) Bijoylaxmi Hota, Amitabh Kant, P.A. Sangama and Sir Mark Tully at the release of Yoga to Preserve Youth and Beauty

S.K. Mehra being felicitated at our Bombay office in 1991

Sunil Gavaskar releasing Gautam Bhimani's Reverse Sweep

Ved Marwah, former governor of Manipur, at the launch of his book, India in Turmoil

Chetan Bhagat, Shashi Tharoor, Pritish Nandy, Aishwarya Rai Bachchan and Anupam Kher at the launch of Again *authored by Pritish Nandy*

I presented Rupa's Charitavali *to Air Chief Marshal Arjan Singh and George Fernandes the then Defence Minister looks intrigued*

And he was pleased when I presented it to him as well...

(From left) General Sundararajan Padmanabhan who served as seventeenth Chief of Army Staff of the Indian Army with Major General O.P. Sabharwal, one of the heroes of 1971 war

On the left is Rashmee Roshan Lall with my niece Akansha and Rashmee's husband in between

GOING GLOBAL

Rupa's stall at London Book Fair

At the Frankfurt Fair, Kapish and A.K. Singh carrying carton of books for display and selling

A.K. Singh, Kapish and Raju Barman at Frankfurt Book Fair

Sir Allen Lane started Penguin as a low-cost reprint publisher and changed the face of publishing forever. Seen here with a Penguin book and a Penguin!

• Chapter 11 •

THE FLIGHTLESS BIRD THAT FLEW AWAY

One of the long-lasting business relationships Rupa had was our association with Penguin Books. Sir Allen Lane had started Penguin in 1935 after quitting his uncle's company Bodley Head. The idea behind Penguin was to make books available at a cheaper cost and, thus, Penguin paperbacks were born. K. Jackson Marshall, who had sold Collins books to D. Mehra, became an agent for Penguin as well and, thus, Rupa became a natural partner for Penguin in India. Penguin titles would be prominently displayed in the showroom of the Calcutta office. At any given time, approximately 500 titles would be showcased. When I was starting out, as I have mentioned earlier, my granduncle, D. Mehra, was very particular that as a greenhorn, I should read and prepare a synopsis of the contents of all the Penguin books that arrived in the office, along with a brief description of the authors. This was a mammoth task, and sometimes it could prove boring if the book wasn't to my taste, but I kept at it—among other reasons, it was a way of impressing the boss.

Rupa had a standing order of 25 copies of fiction and 12 of non-fiction Pelican books with Penguin, UK. Soon enough, I was given the responsibility of selling some of the Penguin titles we had in stock. I well remember my first big sale. I'd been told to go to Oxford Books and Stationers on Park Street and get an order for a paperback edition of Penguin's English Dictionary (American Edition). The Calcutta head of the Oxford, Gulab Primlani, was a meticulous man who liked to be briefed properly on the books being offered to him while his brother Mohan Primlani was the publisher of IBH books and magazines, and only a glass wall separated the office of the seller and publisher. Mr Primlani was a stickler for punctuality. His sales manager, S.G. Motwani, was a living legend.

Oxford Books and Stationers on Park Street, Calcutta

He had a sharp mind and subtle sense of humour. That day, my appointment was scheduled for 4.00 p.m. I got to Oxford showroom much earlier and waited expectantly to be summoned by Messrs Primlani and Motwani. Just a few minutes before the meeting was scheduled to begin, I was told that the office was upstairs and I was waiting at the wrong entrance. I ran around the building to the right entrance and made it to the meeting just in time, panting and perspiring in the humid Calcutta heat. I quickly made myself presentable and began to rehearse my sales pitch. When I was shown in to the presence of Messrs Primlani and Motwani, I was reminded of an old Bengali proverb that went *Daangay bagh, joley kumir*—to be caught between a tiger on the shore and a crocodile in the water wasn't the most comfortable place to find oneself in. I was incredibly nervous as might have been expected, but Mr Primlani possessed an old world charm and he was quick to put me at ease. He offered me a chair and asked, 'What can I do for you, young man?' I pulled out a copy of the paperback dictionary I was carrying and pushed it towards him.

He looked at it and said, 'Sorry. We don't keep paperbacks at all.'

'But there can always be a first time, Sir', I replied, taking my chances.
He was now browsing through the book. As I was about to get up and leave,

he said, 'Okay. I will make an exception. Give us 100 copies.' He wanted them in two lots of 50 each. To say that I was thrilled would be to do injustice to what I was feeling. I wanted to jump for joy and shout myself hoarse and hug the old man. I did nothing of that sort, of course, and continued to maintain a calm and rather an earnest expression on my face. Just then, Mr Primlani noticed another book I had brought along, *The Cultural Revolution in China* by Joan Robinson.

'Let me have a look. Give me a dozen copies of that too,' he said.

When I eventually left their office, I was walking on air. My route back to the office went past a row of cinema halls—Tiger, Light House, Globe, New Empire and Metro. Outside these halls, there were well-turned-out, heavily made-up women who were called 'naughty aunties'. For a price, they would accompany you to a matinee show. I was on such a great high that I smiled benevolently at all of them and they smiled back. All was well with the world!

Soon after this episode, my granduncle called me into his office one day and introduced me to two Englishmen—Christopher Dolley, the managing director of Penguin UK, and David Rogers, the then sales director of the company. Chris was dressed in all white, while David was wearing a suit and sweating profusely in the humid weather. The meeting went well, and that evening, we met again in Mocambo restaurant, where I was invited to London to spend some time for training with Penguin. It was a great opportunity, but, to everyone's surprise, I turned the offer down. My reasoning was simple: I was going to learn my trade in the dust and noise of Indian bazaars. If I was going to make a successful career and contribute to the growth of the company, I would have to train here, not in London. My granduncle did not say anything then, but I took his silence to mean that he approved and later he did commend my decision. It's something I look back on with pride.

Organizing Penguin events. Seen here with Mike Hogben, the then export director of Penguin and M.M. Kaye, the author of Shadow of the Moon *and* The Far Pavilions.

Throughout the violent political turmoil of the 1960s in Calcutta, I continued to learn about books in the Calcutta office. Penguin formed a very large part of the learning curve. I read and sold fiction books by the likes of W. Somerset Maugham, Albert Camus, P.G. Wodehouse, Alberto Moravia, etc., as well as non-fiction by some of the world's greatest writers and thinkers, including John Galbraith, Gunnar Myrdal, Percival Spear, Romila Thapar, K.M. Sen, and many more. Some of the great books of the time that made their mark included landmark biographies of leaders like Hitler, Stalin and Mao. Pandit Nehru's books were in a league of their own. Classic authors, such as Jane Austen, D.H. Lawrence and William Shakespeare, were a mainstay of the Penguin list, and I sold them all. Book lovers, including high profile members of the Calcutta intelligentsia, like Suniti Kumar Chatterjee, Triguna Sen, Desmond Doig and Rev. Fr. Jurius would throng the Rupa store and I would enthusiastically show them the latest arrivals, many of which were published by Penguin.

Rupa's Pataudi House office in Delhi. Penguin paperbacks flew off these shelves.

A young David Davidar at the inauguration of Rupa's Ansari Road office in Delhi in 1991. David was with Penguin then.

N.D. Mehra presenting a replica of Penguin to Peter Mayer, the then chairman of Penguin. R.N. Barman is on the right.

After I moved to Delhi in 1970, Rupa's Pataudi House showroom became the new abode for Penguin books. Delhi was the emerging intellectual capital of the country and an absolutely clean and well-laid-out showroom exhibiting attractive Penguin books became a magnet for journalists, academicians, politicians, booksellers and lovers of books who would spend hours in the shop. Our staff was very knowledgeable and they inculcated the habits that I myself practised—cleaning the books for 10–15 minutes every day and placing them in their right place, genre wise. It made all the difference—a clean, well-ordered space was well-nigh critical to make book-buying a pleasurable experience.

It was here that I met Professor Sukhamoy Chakravarty, who was the chief economic adviser to Indira Gandhi at the time. He would visit the showroom every Saturday, buy books and not leave without having a cup of coffee, our adda peppered with stimulating conversation. Other regulars included Arun Bose, a Marxist professor at Delhi University; Dr Devahuti, a historian;

D.P. Chattopadhyaya, a professor of comparative literature at Jadavpur University and later commerce minister in Indira Gandhi's government; Sham Lal, Dileep Padgaonkar and Jug Suraiya—all three of them former editors of *The Times of India*; journalist S. Prasannarajan; food journalist Sabina Sehgal, and many other stalwarts of the political, academic, journalistic and cultural scene.

Our success with Penguin and others brought many of the UK's largest publishers flocking to us. Collins made us the distributor of their paperback imprint, Fontana. Pan, the UK's second largest paperback publisher, offered us exclusive distribution rights for their books. We started distributing Pan books in 1983. This ruffled some feathers at Penguin and they sent Mike Hogben, their export director, to speak to us, both in Calcutta and Delhi. They brought up matters concerning our old business relationship with them in Calcutta and the future prospects of the business in Delhi. Penguin had a non-exclusive arrangement with Rupa and Pan's new arrangement was exclusive. I asked them just one question. 'Are you satisfied with your association with Rupa?'

The then PM Indira Gandhi at the Rupa stall. R.N. Barman can be seen in white coat and on the extreme right is Sarvepalli Gopal, chairman of National Book Trust, who wrote brilliant biographies of Dr S. Radhakrishnan (his father) and Jawaharlal Nehru.

A philosopher and scholar-politician, Dr Devi Prasad Chattopadhyay in the Rupa showroom

Their answer was a simple 'yes'. My next question was, 'Why did you not consider giving Rupa distribution rights just as Pan did?' Mike had no answer.

In 1986, the Rupa–Penguin relationship hit a major milestone—we completed 50 years of association. I travelled along with my cousin C.K. Mehra to London to felicitate Peter Mayer, the chief of in Penguin those days. On his first visit to India, Mayer had visited my house with his wife, and the couple had their first home-made Indian lunch.

Peter Mayer was a remarkable man. When he had taken over Penguin, the company had been in the doldrums, and he had revived it with some remarkable publishing and brilliant business decisions. He had masterminded the establishment of Penguin India in 1985, in a joint venture with ABP. He had engaged David Davidar as the head of publishing and Khushwant Singh as its literary adviser. Within a few years, the company was thriving. I was a great supporter of the new initiative and applauded the Mayer's foresight and willingness to push the boundaries of international publishing.

Sadly, less than 10 years after Penguin India was set up, the company cut ties with Rupa. In 1993, their export sales director, Max Adam, visited our Delhi office and stated brusquely: 'We do not wish to continue!' A relationship of 57 years sundered with one sentence. There was nothing to be said. Rupa would

Rupa's well laid out showroom displaying the latest Penguin titles was a big draw with readers

scale greater heights in the years to come, just as Penguin would, but our paths had diverged irreversibly. Perhaps, the split could have been handled better, but for me it was a learning experience. It made me greatly determined to not be at the mercy of overseas publishers as a distributor. It was time to ramp up our own publishing.

(From left) Paul Scherer, who was then the president of the Publishers Association of UK, Satyajeet (son of Durga Das), H.N. Kamath, myself and Sir William Collins, chairman of Collins, at the launch of India: From Curzon to Nehru *by Durga Das at Hotel Imperial, Delhi, in 1973. This is the first book we published in India with Collins, and thus began our journey.*

• Chapter 12 •

FROM COLLINS TO HARPERCOLLINS

Rupa has an umbilical connection with Collins. After all, *The Collins English Gem Dictionary* was the first book that D. Mehra sold. We have had a long business relationship with Collins with many memorable moments. I would like to start this chapter stating one such moment. This anecdote has, as its central character, a man who we called 'Madrasi babu'—H.N. Kamath, the representative of William Collins, Sons & Co. A large-hearted personality, he impressed himself favourably on all of us at Rupa. Madrasi babu would visit Calcutta twice a year along with his family. Amidst the discussions of selling and buying books, the family would relish a home-cooked meal and misti doi from Ganguram Sweets. Our *baithak-khana** would always be readied for his visits. The food would be served in a thali laid on a *chowki*. D. Mehra, Mr Kamath and my father would sit on the floor and eat. After a hearty meal, Mr Kamath would take off his tie and smoke his cheroot. On one occasion, we went for an outing to watch a cricket match between India and Australia at Eden Gardens. Kamath babu smoked many cheroots and fed us hot idlis wrapped in banana leaves that he had bought at some local cafe. The aroma of cheroots and idlis mixed with the sight of cricketers playing a thrilling match still lingers in my memory.

A few years later, I moved from Calcutta to Delhi. One day, a familiar visitor, Mr Kamath greeted me at the Rupa office in Daryaganj. He had news to share. His boss Robert Stevens was retiring and going back to England. He was staying at the Imperial Hotel, which was the hotel of choice for many British representatives visiting Delhi. Kamath suggested that we get together at the

---

*An assembly room in traditional Indian households where people sit and relax

Imperial and I went across to meet them. With Robert's departure, Kamath would now be heading the Collins business in India. There could not have been better news for me because I hadn't been a great fan of Robert Stevens, and I had a brilliant relationship with Kamath. Besides, I also had a great deal of admiration for the top man at the company, Sir William Collins.

Sir William was acquainted with many Indian luminaries—Indira Gandhi, Fatehsinghrao Gaekwad aka the Maharaja of Baroda, Kailash Sankhala (a wildlife expert and director of Project Tiger), Raghu Rai (the famous photographer), Durga Das (chief editor of *Hindustan Times*) and so on. I discovered that all of them (except Mrs Gandhi) were writing books for Collins. I asked Sir William how he had managed to put together such a diverse list and he simply replied: 'A publisher must keep abreast of the times'—a key lesson that I have never forgotten.

One day, Sir William and his wife visited me along with Kamath. The day after the couple left, Kamath paid me a visit. 'Divide and rule! This is what the goras did and this is what this couple has done,' he said dramatically.

'What's the matter, Kamath babu?' I asked politely.

'Arrey, they are very impressed with you. They have asked me to ask you if you would be willing to go to London as an apprentice. They will bear all travel and boarding expenses.' Saying this, he went quiet. He thought Sir William was planning to get rid of him and make me their representative in India. I calmed his fears by saying: 'If I ever go to London, it will be on my own coin and I will fend for myself.' Kamath babu informed Sir William about my decision and also wrote to D. Mehra in Calcutta, informing him about my refusal to go to London, which was endorsed by my granduncle as well.

The very next year, Sir William flew to India. He was on his way to Hong Kong along with Paul Scherer, their export director. Paul was quite impressed by what we had been able to do for Collins, and he soon made major changes to the way the company handled its business in India. He appointed Allied Publishers and Rupa as distributors for Collins hardback imprints and Macmillan and Rupa for their paperback imprints. The company's liturgical business was handled separately. Paul retired a little further down the track and began reconstituting the way the Indian operation would be run. Three people in the UK office were now given the responsibility for India—Reg Paine was in charge of hardbacks, David King looked after Fontana, and Peter Henson was responsible for the liturgical list and overall coordination. Collins had a robust liturgical list which was overseen by Lady Collins herself. Instead of exporting the titles as is, she encouraged reprinting them in India through Rupa. Our low-cost model worked well for these books and it was a huge success. Then one day, the legendary Geoffrey Chapman visited Delhi. The Australia-born publisher of liturgical books had transformed Catholic publishing in the '60s and Collins had taken Chapman & Chapman under their umbrella for liturgical publishing. Collins and Rupa's success had caught his attention and he wanted to emulate the same formula for his publishing programme. He met me and disclosed his plans but by then I was already directly dealing with Collins. I politely declined but offered to help by connecting him with Mohan Makhijani of Rekha Printers who readily took up the job. Chapman went back a happy man and sent me a consultation fee of £500, which I refused politely. How could have I accepted the money from Chapman as a consultant while I was working with Collins? And most importantly, the goras would've thought that by giving away some money, they can always buy our services. No sir, not in my world!

Mohan Makhijani of Rekha Printers

(From left to right) N.D. Mehra, Sir William Collins, D. Mehra, Lady Collins and R.N. Barman. On the 400th birth anniversary of William Shakespeare, Rupa sold one lakh copies of Complete Works of Shakespeare. *The Collins flew specially to Calcutta to congratulate us on this phenomenal sales feat.*

Paul and I got on very well, and the Collins business in India soared. We were constantly experimenting with pricing, reprinting, marketing, and so on, and many of our initiatives succeeded. We worked harder than ever. My team and I were travelling 15 days in a month, living out of our suitcases and in railway station waiting rooms. We sold lots of Alistair MacLean, Agatha Christie, Helen MacInnes, Hammond Innes—all printed under the Collins–Rupa imprint with special Indian prices.

Everything was going swimmingly until one morning, in August 1976, I received a phone call conveying the devastating news of Sir William passing away in his sleep. I broke down upon hearing the news. Sir William had been a cherished mentor and friend. Paul left the company soon after. Lady Collins and her two sons, Ian and Mark Collins, took over the reins of the business. Two executives who were promoted to top positions were F.I. Chapman and

John Clement. But the death of Sir William marked the beginning of the end of the Collins family's involvement in the firm. Various members of the family began pulling it in different directions and the Australian media mogul, Rupert Murdoch, took over the majority stake in the company. F.I. Chapman became the chairman. He soon visited India with his wife for a week. Obviously, the Taj was on their itinerary. Kamath, who hadn't yet retired, looked after them. I invited the Chapman couple for a desi dinner at my place, an invitation which the couple accepted graciously. A pure vegetarian, Indian meal was laid out before them with no drinks! The dinner went well, but they had to leave early to catch their flight. Kamath babu and I drove them back to the hotel. Just as they disappeared into the lobby, Kamath and I realized we had forgotten to give them the gifts I had brought them, which were still lying in my bedroom. I drove back home with Kamath, asked him to wait in the living room and went to my room to get the gifts. Just as I returned to the living room, I was overcome with laughter at what I saw—our Madrasi babu was busy wiping off the chole and puris.

'You see, I couldn't eat well because of my boss's presence. Now I will eat my heart out,' Kamath smiled mischievously and winked at me.

~

On the seventh floor of 8 Grafton Street in London was the seat of the Collins Empire. Collins had three offices—one on Grafton Street, the other on Cork Street and a third at Albemarle Street. During a visit in 1983, I made my way to the seventh floor of the Grafton Street office. The purpose of my visit was simple: I wanted to reassure the top brass that their business in India would still be in safe hands despite the demise of Sir William, which I considered a great personal loss. Rupa would continue to look after Collins's interest in India. Between 1983 and 1987, I made a number of trips to the UK, as our business with Collins and other UK-based publishers was growing rapidly. In 1987, HarperCollins proposed we take our business relationship to the next level. They suggested we enter into a joint venture, HarperCollins India, to publish and distribute books in India. A couple of years before, the Penguin India joint venture (set up by Penguin and ABP) had started operations and had been successful. So, this seemed like a logical step forward to HarperCollins. However, we had been tremendously successful in the distribution and reprints business and entering a joint venture would mean a loss of profit. So, initially, I wasn't keen. However, a joint venture would also mean exclusivity over HarperCollins's books. It was worth contemplating.

Terry Kitson was appointed chairman of Rupa–HarperCollins joint venture. His respect for my father can be seen through this picture where he made my father sit while he was standing.

The joint venture moved forward in fits and starts because there was a rapid turnaround among top management in the UK. After F.I. Chapman and John Clement left the company, the joint venture was eventually sealed during the tenure of Terry Kitson. We used to refer to Terry as a son-in-law of India, as he was married to an Indian woman, Barbara, from Dehradun. He was keen on expanding the business in India. I flew to London to meet the UK directors of HarperCollins and signed the papers for the joint venture. There were to be three directors on the board of HarperCollins India. I offered Terry the chairmanship of the firm, even though Collins was the minority shareholder. When the deal was signed, champagne was popped, and, thus, in 1991, I tasted alcohol for the very first time in my life. But I'm sure it was not just the alcohol that was responsible for the entire occasion feeling a bit surreal—my granduncle had sold the first Collins dictionary in India 57 years ago, and now I was launching HarperCollins in India. On 23 August 1991, the first 12 books under HarperCollins India venture, under the imprint Indus, were launched.

(From left to right) Jyoti Sengupta, K.L. Barman, H.N. Kamath, N.D. Mehra, Sir William Collins and R.N. Barman at our Calcutta office

My father, along with R.N. Barman, left for Calcutta the very next day, proud of having hit another milestone. However, he did not live long enough to see us prosper, as he passed away on 8 March 1992. Terry visited my father during his short illness; they had established a wonderful relationship. Terry's involvement in the venture increased. He would visit India at least thrice, if not four times a year. I met his team of brilliant editors, including Stuart Proffit, Christopher Maclehose, Simon King, Richard Rothman and others who were responsible for top-selling authors like Patrick French, Martin Gilbert, Sidney Sheldon, John Keay, William Dalrymple, Philip Ziegler and many more. I would brainstorm regularly with the international group and our team in India to discuss ways in which we could make our list truly world class. Between our locally published list, reprints and distributed books, we had a truly impressive array of books for discerning customers. Moreover, our sales reach also began to expand—we were now exporting books as far away as Africa. And then came the sad news of Terry's retirement in 1994 owing to health-related issues, among other things.

A young William Dalrymple at the launch of City of Djinns *by HarperCollins*

Collins being a Scottish company, Peter Hensen specially flew in to Glasgow to receive me

R.S. Paine (left) and Peter Hensen (right)

Rupa receives the Agatha Christie Award from Collins for outstanding sales. Seen here is our sales team: (from left) A.K. Singh, T.C. Alexander, S.K. Mehra (director), Vinod Kumar, R.N. Sharma and J.K. Bose.

Terry Kitson (red tie) can be seen here interacting with one of our authors as Divya Raina, our editor (second from left) and Poonam our marketing head (in saree) looks on

Eddie's tryst with Nostalgia

Mr. Eddie Bell delivering his speech at the release function.

"Suno choti si guriya ki lambi kahani. . . ." That's how Mr. Eddie Bell, Executive Chairman of HarperCollins UK began his speech at the release function of the book *In Search of Lata Mangeshkar*. For the audience present there it was a real pleasure and a rewarding experience watching Mr. Bell feel at home with Indian ethos and its assimilative nuances. An ardent admirer of Lata Mangeshkar, Mr. Bell gushed about his infatuation with Indian music and its universal appeal. Indeed, his very presence at the function imparted a measure of glory to the occasion and will make any Indian feel proud ,at the cultural importance India enjoys across the globe.

Eddie Bell, executive chairman of HarperCollins UK, charmed the Indian audience when he began his speech with a Lata Mangeshkar song 'Suno Choti Si Gudiya Ki Lambi Kahani' at the launch of In Search of Lata Mangeshkar *authored by Harish Bhimani.*

Eddie Bell took over. Eddie was a remarkable publisher and a great supporter of HarperCollins India and our business scaled new heights. It was at this time that we suffered some setbacks, such as Penguin walking away from us, and a truly irreversible and saddening blow—the passing away of our founder, my granduncle, D. Mehra, in 1997.

As the years passed, we had some major successes at HarperCollins India but the joint venture was not destined to last. Soon after Bell left HarperCollins, his successors ended the partnership with Rupa when they sold their majority equity to *India Today*. Few years later, HarperCollins India became a wholly owned subsidiary of HarperCollins UK. Another long-term relationship had come to an end and although there were some unhappy moments, in the end, it was something to be celebrated.

• Chapter 13 •

THE FRENCH AFFAIR!

'Nothing is more powerful than an idea whose time has come,' the great French poet Victor Hugo said. And the time had come for Rupa to build upon an idea and taste its own share of French. It happened in a language so alien to France: Hindi. It was early 2000, we had published *An Anthology of Hindi Poetry.* It so happened that a French cultural attaché named Mariam was impressed by Hindi. Around that time, her eyes fell on this book of Hindi poetry. Mariam was learning Hindi, and she knew her French! Being a cultural attaché, her mandate was to explore and increase the cultural exchange between her country and India, and she had an idea. Soon, two dignitaries from the French Embassy were sitting in front of me with a proposal for an anthology of French poems along the same lines. When it comes to the love for literature, poetry, art and music, you cannot beat the French. I was on board! Soon, a book of French poetry with translations in English was published. They say that poetry gets lost in translation. But with this translation, we lost nothing. As soon as the book was published, the French Ambassador hosted a gala for the launch of the book at the French Embassy. The French cannot be beaten in the art and aesthetics of hosting an event either. The book was launched by the Spanish Ambassador who was a poet himself. Naturally, the usual stiff lipped and politically correct diplomacy gave way to free expression, as the Ambassador was rediscovering the poet inside him. Poetry was flowing like wine and champagne, albeit in a language unknown to me. The speeches were awfully long, and even though I could not comprehend a word of what was spoken, I joined the applause and nodded or clapped when others did. Suddenly, I realized that the French Ambassador had said something and everyone was clapping, looking at me. I, too, was clapping, but it looked odd. *Why are they staring at*

With the French cultural attaché Maraim, whose interest in India and in Hindi led to the Rupa–France initiative

At the launch of The Book of French Poetry *at the Embassy of France*

me? Have they found out that I am only acting that I know French? I kept sitting there, smiling and applauding as everyone did. Soon, the Ambassador started speaking in Hindi and he called my name. *Oh, they want me to deliver the publisher's address!* I realized. In my kurta–pyjama, I walked towards the podium and commenced my speech in Hindi, which the French cultural attaché was translating into French. It was a confluence of two worlds, of Hindi and French, and a heralding of a long and propitious partnership between Rupa and France.

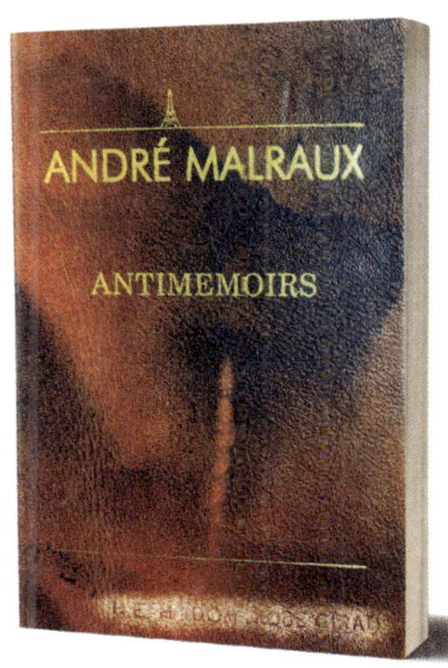

The autobiography of arguably the most influential figure of the enlightened militant conscience in the 1930s.

The book launch ended and a partnership began. The French Ambassador and the cultural attaché offered to get the English translation rights of French authors for Rupa and to publish them locally. A new list called 'Rupa France' was born, boasting of titles like *Blues for a Black Cat and Other Stories* by Boris Vian; *Book of My Mother* by Albert Cohen; *Female Deities in Buddhism* by Vessantara; *Murder in Memoriam* by Didier Daeninckx; *My Big Apartment* by Christian Oster; *Ostinato* by Louis-René des Forêts; *Porporino or the Secrets of Naples* by Dominique Fernandez; and *Sans Moi* by Marie Desplechin.

It was in Chandernagore, Bengal, that the first French settlement had been established in 1673 and, within a year, the French had acquired another settlement, Pondicherry (now Puducherry) in the south. The French have long gone from these geographies, but the connection has stayed on. The Rupa France list immediately caught the attention of these two erstwhile French areas and the demand there increased. Soon, the French PM visited India and the Ambassador hosted a lunch at his residence for a few select invitees. I was one of them.

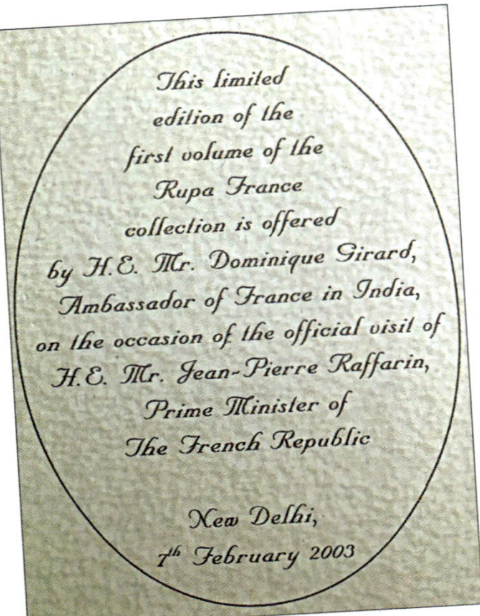

This limited
edition of the
first volume of the
Rupa France
collection is offered
by H.E. Mr. Dominique Girard,
Ambassador of France in India,
on the occasion of the official visit of
H.E. Mr. Jean-Pierre Raffarin,
Prime Minister of
The French Republic

New Delhi,
7th February 2003

Rupa published An Anthology of French Poetry *and thus began Rupa France*

There was no full stop thereafter. I suggested to my French counterparts my desire to publish *Anti-Memoirs* by André Malraux, a French novelist, art theorist and the minister for cultural affairs. The book covered a lot about contemporary and ancient India vis-à-vis our French connection. Publishing *Anti-Memoirs* was but a natural extension of our collaboration with France.

The French Ambassador got a leather-bound edition of several hundred copies for free distribution in India and abroad. Ambassador Dominique Girard and his wife surely loved India, its heritage and culture!

Rupa published another book *Ardhanarishwar* by Dr Alka Pande, an art curator. Again, the book launch was a gala affair where a dance invoking Shiva was performed at the French Embassy to showcase Indian culture. The Rupa France list was soaring new heights. I was invited to visit France during Paris Book Fair, but I preferred to be on my own. The following year, France was invited to be the guest of honour at Calcutta Book Fair. To mark the occasion, the French placed four replicas of the Eiffel Tower at the four entry gates. A special Rupa France stall was put up, with French authors visiting the fair and giving talks about their books.

Additionally, this time, the book fair was special for me for another reason. A month prior to the book fair, I had received a personal message from the French Ambassador informing me that I was to be decorated with the Chevalier de l'Ordre National du Mérite, which is a French order of merit awarded by the President of France. I was invited to be in Paris to receive the honour. I graciously accepted the French honour but on one condition. I would only accept the award if the city of my birth, the city I loved and adored, could witness the

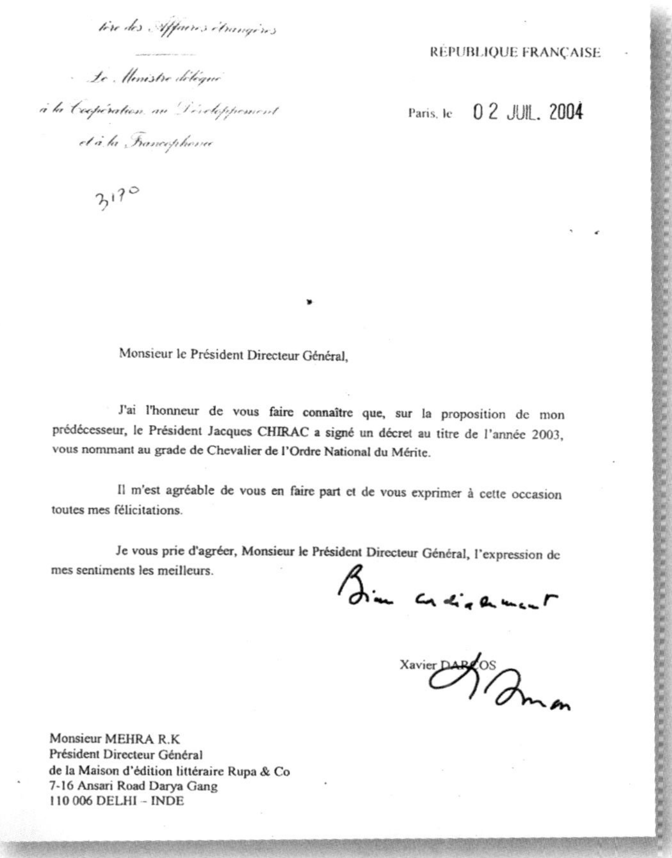

Ministère des Affaires étrangères

Le Ministre délégué
à la Coopération au Développement
et à la Francophonie

3170

RÉPUBLIQUE FRANÇAISE

Paris, le 02 JUIL. 2004

Monsieur le Président Directeur Général,

J'ai l'honneur de vous faire connaître que, sur la proposition de mon prédécesseur, le Président Jacques CHIRAC a signé un décret au titre de l'année 2003, vous nommant au grade de Chevalier de l'Ordre National du Mérite.

Il m'est agréable de vous en faire part et de vous exprimer à cette occasion toutes mes félicitations.

Je vous prie d'agréer, Monsieur le Président Directeur Général, l'expression de mes sentiments les meilleurs.

Bien cordialement

Xavier DARCOS

Monsieur MEHRA R.K
Président Directeur Général
de la Maison d'édition littéraire Rupa & Co
7-16 Ansari Road Darya Gang
110 006 DELHI - INDE

I was conferred with Chevalier de l'Ordre National du Mérite by General Kelche and I became Monsieur Mehra R.K.

award ceremony. In short, I wanted to receive the honour in front of my own people, in my city, Calcutta. The Ambassador seized the opportunity and, with the permission of the French government, it was decided that the award would be conferred on me in Calcutta on the inaugural day of Calcutta Book Fair.

The convention hall of The Oberoi Grand was the venue. The august gathering of 400 people included the who's who of the City of Joy. The moment came, and I was invited to the dais with my wife. I was in my usual silk pyjama–kurta and Kaminee was in an elegant white sari. Amidst the applause of my fellow

RÉPUBLIQUE FRANÇAISE

ORDRE NATIONAL DU MÉRITE

LE PRÉSIDENT DE LA RÉPUBLIQUE FRANÇAISE
GRAND MAI'RE DE L'ORDRE NATIONAL DU MÉRITE

nomme Monsieur R.K. MEHRA
Prés dent-Directeur Général d'une Maison d'Edition
de nationalit indienne

CHEVALIER DE L'ORDRE NATIONAL DU MÉRITE

Fait à PARIS, le 17 Juin 2004

Scellé du sceau de l'Ordre sous le n° 306 E 04
P Le Secrétaire Général adjoint,

Par le Président de la République :
LE CHANCELIER DE L'ORDRE NATIONAL DU MÉRITE

Général KELCHE

The certificate of honour I received from the French government

French order of merit award. I requested the government of France whether I can receive this award in Calcutta and not in Paris, and they graciously obliged.

Calcuttans, my adda people, the friends and authors I love to meet and talk to, I was conferred with Chevalier de l'Ordre National du Mérite by General Kelche. It surely was a momentous occasion for me, one that has been framed and now hangs in my son Kapish's office in Daryaganj.

Although this was a proud moment for me, what is life without its share of unexpected awkward moments? As soon as I received the award, I was expected to kiss my wife on stage. French customs beckon! I was now sweating and fretting and looked at Kaminee who looked equally bewildered. *What next Monsieur Mehra? Are you going for that kiss?* The French seemed to be demanding. But I could not do anything and left the dias. I surely could not have kissed her and let all of Calcutta tell. So, I held her hand and let the warmth of our relationship do the rest; it was a display of mutual respect and love, of having her by my side forever. My acceptance speech was neither in Hindi, nor English, nor French because I hardly knew the language. It was in a language I had grown up with, the language of my friends and addas, of the bhadralok sitting in that convention hall. It was in Bengali. The French Ambassador could not understand a word but was in awe. I was speaking to my roots.

Author Alka Saraogi with the representatives of French embassy at the France stall at Calcutta Book Fair

A year later, Ambassador Girard and his wife completed their term and left for France. The Rupa France collaboration gradually disappeared because people changed and so did the warmth of the association. But what remains etched in my mind is this little literary 'affair' with France. It was good. It was warm. It was so French.

• Chapter 14 •

HYDERABAD HAZIR HAI

Hyderabad, the city of Chowmahalla Palace, the Charminar and Golkonda Fort is one of my favourite cities. I first visited Hyderabad in December 1968, when I was 21. I explored Laad Bazaar, Madina Circle, Begum Bazaar and Sultan Bazaar, soaking in the city's language, culture and distinct personality. The aroma of Hyderabadi biryani and *haleem* still linger in my memory after all these years.

Hyderabad has been the meeting place of many different cultures and traditions and has developed its own distinctive Ganga–Jamuni culture. It is a cosmopolitan city where people never identify themselves by their religion but as Hyderabadis. Dussehra, Diwali or Sankranti are enjoyed by Hindus and non-Hindus alike. And Eid is not a celebration for a single community but for the entire city. Faith is a personal matter and what unites everyone is the sense of belonging with Hyderabad. (At present, people say all this is a thing of the past, but I believe such pessimism is unwarranted.)

Language is never a problem in the city. The unique lingua franca, Dakhni, is one of the most identifiable markers of Hyderabad. It is a delicious blend of Hindi, Urdu and Telugu, laced with old Marathi. The plural character of the city dates back to its founder Muhammad Quli Qutb Shah, who was also a Telugu scholar. Geographically, too, it is inclusive: the twin cities, Hyderabad and Secunderabad, do not exhibit the cleavage in environment that divides, say, South Bombay and the suburbs, or the Calcuttans whose lives are demarcated along the south of Park Street. And now, there is also Cyberabad, as the 400-year-old city is constantly reinventing itself.

Hyderabad is not only a cosmopolitan but also a pan-Indian city. Since the city was never directly ruled by the British (there was a Resident stationed there), it owes its pluralism not so much to the British but to the Nizams who encouraged Parsis, Kayasthas and Maharashtrians to join the civil service. The inclusive nature of the city blended all these communities into a harmonious whole, distinguished by the adoption of what is known as the 'Hyderabadi tehzeeb'—the traditional composite of civility, hospitality, courtesy and grace in social interaction, the hallmark of which is respect and consideration. An outsider in Hyderabad (though I believe that the city does not treat anyone as such), does not jar. There is no need or wish to retain separateness—all willingly and happily submit to the warm embrace of a city, which even visitors as far back as 400 years were in no hurry to leave once they had arrived.

During my first visit, I stayed at the Taj Mahal Hotel at Abids. The hotel, one of the oldest 3-stars in the city, had an unassuming building and exuded an old-world charm that is difficult to find these days. I remember sitting on the floor to eat the rice and sambhar, which was served on a banana leaf. However, since I had not developed a taste for such food, I wasted most of it. This elicited disapproving looks from the staff, who showed their resentment at what they took to be a slur on their cooking. I decided to look for a place more suited to my palate and found one Kwality Restaurant, run by (wonder of wonders!) my namesake, a certain Mehraji. I used to like the fare on offer at Kwality Restaurant in Calcutta's Park Street; if the Hyderabad branch was even half as good, then my quest for a meal more suited to my tastes would end. I looked forward to a good meal in prospect but fate decreed otherwise.

I had tasted red chillies many times before, but I became aware of the dynamite that Hyderabadi red chillies were that day. Perhaps the chef was in a bad mood

Meetings with M.L. Jaisimha were fun and 'high spirited'

and added more than a healthy dose of chillies to the food. Whatever the reason, my insides were soon on fire. I can never forget that burning sensation. The May heat, a scorching 40-degree Celsius, only added to the miseries of my alimentary canal! I ran out of the restaurant and hired a cycle rickshaw—the only means of transport available at the time. I needed some fresh air. Hyderabadi rickshaws make one feel like a true Nawab. One does not sit in them, one lies back. The seats are such that you become horizontal, looking up at the sky. I did some gallivanting: the streets from Abids to Sultan Bazaar were full of cinema halls and hoardings with charismatic movie stars looked down at the populace. But sitting, or rather lying down, in the rickshaw, I could only see the puff of the heroes' hair!

In those days, Hyderabad was a publisher's delight. It had a flourishing publishing business and the bookshops included J.C. Pinto & Co. and A. Hussain & Co. at Abids, along with the the Book Selection Centre and Book Syndicate near Arya Samaj Mandir at Sultan Bazaar.

It was in Hyderabad that I made the acquaintance of the dashing Indian cricket opener, M.L. Jaisimha, whose cultivated roguishness and unmatched sartorial sense charmed me. We became friends and lunch with him used to be a long affair—he was almost always on a 'liquid diet' and would guzzle large quantities of beer. Unsurprisingly, conversations with him proved to be 'high spirited', both literally and metaphorically, and on these occasions, the flamboyant cricketer used to be in his element.

During one such luncheon meeting, Jaisimha kept drinking beer and the lunch never arrived. I thought I would miss my flight but thankfully Salim Durani, the heart-throb of yesteryear who used to hit sixes on demand, was also there and he drove me to Begumpet airport at breakneck speed. '*Agli bar saath mein lunch zaroor karenge*,' was Jaisimha's usual parting line. It became something of an amusing routine. Meeting Jaisimha and Durani, and the latter rushing me to the airport with a smiling and tipsy Jaisimha saying, '*Agli baar saath mein...*' The lunch never materialized but the memory of these entertaining meetings has stayed with me forever.

Years passed and Hyderabad kept growing on me. The city gripped me and I developed a circle of friends there. In 2007, my friend and author, Bakhtiar Dadabhoy, now an additional member of the Railway Board, was posted to Hyderabad from Bombay. We would invariably meet over drinks and dinner. Bakhtiar had done four books with Rupa by then, including *Jeh: A Life of J.R.D. Tata,* which continues to sell well. I can proudly say that it was on my prodding that he wrote it. The year 2004 marked J.R.D.'s birth centenary and I thought that it would be a good idea to have a new book on the former Tata chairman in his centenary year. Bakhtiar was diffident at first but finally acquiesced to my request. By the end of that year, he delivered his manuscript and the coffee-table book was published in early 2005. Apart from a lucid exposition of the main events of J.R.D.'s life, it owes its success to an attractive cover and some excellent photographs. The fact that it has run into numerous editions is testimony to its popularity. We have recently published *Homi J. Bhabha: A Life,* written by Bakhtiar, which has been critically acclaimed and is also selling well.

Later, Vanaja Banagiri, a former journalist, joined our group in Hyderabad. Rupa has published two of her books—a novel and an anthology on Hyderabad called *Hyderabad Hazir Hai: Writings from the City of Nizams*, which has inspired

Bakhtiar Dadabhoy, my long time friend and a cherished author

Vanaja Banagiri, another gem of a person from Hyderabad who became our author and my good friend

the name of this chapter. The three of us used to meet at the Secunderabad Club (and sometimes at the Taj Deccan, where I would reside when I was in the city), where the tranquil evenings often stretched into the night. There is nothing like good food combined with lively conversation. I greatly enjoyed these evenings and always looked forward to my visits to Hyderabad. *Hyderabad Hazir Hai,* which was released at an elegant function in a five-star hotel, had contributions from many well-known personalities of Hyderabad. It was a modest success commercially, but, to my mind, it is an excellent compilation that has captured through the writing of its many contributors, the Hyderabadi ethos. Bakhtiar contributed an article on the Salar Jungs of Hyderabad and the eponymous museum.

Bakhtiar, meanwhile, had completed his fifth book *Sugar in Milk: Lives of Eminent Parsees*, which consisted of detailed biographical profiles of 12 of the greatest Parsees of all time. While discussing alternatives for the formal launch of the book, it suddenly struck me that the Raj Bhavan would be a good option. I was on friendly terms with N.D. Tiwari, the then governor of Andhra Pradesh. I called on him, taking Bakhtiar with me. Bakhtiar, awestruck at first, was soon put at ease by Tiwariji. The veteran Congress leader who combined the graces of a bygone era with a most amiable and courteous disposition had a way of disarming you. I made it a point to meet him on every visit to Hyderabad. He always welcomed me with a bouquet of flowers, and tea and refreshments followed. The governor was partial to cashews and almonds, especially the latter. He probably realized the strength almonds would provide where it was needed the most!

The then Governor of Andhra Pradesh N.D. Tiwari and historian Narendra Luther launching Sugar in Milk *by Bakhtiar Dadabhoy*

Sugar in Milk was released by Tiwariji at the Raj Bhavan in February 2008. Given the venue, the who's who of Hyderabad were in attendance. They included the former Chief of Air Staff and former governor of Maharashtra, Air Marshall Idris Latif, and his gracious wife Begum Bilkiz Latif. They had been invited by Bakhtiar's father, Keki Dadabhoy, a former director general of police. The launch provided me with an opportunity to meet Bakhtiar's parents for the first time. His father, a genial extrovert was great company, while his mother the gracious and aristocratic, Rati, was more reserved, but exuded a quiet charm.

The function, which was a huge success, had its share of amusing moments. I will narrate two here. Narender Luther, a retired chief secretary of Andhra Pradesh and a historian of Hyderabad, introduced the book. Bakhtiar and I gave brief speeches, and then it was time for Tiwariji's address. As is customary on such occasions, Tiwariji praised the book and its author. What perhaps many did not realize was the fact that a few minutes into the speech, Bakhtiar Dadabhoy became 'Jamsetjee Jejeebhoy', and by the end of the speech, if I recall correctly, had become 'Dadabhai Naoroji'. Bakhtiar later told me that some of his colleagues who had attended the launch still tease him about it.

Tiwariji was an old man in his eighties at the time and physical infirmity was knocking on his door. He needed help while walking and to stand up after sitting. One of the guests wanted his autograph and Tiwariji, after having risen for the national anthem at the end of the function, was obliged to sit down again. After having satisfied the autograph hunter, he attempted to stand but seemed unsteady and his aide-de-camp rushed to his assistance. This prompted a lady to remark in typical Hyderabadi Hindi that the governor could not even stand. It was meant for her immediate neighbour, but she ended up stating it in a voice louder than she had intended. Its delivery, and more importantly, the unintended sexual innuendo, were not lost on anyone. It was my first taste of Hyderabadi Hindi! The limitations of the lady's Hindi caused unintended merriment.

Tiwariji was hard of hearing in one ear. It was not an infirmity associated with age but an affliction he owed to a British jailor who had slapped him on the ear, damaging his ear drum. Notwithstanding this handicap, he had guessed that someone had said something. When he asked me, I gave him an evasive reply. Bakhtiar kept a straight face and maintained a stony silence. Bakhtiar later told me that Tiwariji kept in touch even after the launch and invited him to the Raj Bhavan frequently. He gave him mementoes and displayed great courtesy—he would even see him off to his car—something that

Sudhakar Krishnamurti's book created so much buzz that I started getting calls from anxious men to 'fix' their problems.

a relatively junior officer could never expect from a governor. Tiwariji wanted to write his memoir and Bakhtiar had agreed to help him. Unfortunately, Tiwariji's gubernatorial tenure ended in a scandal and the autobiography proved to be stillborn.

I recall another amusing anecdote that provided a few good laughs. A little before *Sugar in Milk* was launched, we published a book called *Sexx Is Not a Four-Letter Word* by a famous sexologist called Dr Sudhakar Krishnamurti. The doctor and his wife Kavita (a paediatrician) have been a charming couple who, if I remember correctly, were often on Page 3 in Hyderabad. They invited me for a dinner after the book was published and wanted it to be aggressively marketed. We went around town and ensured that every bookseller was made aware of this new title. The book was well-received. Khushwant Singh, the high priest of unconventional wisdom and famous for his risqué jokes, wrote in *The Telegraph*, 'The book makes good reading and is packed with useful information.'

One of the booksellers, a young man, wanted me to fix an appointment with the high-profile sexologist whose book he was now selling. Apparently, he had a few concerns that he wanted the learned doctor to address. I arranged the appointment, happy to play a role in alleviating this bookseller's 'manly' anxiety. But things didn't go well, at least initially. After a few days, I got a call from him in which he expressed his great displeasure using some of the choicest abuse while referring to the doctor. The prescribed dosage had not worked and his frustration knew no bounds. He shouted into the phone, '*Ye kya hua, mai to bekaar ho gaya*' or words to that effect. I advised him to go back and share his misgivings with his doctor. Luckily, there was a 'happy' ending. I was gladdened when, a few weeks later, he called me again with a cheerful '*sab theek hai ab* (everything is okay now)'. I was more relieved than he was. I had never even dreamt that I would play such an important cameo is someone else's climax!

The things we publishers have to do!

Intizar Hussain (left) receiving the first Yatra Award from Ashok Mitra, the then finance minister of Bengal, at Park Hotel, Calcutta, in September 1993

• Chapter 15 •

A DIVIDED HEART

The year 1993 was special in more ways than one. It was the year our joint venture with HarperCollins became fully operational, but it was meaningful to me for another reason. It was the year I took my first trip to Pakistan, the land of my forefathers. A.K. Singh—my long-time colleague who had been to Pakistan before, attending book fairs and getting to know local booksellers—accompanied me. Besides sentimental reasons, I was crossing the border to invite one of Pakistan's greatest writers Intizar Hussain to India to accept the inaugural Yatra Award that we had instituted in memory of my father, N.D. Mehra. Hussain sahib had migrated from Basti, a small district of UP in India, to Lahore in Pakistan. The jury, which had chosen Hussain sahib as the first recipient of the award, was a very distinguished one, comprising Sham Lal, Dileep Padgaonkar, Ashok Vajpeyi, U.R. Ananthamurthy and Alok Bhalla.

As the flight took off from Delhi and headed towards Karachi, wave after wave of memories and emotions broke over me. I thought of my granduncle D. Mehra, his brothers and their families, their origins in Peshawar, their move to Lahore and India. I thought of my father and his belief that India and Pakistan would be unified, a hope he lived with until his death, just a year ago. I imagined how I would feel upon my arrival in a part of the subcontinent that had always held a special place in my heart. Our arrival in Karachi was uneventful. Iqbal bhai of Paramount Book Store had arranged transport for us from the airport to the Pearl Continental Hotel where we would be staying. We passed through Customs and immigration in less than 10 minutes. When the immigration office asked us the reason for our visit, I said, 'I have come here to invite your writer, Intizar Hussain.' He responded with a proud smile and said, 'He is magical. Welcome to

Meeting Intizar Hussain at the Pearl Hotel in Lahore, Pakistan. I went there to formally invite him to receive the Yatra Award.

Pakistan.' In fact, we cleared the immigration formalities in no time and we were out of the airport and in our car even before the Paramount manager deputed to receive us got there. He eventually met us late at night at the hotel and asked in puzzlement, 'Sir, how did you clear the airport formalities so quickly?'

'Because we have brought love from India for your great writer Intizar Hussain,' I said with a smile.

~

Our first meeting the next day was not with any bookseller but with a police officer. As visiting Indians, we had to present ourselves before the local police and get our passports endorsed. Both A.K. Singh and I were nervous but our anxiety vanished the moment we met the officer. He was cordial and polite with his Indian guests—a great ambassador of his country's warmth and hospitality. I requested him to waive the mandatory trip to the Lahore police station when we visited the city. He accommodated my request without any fuss. Emboldened by this, I had another request—would we be able to take the Lahore–Amritsar bus route on our way back? He politely replied that this could be done only at the time of applying for a visa and not now. No further argument—I had got what I wanted and that was avoiding a trip to the Lahore police station. I was keen to visit Peshawar, the city of my ancestors but permission was only granted for a limited number of cities.

Kickstarting our business trip, we met our first client, Paramount Books. Iqbal Hussain, the owner of Paramount, had hospitably sent his car for us; at his office, his two sons, himself and a manager were waiting to welcome us. Before entering the room, we took off our shoes and after the customary handshakes, dua-salaam and other pleasantries, we began talking in right earnest, sometimes in chaste Punjabi, sometimes in Urdu mixed with Hindi and Hindustani. We talked for hours—there was so much we had in common. Iqbal bhai had many

A meeting of two greats: Intizar Hussain with D. Mehra

friends in India and asked after all of them. We hardly discussed business. When he asked us to choose a cuisine for lunch—Chinese, European, American or Mexican—I surprised him by saying 'dal–roti'. Ever the perfect host, Iqbal bhai phoned his wife and said he'd be bringing some guests over. We were served a superb vegetarian meal at his well-appointed dining table. As the lunch was being served, Iqbal bhai excused himself for his afternoon namaz. In the background, Rajendra Kumar and Waheeda Rehman were swooning over their admiration and love for each other through the songs of the famous film *Palki* (1967), which was playing on Iqbal bhai's music system. We continued to talk at great length about the situation in both countries.

His daughter had served us lunch and, mustering great courage, I asked Iqbal bhai why his wife hadn't joined us for lunch. 'Babri masjid', whispered Iqbal bhai in my ears. The controversial mosque had just been demolished in Ayodhya, much to the hurt and anger of some of the Muslims, Iqbal bhai's wife being one of them. She welcomed us with her warm home-cooked food, but her heart had gone cold! Years later, an interesting event mellowed her bitter heart.

Iqbal bhai was scheduled to visit Delhi for the book fair but was denied visa. Pulling a few strings, we were able to secure visa for him. On the day of his arrival, he informed us that he could not travel, since his wife had no visa! Needless to say, this too was arranged and the couple happily crossed the Radcliffe Line. The staunch Muslims stayed in Delhi with Manish Jain, a devout follower of Jainism and the owner of BPB Publications. Our hearts converge at odd angles.

Finally, it was time to get going. Iqbal bhai dropped us off at the office of his biggest business competitor, Liberty Books. Saying goodbye, I invited him and his two sons and the manager for dinner at Pearl. The invite was graciously accepted.

Once inside Liberty Books, we were surprised to learn that the family was originally from Hyderabad, India. Shaukat Hussain, Saleem Hussain's brother and co-owner of Liberty Books, had business interests in Bombay but later, they migrated to Pakistan, albeit 18 years after Partition. Once the business discussion was over, it was time to get a feel of the city. Shaukat bhai took us around the port city, which is now one of the bigger metropolises in the world. While navigating through a busy Karachi road, my attention was riveted by a shopfront that proclaimed it was the 'Banarasi Silk House'. It piqued my curiosity and I requested my host to stop the car, so I could visit the shop. The owner's ancestors were from Banaras. Once a Banarasi, always a Banarasi, even in Pakistan! As I spoke to him, memories of my late father came flooding in. My father loved Banaras with every ounce of his being. His mother had been a native of the holy city, and he had spent a lot of time in its alleys and on the ghats of the great river Ganga. As the shopkeeper continued to reminisce fondly about Banaras, I teared up. Why did our countries have to part ways when we had so much in common, so much about this land that we loved!

That evening, Iqbal bhai and his sons came over to the Pearl Continental hotel for dinner. After a vegetarian dinner of paneer, fried potatoes, salad, dal and Afghani naan, which we had in the hotel room, we bid each other farewell. I

(From left to right) Terry Kitson, Ashok Mitra, Alok Bhalla and Intizar Hussain at the 1993 Yatra Award, which we instituted in memory of my father

wanted to see them off to their car but Iqbal bhai was against it—ISI surveillance was always on everyone's mind in Pakistan.

Next morning, the hotel car dropped us at the Karachi Airport. On our way, we could see streets lined with beggars on one side and fleets of Mercedes cars on the other. This paradox was no different from anything to be seen in any big Indian city.

The flight to Lahore was delayed by an hour but once the aircraft arrived, I was impressed by how well-maintained and clean it was. Pakistan International Airlines, in those days, was a quality airline. We were in Lahore in an hour. During the journey, I was amused to overhear snatches of conversations in undiluted Punjabi, peppered with *tussi* (you) and *ithe* (this side). 'We could be in Amritsar or Chandigarh,' I quipped to A.K. Singh.

In Lahore, we were to stay in Hotel Fariyad. Unfortunately, the hotel lived up to its name, which means whimpering or whining in English. It was a shabby old hotel with large rooms, furniture and beds. However, the huge size of the furniture was not able to compensate for its dilapidated state. The sofas creaked mightily when one sat on them and the beds were equally rickety. We quickly checked out and implored the taxi driver who had just dropped us off, and fortunately not driven away, to take us to Pearl Continental instead. What a world of difference greeted us when we walked into the lobby of Pearl Continental. In many ways, it was even better than its sister hotel in Karachi. The lobby had a magnificent painting of a maharaja and it set the tone for the rest of the hotel. The fittings and décor were world class and the staff was courteous and professional. The rooms were comfortable and well-appointed.

Once we had settled in, it was time to call Hussain sahib. He was waiting for our call and arrived at the hotel soon, as he lived nearby. I invited him to visit India and accept the Yatra Award. He asked for a week-long stay in

Saleem Hussein, the owner of Liberty Books in Karachi, whose family originally hailed from Hyderabad, India

Iqbal bhai of Paramount Publishers who was generous and hospitable during our visit

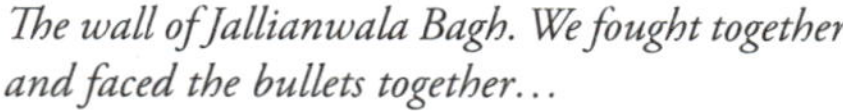

The wall of Jallianwala Bagh. We fought together and faced the bullets together…

But our heart has been divided forever…

India in order to visit his hometown Basti, near Meerut. It was a small price to pay to have this peerless chronicler of humanity with us as our guest, and I unhesitatingly acceded to the request.

Our next destination was Ferozsons Book Store and, for the first time during our trip, the enmity between the two countries reared its ugly head. We were only allowed to meet the manager, as the proprietors refused to meet us in protest against the demolition of the Babri Masjid in Ayodhya the previous year. They were hurt because they felt that Muslims in India had been wronged. I empathized with their stance and did not take umbrage at their refusal to meet. We then met a few booksellers in the Urdu Bazaar to get some orders—even though they had a reputation for not paying their bills. I then wanted to meet Sang-e-Meel Publications, as I had heard a lot about them. We were told that the best person to organize the meeting was Hussain sahib, as they had published all his books. We didn't have much time, since we were due to fly out the next afternoon and had quite a packed schedule already in Lahore. Nevertheless, I spoke to Hussain sahib and a meeting was arranged. We took a taxi to the Sang-e-Meel office. There was a power cut in the area, another phenomenon common to big cities on both sides of the border. A narrow staircase led up to the Sang-e-Meel office. *Vastu shastra*, in Hindu philosophy, considers a narrow entrance leading to a large courtyard auspicious. The building plan of Sang-e-Meel suggested prosperity and it underlined the success this publishing company had achieved since it had been established. The owner Afzal Ahmad and his two sons were exceedingly gracious hosts. An enormous plate of Lahori sweets was placed before us and we were invited to help ourselves. This was my first experience of this form of Pakistani hospitality, and I was charmed by it. Although we were not visiting Sang-e-Meel for business, unfortunately, the demolition of the Babri Masjid cast a shadow over our meeting. The owner clarified that he could never do business with us because of the incident. The event had made a section of Pakistanis even more hostile towards India, but this political gulf between us did not stand in the way of the gracious hospitality we received from the owners. Once our meeting was over, the owner drove us to a sweet shop on the famous Mall Road, called Nirala. He presented to A.K. Singh and me a packet of Lahori sweets as a parting gesture. We all hugged and bade each other goodbye, saying, '*Khuda hafiz, salamat rahen.*'

Soon after, we met the owner of Vanguard Publications, Najam Aziz Sethi, the businessman and journalist who also served as the CM of Punjab (Pakistan) for a short tenure. Najam is a prominent intellectual voice in Pakistan and, as the editor-in-chief of *The Friday Times*, has always called spade a spade.* Najam's wife had also visited Delhi a couple of times and he was outspoken on Indo-Pak relations. He had invited a professor from Lahore University, an expert on Greek philosophy, to our meeting and we discussed both these subjects at length. We discussed Greek tragedy and drew parallels to our

---

*Najam also served as the chairman of Pakistan Cricket Board and later as the chairman of Pakistan Super League.

equation with Pakistan. We discussed what a tragedy this equation had been, and what a long shadow it had cast on the relations between the two countries.

We left Pakistan the next day with mixed emotions. We loved the time we had spent in the country and were delighted to have met many of its illustrious publishers and intellectuals. But the enduring animosity between our countries saddened me. When would things get better? Would leaders on both sides have the courage, imagination and good sense to bridge the divide? I certainly hope to witness this in my lifetime. Will I?

But if barbed wires and concrete walls divide the two nations physically, it is the ink that makes them porous. While we went to Pakistan to extend invitation to one of their acclaimed authors, we came back with one more—the novelist, poet, critic, diplomat and scholar Ahmed Ali. He was born in Delhi in 1910 and had taught at the universities of Lucknow, Allahabad, Agra and at Calcutta's Presidency College. A pioneer of modern Urdu poetry and a co-founder of All Indian Progressive Writers Movement and Association, Ali became a household name when he, along with Sajjad Zaheer, Rashid Jahan and Mahmud-uz-Zafar, published *Angaaray*, a collection of Urdu short stories and a play, in 1932. An unconventional book that challenged the orthodoxy in Islam as well as the then colonial ecosystem, it was denounced both by Islamic society as well as by the political establishment represented by the British government. But it heralded the onset of a new form of writing that moved beyond the

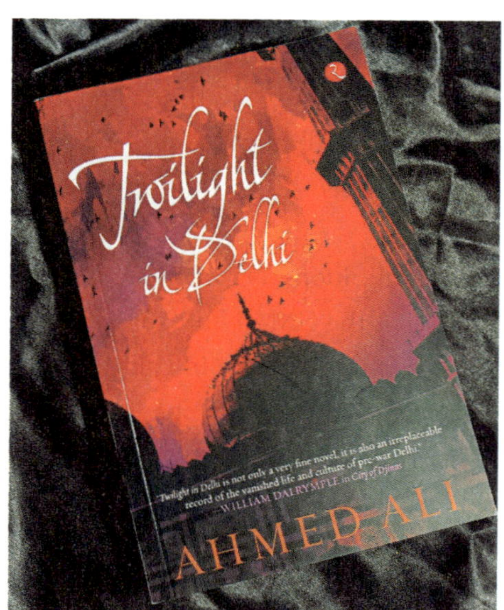

A literary masterstroke, the book displayed India's agony and British apathy towards her

paeans of Urdu literature and questioned the existing state of affairs. After facing backlash at home for writing *Angaaray*, Ali wrote his most famous novel, *Twilight in Delhi*, not in his native Urdu but in the language of the Crown, which was a literary masterstroke. Ali wanted to present India's agony and the injustices she had faced to a wider audience. Upon its publication in 1940, a critic wrote: 'It may well be that we shall not understand India until it is explained to us by Indian novelists of the first ability, as it was that we understand nothing of British before we read Tolstoy, Turgenev and the others. Ahmed Ali may well be vanguard of such a literary movement.'*

The book was first published by Hogarth Press in 1940, by Oxford University Press in 1966, 1984 and 1991, and by New Direction Inc., in 1994. Iqbal bhai gave us Ahmed Ali's contact details. We got in touch with the family and published *Twilight in Delhi* for the Indian readers in 2007. In his life, Ali lamented the loss of his past and his banishment from his city of birth. By publishing the book in the author's city of origin, we believe we brought some part of the Ali back to his *janmabhoomi*, his beloved Delhi.

*Ali, Ahmed, *Twilight in Delhi*, Rupa Publications, New Delhi, 2007.

• Chapter 16 •

NEPAL: THE LAND OF MAHADEVA

It boasts of the world's highest mountain, the Mount Everest, acting as its crown. Fascinating and mythical creatures like the Yeti (snowman), Khyah (small hairy demons), Gurumapa (mythical man-eater) and Garuda (half man-half eagle) inhabit its cultural landscape, making Nepal a land of rich history and stories. And stories are what we fetch. R.N. Barman made inroads for Rupa's business in Nepal. Nature has endowed Nepal with beauty, making it a haven for tourists who also camp there for months. By the early '70s, Rupa published a pictorial book on Nepal, in collaboration with a French publisher. Titled *Nepal: Moments of Life*, the book had pictures corresponding to the text, which conjured up 'the poetry and harmony of the people and things which make up the everyday life of the country with their looks, colours, luminosity and movement'. The book truly captured the soul of Nepal and was an instant success, with one bookstore ordering 4,000 copies at once.

This paved the way for Mr Barman to make frequent trips to Nepal from Calcutta, establishing Rupa's significant presence in Nepal. By mid-'70s, Delhi was emerging as a business hub and its connectivity with Kathmandu was also improving. Mr Barman persuaded me to visit Kathmandu and explore more business opportunities. Thus, Rupa's trade link with Nepal was was established by A.K. Singh and me.

An instant hit in Nepal, this book started our publishing relations with the Himalayan kingdom

One day, during one of my trips to Kathmandu, Mahadeva blessed me, albeit in a different way. In Nepal, the work week starts from Sunday, and it is always better to reach an evening before and plan the upcoming day. During that trip, I landed in Kathmandu late on a Saturday afternoon. Mohan Shreshtha of Educational Book House had very kindly sent his driver to pick me up from the airport. They had been our distributors in Nepal. Our association was going strong, and so was my association with Mohanji's driver, a cheerful and talkative person. Visiting the Lord Pashupatinath Temple was a ritual during my visits and it was no different this time. As I was walking towards the temple's sanctum sanctorum, I heard some commotion. Before I could realize, I was in the line of attack of a raging bull and, in no time, I had fallen and hurt myself. My trousers were torn from the knees, which were now bleeding. My hands were also bruised and I was in agony. '*Khoon nikalto…khoon nikalto* (He's bleeding)', shouted the devotees there, who were all advising me in unison to go back. *I have to complete the puja*, I told myself. Limping, bleeding and in pain, I stoically paid my respects to Lord Pashupatinath.

More drama was to unfold. An otherwise still evening suddenly broke into a downpour and it grew dark. I somehow reached my hotel, The Everest, with Mohanji's driver skillfully navigating Kathmandu roads in such a deluge. The staff at the hotel knew me. They provided me with first aid and, in no time, I fell a sleep. Waking up in immense pain the next day, I completed my planned morning meetings but had to cut short my trip. I returned the same afternoon, battered, bruised and in shock. Couple of months passed but my pain persisted. I was surviving on painkillers.

Then one day, I went to Bangalore, unbeknownst that a happy twist in this painful tale was awaiting me. Near our office on Ranganathan Street is the Vinayak Temple and on the other side is a 400-year-old Bull Temple. After polishing off idlis, which my manager in Bangalore knew I relished, for breakfast, I went to offer my obeisance at the Vinayak

Lord Pashupatinath Temple where I came in the line of a raging bull

Temple. While I was going back to the office, my driver asked me politely, in his charming Kannada accent, 'Sir, you always visit Vinayak Temple. Why don't you go to the other side of the road? There is another very famous temple there.' His excitement had already piqued my curiosity, so I went to see this temple. And lo and behold! Carved from a single stone of granite stood the mighty, black-coloured bull in front of me. This was the famous Bull Temple of Bangalore, but I had been ignorant of its presence! I touched Nandi baba's feet and only said, 'Baba, what have I done to deserve so much pain?' My knees still ached from that bull attack in Nepal. I returned to Delhi and life went on as usual. After a couple of days, my wife pointed out that I had not been taking my painkillers. I realized that she was right. I had not been taking the medicines because I didn't feel any pain! In the next 48 hours, my wife and I were at the feet of Nandi baba in the Bull Temple in Bangalore. How else could a mortal soul pay its respect and thank this miraculous and divine pain killer? Incidentally, the same year, we did a majestic book on the landscapes of Bangalore by Anuradha Mathur and Dilip da Cunha. Titled *Deccan Traverses: The Making of Bangalore's Terrain*, it has a venerable mention of the Bull Temple.

(From left) Dilip Da Cunha, H.D. Kumaraswamy, the then CM of Karnataka, Governor T.N. Chaturvedi and Anuradha Mathur at the release of the book

With Jug Suraiya, an old Calcutta pal, our author and the man who introduced us to Dubby Bhagat

Our list of books on Nepal and by Nepalese authors in English was increasing. While in Calcutta, like every native of the city, I had heard about Desmond Doig (which native of Calcutta hasn't!) and his remarkable book on the city called *Calcutta: An Artist's Impression*. Desmond was a journalist par excellence, an observant writer, an immersive artist and a free-spirited adventurer. Being of Anglo-Irish descent, he was also the first Indian journalist to write about a certain nun from Albania who was helping the poor and the destitute on the streets of Calcutta. He later wrote a heart-warming biography on her, *Mother Teresa: Her People*

Desmond Doig (fourth from right), the maverick who loved Kathmandu and Calcutta, seen here holding his adda in Kathmandu

and Her Work. Desmond loved Calcutta and, during the latter part of his life, Kathmandu. Peter Hensen one day informed me that Desmond had made some beautiful sketches of Kathmandu and that we should publish them. The only problem was that Desmond was no more and no one knew where these sketches were. However, if something is destined to happen, it will happen. The maverick Desmond had started *Junior Statesman* in Calcutta and Jug Suraiya was one of its editors. I knew Jug and thought that he could be the one holding the key to Desmond's world. I was right! Jug told me about a man living in the Himalayan kingdom, who had once worked with Desmond and who was living in Nepal and to whom Desmond had bequeathed all his writings and sketches. This man's name was Dubby Bhagat. He ran a travel agency at the Everest Hotel in Kathmandu, the same hotel where we always stayed. Immediately, a trip was planned to Kathmandu, with my wife and our 11-year-old son Kapish accompanying me. During this trip, I met Dubby at the Everest Hotel. He showed me Desmond's will and told me how he has kept all the sketches that Desmond drew safe. Perhaps he knew some publisher would

(*Top*) *At the launch of* My Kind of Kathmandu, *which was published the same year as* Peak Hour (*Bottom*) Peak Hour, *which was released by Nepal's tourism minister, was an accidental book that came out while I was pursuing Dubby Bhagat to finish Desmond Doig's* My Kind of Kathmandu.

come to him one day, looking for them. Dubby then took us to Far Pavilion, a rooftop restaurant in Everest Hotel from where you could quietly soak in the breathtaking view of the city of Kathmandu. It had been a perfect evening till I broke its calm with my lamentation of not being able to go on the one-hour flight that would provide majestic views of the 21 peaks of the Himalayas. It was a cakewalk for Dubby, who ran a travel agency, to organize this. By the next morning, we were to take an early morning mountain flight. The experience became more special because we were booked on a flight with just the three of us and a Chief Justice of Pakistan. We were all set for an exclusive tête-à-tête with the Himalayas! Several peaks of the mighty Himalayan range stood before us, unfolding their grandeur with every turn of the plane. It is said that whatever you feel when you see the Himalayas is yours and yours alone; your memory of the mountain never fades. Young Kapish was excited to see the cockpit and the pilot was more than happy to oblige. Emboldened by this invitation, Kapish asked the pilot, 'Can you take one more round?'

Desmond Doig's
My Kind of Kathmandu

'The fuel is limited, but I think it can be done young man,' replied the smiling pilot. Despite the limited fuel, he completed another round while my wife and I were only praying to the Almighty until we landed. The experience of witnessing the Himalayas was ethereal and I asked Dubby to write a book on these Everest flights. Thus, *Peak Hour* was born. It is a beautiful, four-colour book on the 21 peaks about which Sir Edmund Hillary said, 'If you want a fascinating romantic story of Nepal and its great mountains you will undoubtedly find it in Dubby Bhagat's narrative.' To be honest, *Peak Hour* was an accidental book that came out while I was pursuing Dubby to finish Desmond Doig's enchanting book, *My Kind of Kathmandu,* which was also published the same year.

Mohan Shrestha of the Educational Enterprise

Rama Tiwari of Pilgrims Book House

Anjan Shrestha of Educational Book House

Ramchandra Timothy of Ekta Book Distributor

Bidur Dangol of Vajra Bookshop

Madhab Maharjan of Mandala Book Point

The Everest Hotel in Kathmandu

Our business in Nepal was picking up pace and soon we realized we required a full office there. Mohanji's uncle was kind enough to lend the front portion of his house for our office and thus was established Rupa's Educational Book House in Kantipath, Kathmandu, in 1994. Over time, our distributors in Nepal increased. Ratna Book Distributor, Mandala Book Point, Ekta Book Distributors, Tibet Book Store, were all populated with Rupa books. Pilgrim Book House was another great place for Rupa books. Its owner, Rama Tiwari, lived in Banaras, and his daughter and son-in-law looked after the shop. Our list of authors from Nepal was also increasing and becoming heterogeneous. While Desmond's and Dubby's books talked about the social and cultural imprints of Nepal, we also did Prakash A. Raj's *The Dancing Democracy: The Power of the Third Eye*—an incisive commentary on Maoism in Nepal, and Sagar Rana's history and politics of the country as the Rana kingdom and thereafter.

I always got an audience with the then PM Girija Prasad Koirala and his ministers and associates

The Everest Hotel in Kathmandu was where we always stayed and it became our home away from home, considering the frequency with which we were travelling to Nepal. The hotel housed one of the best casinos in the country, and was looked after by an affable man Rakesh Wadhwa and his colleague Kalyan. Rakesh was particularly fond of young Kapish, so much so that he took our son to a casino when he was only 11 years old!

Whenever I was in Nepal, I always got an audience with the then PM Girija Prasad Koirala and his ministers and associates. During one of my meetings with him, I confessed to the PM about having smuggled something from his country. Amazed at my boldness and confused as to what he should do, he politely asked me what it was.

'Sir, a few illustrations of Desmond Doig for our book on Kathmandu,' I replied.

He was relieved that the artistic impressions were in safe hands and not with Nepal Customs! PM Koirala's daughter took keen interest in the development of publishing in Nepal, and she foresaw a longer strategic partnership between Rupa and the booksellers and authors in Nepal. Unfortunately, the Himalayan kingdom witnessed a massacre that shook its very roots, particularly the monarchy. In 2001, Crown Prince Dipendra killed King Birendra, Queen Aishwarya and several members of the royal family, before shooting himself in a horrendous tragedy that left everyone numb. Maoist influence over the political arena also increased and soon, Girija Prasad Koirala had to resign. Over the years, Nepal has witnessed political turbulence, which always spells doom for any enterprise. Then, in 2015, the country witnessed a seismic shock that killed thousands and rendered millions homeless. The book business is always a casualty in a human calamity of such scale. Covid-19 further froze our trade in the country. As the country has been rebuilding itself from the aftershocks of political and natural disasters, I hope that our business relationships thaw soon, and we are once again drawn to the land of mountains, mythologies and Mahadeva.

'We swim and sink together' was D. Mehra's ethos for the company and his staff. This is a rare photo of 1972 wherein on the extreme left (sitting) is B.P. Patel, our Bombay manager and on the extreme right is B.D. Khatri, who was our manager in Allahabad. Both Mr Patel and Mr Khatri were the icons of loyalty, having spent their entire professional lives at Rupa.

• Chapter 17 •

THE PASSING OF AN ERA

Three years before the dawn of the new millennium, my granduncle, D. Mehra, passed away in his home in Calcutta. He led a long life, full of achievements, adventure and fulfilment, and left behind a lasting legacy through the publishing house he founded. In many ways, his passing marked the end of an era, not just for Rupa but also for the Indian book world. As I look back in time, I am filled with wonder; starting from a small street corner in 1936, we branched out to Allahabad in 1939, then Bombay in 1954 followed by Delhi in 1970. I wonder how we managed to sell books, first all across India and now globally. What started with importing foreign titles, then acquiring rights for the titles, reprinting, joint ventures with global giants and finally to independent publishing, Rupa's metamorphosis elicits both awe and humility in all of us. Rupa now has more than 2,000 front list titles and the list is only growing. The birth of Aleph Book Company as part of the Rupa family has added to our joy and wonderment. The principles and foresight of D. Mehra have been our guiding light and they continue to be so.

(From left) N.D. Mehra, D. Mehra, R.N. Barman and Mike Hogben. D. Mehra was a reluctant socializer, hence this photo is rare.

Rupa book fairs and events were always crowd pullers

When D. Mehra entered the world of books, it was a very different place. The world of publishing was small, authors remained largely invisible, thus leaving an aura of mystique, charming the readers with their anonymity. The term 'marketing' was looked down upon, considered an exercise more in self-promotion rather than the product. However, evolution is how species become a better version of their previous selves and this principle of biology applies in all aspects of our lives. The Mehras have a reclusive gene that I have inherited. I am an extremely reticent person. However, when it came to highlighting our books and authors, I knew how to blow that trumpet. A book on Hyderabadi cuisines had a launch at a five-star hotel with a nine-course meal for 700 guests, with an M.F. Hussain painting on one side of the hall and the city's who's who sharing culinary tales; *Sunny Days* witnessed Gavaskar's teammates as well as opponents coming together under one roof—laughing, eating, drinking, celebrating; the launch of Gayatri Devi's memoir *A Princess Remembers* was brimming with royalty; and for the launch of L.K. Advani's autobiography, *My Country, My Life*, we turned Siri Fort Auditorium into a citadel hosting the most powerful politicians of the day. If fancy book launches were about the glamour and glitterati, Rupa's book fairs in non-metro cities became a haven for the literati. By the early '90s, we realized the latent demand for books in the then Tier 2 cities of Lucknow, Chandigarh, Jaipur and Dehradun. Rupa started its own book fair in these cities and it became a talking point among authors and book lovers. This was an age before e-commerce had entered our lives and bookshops were the only place to buy books. Naturally, a huge fair dedicated exclusively to books would be a big draw and Rupa's book fairs were received enthusiastically. We ensured that a prominent person from the city inaugurated the fair, that a pocket-sized Rupa stocklist was placed on the window of every car parked, that a flyer displaying latest offers from us was handed over to each and every soul visiting the fair, that news about Rupa's book fair was on the ticker of the local cable TV. Transporting books to these cities and creating a fair from scratch was a massive logistical exercise, but the prospect of finding new readers and buyers and making our books available to the widest possible section of population was our driving force.

However, by the early 2000s, things changed both on the publishing end and the way books were distributed and sold. On the retail front, the advent of e-commerce platforms was a game changer. When Flipkart entered the e-commerce fray around late 2006–07, followed by Amazon, bookselling in India underwent a seismic shift. Short circuiting geographical limitations, it has helped publishers reach readers residing in the deeper pockets of the country and service pin codes that were earlier unreachable for distributors. It also encouraged buyers, who were otherwise reluctant to visit a bookshop, to look for books online, thus opening up a new channel of communication between publishers and readers.

Over the last 20 years, Amazon and Flipkart have dramatically changed book distribution in India and retail today exists parallelly with these e-commerce giants. This fairy tale, however, had its own share of controversies. In December 2014, we published the then President Pranab Mukherjee's autobiography *The Dramatic Decade: The Indira Gandhi Years*. Taking an unconventional route, we signed an exclusive deal with Amazon to make the book available on the platform only for the first three weeks post-publication. It was a masterstroke in marketing and with just the pre-orders, the octogenarian's autobiography was the third bestselling title after Chetan Bhagat's *Half Girlfriend* and Sachin

Tendulkar's autobiography *Playing It My Way* (Hachette). Respecting the new market realities, we really played this one our way, but the traditional distributors threatened to boycott us. Imagine getting boycotted for selling one's own product! This was a wake-up call for all stakeholders to recalibrate and realign our relationships with the changing market conditions. I can safely say we have been able to achieve that.

If Calcutta lives in its bookshops, Bombay revels in them. New Book Company, Strand Book Stall, Pocket Book Centre, Excelsior Book Centre, to name a few, are booklovers' hubs. Crossword has spread its wings across Bombay, and Kitabkhana is also a noticeable addition to this long list of brick-and-mortar outlets. While these stores fill their shelves with the books that are fresh off the press, there is a rich culture of second-hand bookshops in Bombay, catering to customers with a deep love for reading but not-so-deep pockets. The New and Second-Hand Book Shop is notable among them. Started in 1905, with its cramped shelves and two floors, it continues to robustly sell old, obscure and unique books. Talking about second-hand books, one Mr Saha in Calcutta used to sell these books at his almost dilapidated kiosk on College Street. If

Connaught Place in Delhi was once dotted with bookshops and was a literary wonderland

for any reason a title was not available, he would make it available within 24 hours. It was no mean feat to carry out such tasks without Google or even a mobile phone at one's disposal.

Gangaram, Higginbothams, Sapna, Landmark are some of the stores in Bangalore that are a reader's delight. The owner of one such bookstore, Premier Book Store, Mr Shanbaug, was a human encyclopedia on all the classic and current books. Unfortunately, after his death, the store closed down and Bangalore lost one of its remarkable literary outlets. Similarly, Nalini Chettur's Giggles at Taj Connemara, a major stopover for bibliophiles in Madras had to shut shop. But Nalini being Nalini, the master bookseller still continues to buy books from us and sell them to her old customers. After being in the books business for more than four decades, she has cultivated an army of loyal customers who stand behind her, with or without Giggles. But Higginbothams, Starmark and Odyssey are still around and rocking.

Connaught Place in Delhi was once dotted with bookshops like Ramkrishna & Sons, Galgotia Book Shop, New Book Depot, Bookworm, Piccadilly, Amrit Book Company, St Paul's, Delhi Book Company and many more. My sepia-tinted memory takes me to these shops where I see Dev Kant Barooah (the man who sycophantically proclaimed 'India is Indira and Indira is India') picking up a book on Picasso; Babu Jagjivan Ram rummaging through a shelf and coming out victorious with a book on agriculture; or Dom Moraes on a ladder, taking out his book from the upper shelf and keeping it within the customers' eyesight at Galgotia Book Shop. More bookshops have emerged across the city with Khan Market, South Extension and Aurobindo Marg becoming the new hubs for buyers. Bahrisons, Faqir Chand, Midland, Om and K.D. Singh's are popular names among the book buyers, with their owners running the show. Changing times have forced some of these shops to lower their shutters; yet, some still exist like candles in the wind, their pale light trying not to fade away.

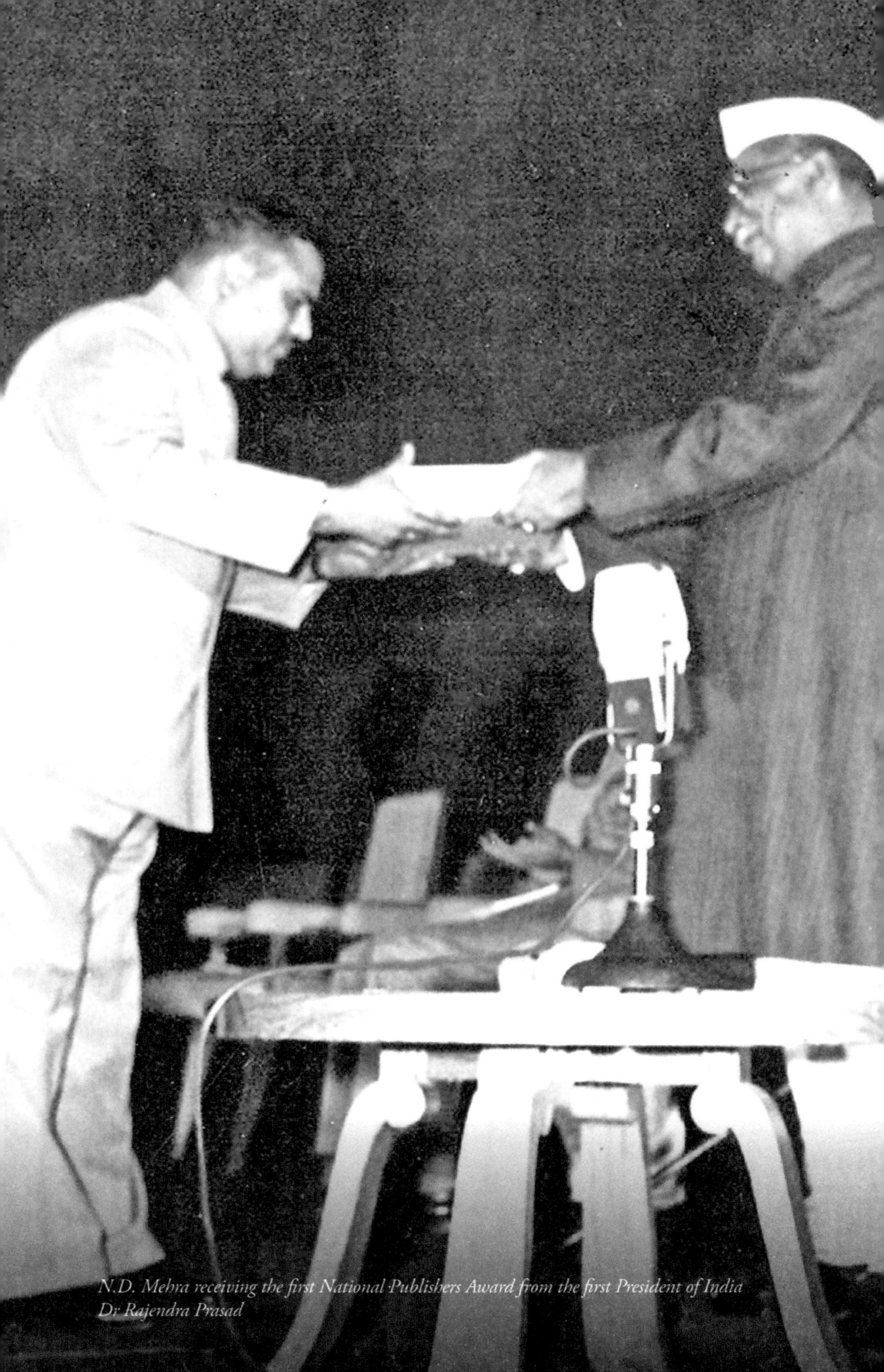

N.D. Mehra receiving the first National Publishers Award from the first President of India Dr Rajendra Prasad

• Chapter 18 •

THE BOOKKEEPER WHO COULD DO ANYTHING

How to Win Friends and Influence People is a twentieth-century bible of self-help books written by Dale Carnegie, the cheerleader of individual victory, charm and persona. Publishers across the world have been publishing Dale Carnegie, readers after readers hoping to get this talisman of success. Carnegie writes in the book:

> If you believe in what you are doing, then let nothing hold you up in your work. Much of the best work of the world has been done against seeming impossibilities. The thing is to get the work done.

My father, N.D. Mehra, was winning friends, influencing people and at the same time getting the work done; he was the closest person I know who lived up to Carnegie's dictum without ever having read him. Born in Banaras on 13 October 1924, he was only 12 years old when he saw his uncle, D. Mehra, start Rupa. The young boy was blown away by his uncle's indefatigable spirit in selling books; his future was sealed right then. By the time he turned 18, the young N.D. Mehra had joined Rupa, working with his uncle. If D. Mehra was the visionary, N.D. Mehra was the executor; if the uncle had imagination, the nephew marshalled all the resources to turn that imagination into reality; if one saw a dream, the other made it possible. The uncle–nephew duo complemented each other in more ways than one.

My father was Rupa's bookkeeper. He knew his pennies and pounds. He could decode the most complex and esoteric income tax clauses and could unravel the

N.D. Mehra, at the Rupa cash counter in Calcutta

financial mysteries of our banking system. Allahabad Bank on College Street was his regular adda, where he was often seen chatting with the bank manager, giving the bank more business by opening accounts of known people. He knew every clerk and cashier and what was going on in their lives. He banked on people and they loved him for that.

As a father, he was a strict disciplinarian, and my first memory of him is him holding my hands and taking me to an unfamiliar place, which made me anxious. But with my father by my side, I conquered my fears and started loving the place—my first school. To be honest, till the age of eight or nine, I didn't know my father much, as I used to spend more time with my mother and grandmother. Until then, I only knew that father goes to 'office' every morning which we called the showroom; that this place was full of books, which were very colourful and looked very different from my school books;

that in father's showroom, we were always served cold coffee or ice cream, and I always wondered who read these books. Sunday was the day when all the children were packed in our family's old second-hand Volkswagen, bought at a princely sum of ₹8,000, and driven to Victoria Memorial and Maidan, gorging on phuchkas, jhal muri and ice cream. I also have a faint memory of him taking me to buy vegetables in the neighbouring Nuton Bazaar and Chaatu Bazaar and haggling so hard with the vendor that the poor chap would almost give him the vegetables for free. That's where my bargaining powers have come from!

Distance makes the heart grow fonder, the cliché goes. And I, too, couldn't escape it. I grew closer to my father when he was away from me. When I was leaving Calcutta to establish Rupa in Delhi, there were teary eyes all around me—after all, I was leaving the family home. My father's stoic presence comforted me a bit and he gave me a cheque of ₹50,000, his entire life's savings. 'This is all

Philip Zeigler, son-in-law of Lord Mountbatten, with C.K. Mehra and N.D. Mehra

N.D. Mehra distributed bonuses to his staff himself to bring a sense of personal touch

I have'; he said, 'this step that you are taking will give you benefit in the long run.' He didn't shed a tear; at least I didn't see one.

Delhi was not a new city for me, but this time it was. I was all by myself, my own small boat trying to sail away from the mother ship. And the very first experience stormed me. I negotiated for an office space on Ansari Road; it had been Indian Telephone Industries office and they were vacating it. The place was decent and the lease was settled for ₹1,500. I telegrammed our Calcutta office from where the bank draft was to be issued. Feeling elated over this first victory, I went to the landlord's place with the draft, only to be told that they had found a new buyer. This left me baffled and betrayed. The deal couldn't go through and it was my first defeat in the new city. Soon after, I did manage to get an office at Pataudi House Road. My father came and ensured that the deal was finalized, the office was set up and a small function marking the occasion was hosted. But there was nothing 'small' in

N.D. Mehra's world. So many people turned up that we fell short of snacks and refreshments. My father surely had built his own world—engaging, immersive and full of people.

A gastronome at heart, he loved his raj bhogs, chhappan bhogs and rosogullas. I once witnessed him gulping 32 rosogullas because he had a bet with his friend! His love for culinary adventure landed us our landmark and current office in Daryaganj. One afternoon, during one of his epicurean pursuits, he chanced upon a shop selling the ubiquitous Delhi snack, dahi bhalla. He fell in love with the concoction and became a frequent visitor at this very famous eatery in Old Delhi, called Natraj. During one such visit, he asked a broker who knew him (one of his many known people) if an office space was available near this place that served such delicious dahi bhallas. And thus was discovered the building 7/16 Ansari Road, which became Rupa's trademark Daryaganj address—a result of someone's pursuit of happiness.

He not only loved his food but also loved treating people around him. Back in Calcutta, hardly an evening went by when he would not return home with *besan ka sev* or *mota sev* from a shop set up by a family from Bikaner. This is how the Mehra household was introduced to Haldiram's, a tradition which has seen a few hundred kilograms of bhujia be consumed over five generations!

My father's cheerful persona masked a shrewd business sense. Much before the fancy financial terms we use today—venture capitalists, angel investors, incubators and accelerators—there was N.D. Mehra who knew exactly where and how to invest the company's money. He knew how much royalty went to an author, how much money was due from a distributor, how many copies a title sold, the remainder stock, etc.

Though he could never attend college, my father had a great economic and

My father's last public appearance in December 1991. He had been admitted in AIIMS with a fractured hand. We took special permission from the doctor to ensure that he attends the launch of one of our books, The Scarlet, *at The Lalit. On his right can be seen, Sunil Goel and Ratanji of Gopsons.*

financial insight. The election in 1991 resulted in Congress winning without a majority but still as the largest leading party. P.V. Narasimha Rao, the Chanakya of politics, became the PM. He appointed Manmohan Singh as the finance minister to bring the country's economy out of the woods. It was profusely debated whether Manmohan Singh was appointed under the diktat of foreign powers, as the Indian economy was in shambles and needed World Bank funds and support from the US. Once the government was in place and the first budget presented, the rupee was devalued twice in three days. Foreign currency became expensive and so did import. My father saw the first budget drafted by Manmohan Singh on 29 February 1992 and remarked that it was 'destructive'. And it surely was the beginning of a long period of struggle for small, independent and indigenous business entities.

A man of the world who was genuinely interested in the life of others from cradle to grave, a man who had the loudest laugh in the room and who could laugh at himself, N.D. Mehra was the rainmaker, even he never acknowledged. Once, an Australian publisher visited us in Delhi. To make the Australians feel at home, I ordered a crate of Heineken beer. My teetotaller father, trying to impress his guests, vigorously shook a beer bottle and opened it. Foaming and frothing in beer, our Australian guests remarked, 'Mr Mehra, you are the first person who made champagne out of beer.' Realizing his spirited faux pas, he said, 'I can do anything.'

N.D. Mehra sure could do anything.

GRATITUDE UNBOUND

Honouring our booksellers, without whom a publishers journey is incomplete

Ram Advani (left) of Advani Booksellers, Lucknow, with A.K. Singh. Ram Advani was an icon of knowledge and his lifelong love for books is his true legacy to the publishing world.

K.D. Singh, in his bookshop. The keeper of tales, his endless passion and knowledge about books was a lesson for booksellers and publishers.

K.G. Nayak (second from left) of Vinayak Book Distributors with M.K. Srinivasan (third from left)

Chaturbhuj (left) with Atmaram of Gangaram, Bangalore

S.K. Mehra (right) in conversation with Naveen bhai of Rajesh Book Centre (white T-shirt) along with his younger brother

Rajiv Chaudhary (left) of English Book Shop, Chandigarh

Anup and Mamata of Faqir-Chand Book Shop. The family migrated from Pakistan.

Shanti Bhai, a well-known trade personality from Bombay

Jay and Hemu Subramaniam of Landmark, Madras

Nalini Chettur of Giggles, Madras

Qadir bhai (left) of Ensign Book Shop, Bombay, with S.K. Mehra

S.K. Mehra with Mani bhai (right) of Book Lovers

(From left) Ramesh Patel with Kalyanji bhai of Student Agency and T.N. Shanbaug of Strand Book Stall

(From left) Mirza Afsar Baig of Midland with Sanjeev Mago, Sanjay Mago and Ajay Mago of Om Book Shop

Om Mago with Vedant (grandson) and Sanjay Mago (son)

Randhir Arora and Siddhant Arora of Bookworld Dehradun

O.P. Arora of Capital Book Depot, Chandigarh

Pankaj Singh of The Browser, Chandigarh

C.M. Chawla of UBS Publishers and Distributors

With Prakash Krishna (left) of Ramakrishna & Sons. They were four brothers and their family had migrated from Pakistan.

Bhupinder Chowdhury of English Book Store

Dinesh Gupta of Crossword Bookstore

(From left) T.C. Alexander with J.K. Bose and Ajit Bikram Singh of Fact n Fiction, Delhi

Harish C. Lal of UBDC, Lucknow

Jagath of Kitab Khana, Bombay

(Sitting from left) B.R. Chawla, Sunil Sachdeva, M.G. Arora, S.C. Sethi, Bhupinder Chaudhary and S.K. Ghai
(Standing from left) J.L. Kumar, Vinod Vashisth, Ravindra Saxena, Himanshu Chawla and Manas Saikia on the occasion of ninetieth birthday of M.G. Arora

Ashwin of Odyssey, Madras

Om Arora of Variety Book Depot

Barman brothers—Ashok and Pramod—of the Family Book Shop

(From left) Manav Prakash, Chandar Prakash, Bishan Prakash and Gaurav Prakash of Universal Booksellers, Lucknow

Universal Book Centre, Lucknow

Minoo and Dinshaw Booksellers

Om Prakash of Modern Book Depot, Bhubaneshwar

Hira Primlani (left) of India Book House and R. Manoranjan (right), our Madras manager, with a customer

Sukhdev Arora of Book World, Dehradun; a familiar name among writers, publishers and readers

D.C. Kizhakkemuri of D.C. Books, Kerala, and one of the most well-read booksellers in the country

Satheesan of DC Books, Koytayam

With Shaukat Bhai of AA Hussain Booksellers, Hyderabad

R.K. Gupta, director at S. Chand & Company, was a dear friend

Snehlata Arora of English Book Depot in Dehradun. In her early 80s, she still reaches her shop at 10.30 a.m. and stays till the very end of the day

A.S. Dutta, owner of Dutta Book Center

With Nitin Shah and Deepak Shah of Sapna, Bangalore

An enduring partnership:
Authors weave tales,
publishers weave success
and readers weave
memories.

·PART TWO·

PLAIN TALES OF AUTHORS AND BOOKS

There never was and never will be anyone like Don

• Chapter 19 •

CRICKETERS

May cricket continue to flourish and spread its wings.
The world can only be richer for it.
—Sir Donald Bradman

Many years ago, at London Book Fair, a British publisher friend remarked to me that a publisher was only as good as his last list. I must admit that this so-called 'insight' startled me because it seemed to me that it classified authors as dispensable commodities who would only be cherished for a brief while and then be cast aside when the next season's stars were ushered into the spotlight. My riposte to my friend was swift, 'At Rupa, we try to value our authors; they are not just the flavour of the month or year. Without our authors, Rupa would not have lasted as long as it has.' In this section of the book, I'd like to briefly recount stories about some of our memorable authors and books.

First up are our books on cricket. Rupa's cricket list was launched in 1962—a memorable year on many counts: America put an astronaut in space; Bob Dylan sang 'Blowin in the Wind'; Nelson Mandela was arrested; and James Bond made his first appearance on screen. In our country, three-time PM Jawaharlal Nehru, was betrayed by the Chinese, who invaded our borders and slaughtered our brave soldiers. Even as the Indian Army fought bravely against the invaders, civil societies organized a host of fundraisers to send money and supplies to the armed forces. One such event took place in Calcutta, where a charity cricket match was played in Eden Gardens with Lala Amarnath, Dattu Phadkar, Polly Umrigar, Mushtaq Ali, Pankaj Roy and Vijay Hazare sweating it out for our men in olive green to raise funds

Rupa's Calcutta office where several Indian cricketers attended the event that started our journey of cricket publishing. On the extreme right can be seen Lala Amarnath with his trademark pipe (December 1962).

for the National Defence College. This was also the beginning of a series we published called *Rupa's World of Cricket*.

Rakhal Bhattacharya, sports editor with the venerable newspaper *The Statesman*, was a household name in the city for all things sports. When he suggested that we publish autobiographies of some of the stalwarts of the game, we were quick to act on the suggestion. In those days, sports books and autobiographies were rare, and my granduncle and his foster son, R.N. Barman who himself was a sports enthusiast and an avid consumer of all Raj Kapoor movies, immediately saw the potential in the idea. In no time, Rupa organized an event to welcome the legends of cricket who would be playing in the upcoming charity match in the city. Unlike the glitzy events organized by the publishing industry today, this event was devoid of any razzmatazz, with players being served coffee, sandwiches, idlis and dosas in the 'Koljepara Coffee House' as Calcutta's Coffee House was popularly called. Lala Amarnath, Dattu Phadkar, Polly Umrigar,

Pankaj Roy, Mushtaq Ali and Vijay Hazare turned up. Amidst the free-flowing coffee and club sandwiches, ideas for cricket books brewed and the first cricket autobiography we signed was *Cricket Delightful* by Mushtaq Ali.*

Syed Mushtaq Ali was a popular hero, the first Indian cricketer to have scored a century overseas (against England at Old Trafford in 1936), 'a romantic figure of the game' (as stated in his obituary in *The Guardian*†) and about whom the great cricket writer Neville Cardus wrote, 'At times his cricket was touched with genius and imagination.'‡ No sooner had Mushtaq Ali agreed to write his autobiography for Rupa than we found ourselves on a sticky wicket. This daring batsman, who would awe spectators by dashing down the pitch to belt even the fast bowlers, was no writer. Although a daredevil batsman and a great talker and charmer, he would need assistance to get his life story down on paper. Our frantic search for a ghostwriter finally ended at the door of Rakhal Bhattacharya, the versatile editor of *The Statesman* who had suggested the cricket series in the first place. Bhattacharya agreed to write the book with Mushtaq Ali but refused to travel to Indore, and insisted that Mushtaq bhai come to him instead. It's a telling comment on the humility and stature of Mushtaq Ali—a

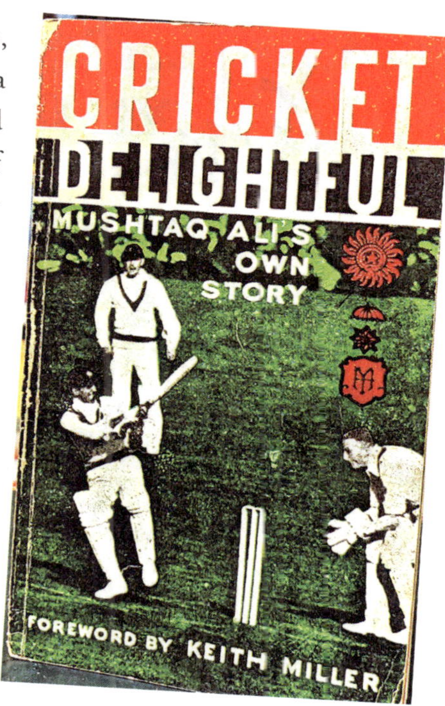

The first cricket autobiography we signed

*Though the first cricket book that we imported and sold in the Indian market in 1962 was *Cricket Crossfire*, an autobiography of the Australian cricketer Keith Miller, originally published by Oldbourne Press in 1956.

†Pandya, Haresh, 'Syed Mushtaq Ali', *The Guardian*, 20 June 2005, https://tinyurl.com/2s4zzyw6. Accessed on 25 July 2023.

‡Ibid.

Vijay Mehra, India's opening batsman with Rakhal Bhattacharya at Rupa's office in Calcutta. Vijay can be seen with Cricket Crossfire, *an autobiography of the Australian cricketer Keith Miller published by Rupa.*

legend in his own right, whom the Government of India had awarded a Padma Shri at that time, and who enjoyed the patronage of the royal household of the Holkars— that he complied with the request of the eccentric editor. This would be unthinkable in this day and age of sporting superstars. But that was a different, more gracious age. We made arrangements for the cricketer to stay at Hotel Broadway on Ganesh Chandra Avenue. Work on the book went smoothly till one day, when the fearless cricketer found himself locked in our house for three days. Every once in a while, Mushtaq bhai would come over to our house to spend time with us. On one such occasion, when he was visiting, communal riots broke out in the city. We refused to let him go back to his hotel until it was safe to venture out. This is how the staunch meat-eating cricketer found himself grazing on vegetables in the Mehra household. He stayed with us for three days, sleeping on a charpoy on our terrace.

Cricket Delightful was published in 1967 and with it, Rupa made its debut as a

R.N. Barman alongwith a display of Rupa's World of Cricket

publisher of cricket books. One of the biggest crowd-pleasers in Indian cricket, Mushtaq bhai's autobiography was in keeping with his character—it was a reader's delight with its colourful anecdotes and no-holds-barred storytelling, just like his batting. The Australian all-rounder, Keith Miller, in his foreword for the book called him 'the Errol Flynn of cricket—dashing, flamboyant, swashbuckling and immensely popular wherever he played'.* In the book, Mushtaq bhai narrated how he first started as a left-arm slow bowler; his debut was unimpressive except that he took Douglas Jardine's wicket; he told the story of how a mix-up of letters resulted in his being dropped from the team and unfortunately labelled a 'rebel' by the cricket authorities; how he was perceived as a perennial bad boy for cricket administrators even when his popularity with the crowds was unmatched. Once, just after the Second World War, the Australian Services Team was touring India and Mushtaq bhai was dropped from the Indian XI team for

*Ali, Mushtaq, *Cricket Delighful: Mushtaq Ali's Own Story*, Rupa Publications, 1967.

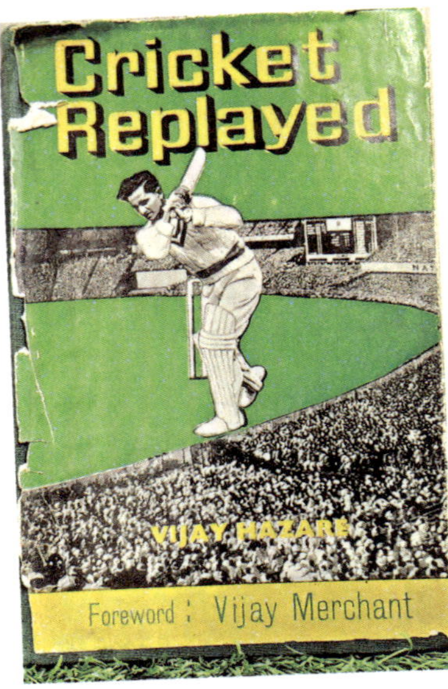

Hazare's autobiography was a great tribute to the game itself

the unofficial Test at Calcutta. The story goes that the passionate Eden Garden's crowd protested in anger, carrying placards reading, 'Bring Back Mushtaq. No Mushtaq, No Test.' They even manhandled the chairman of the selectors who was present in the pavilion and forced him to include Mushtaq bhai in the team.

If our first cricket autobiography was that of a debonair and flamboyant cricketer, our next was of a Test captain whom Vijay Merchant called 'Mr Concentration of Indian Cricket', the ever so accurate, meticulous and mild-mannered Vijay Hazare. *Cricket Replayed*, which was the title of his autobiography, was an aesthetic and detached replay of Vijay Hazare's recollection of his cricketing days. Hazare was renowned for the centuries he had made in Indian cricket, which made him a staple response in crossword puzzles. Many puzzles would use his name, as it could be used as a pun—his name, meant centuries in Hindi. In his foreword to the book, Hazare's contemporary, Vijay Merchant, spoke of how his cricketing career had been cut short:

> The tragedy of Hazare's life was the manner in which he went out of Test cricket. I have not the slightest doubt that he was good enough to play for India, for at least another couple of years, but cricket politics of a dirty nature was responsible for his being ousted. Cricket politics has been the bane of the game in our country. The loss was that of India, not of Vijay Hazare. He has left a mark on Indian cricket which nothing can ever erase.*

Vijay Merchant and Vijay Hazare were unnecessarily dragged into a contest for the Test captaincy in 1951–52, and while Hazare won the race, there was

*Hazare, Vijay, *Cricket Replayed*, Rupa Publications, 1974.

Vinoo Mankad, a cricketer par excellence

Mankad's book, How to Play Cricket

never any animosity between the two. In fact, Merchant candidly told the press that if he had known that the Cricket Control Board wanted Hazare as a captain, he would have withdrawn and played under him.

It was my pleasure to meet Vijay Hazare during the publication process. He was a thorough gentleman, humble in his success, never downcast in defeat and a great ambassador of the game.

Soon, we had several cricketers as our authors. Rakhal Bhattacharya introduced Rupa to Denis Compton, and he too became our author. Then came Vinoo Mankad. I once had a rather comic encounter with this great man. On arriving at his house at 26 Marine Drive, in Bombay, I rang the doorbell. Out came a man clad in a white dhoti and white banian. He said in chaste Gujarati, '*Bai*

Ramprakash Mehra (left), president of the BCCI, releasing the paperback edition of Mushtaq bhai's (right) Cricket Delightful

sooh rahi hai (The woman of the house is sleeping)', trying to shoo me away, probably thinking I was some shopkeeper who had come to settle his bills. When I told him who I was, he was graciousness personified.

A versatile all-rounder, Mankad batted at every position, from number 1 to 11 in his Test career, a truly remarkable feat! Any cricket fan or historian would remember the Lords Test of 1952, which, even though India lost, is remembered as 'the Mankad Test'. Vijay Hazare, captaining India in this dramatic match has called Mankad's innings his pièce de résistance and compared him to a Trojan warrior. Mankad was on the field for all the five days, batting, bowling or fielding. He scored an audacious 70 in the first innings, followed by bowling more than 70 overs and removing half the English side, followed by scoring a brilliant 184. His innings, in the words of his captain, was 'full of belligerence and open defiance'*. Unfortunately, Mankad is more remembered today for a bizarre dismissal of a batsman he was playing against. In 1947, when an Australian side toured the

*Ibid.

country, Mankad removed the bails of non-striker Bill Brown who was out of his crease before bowling the ball. All hell broke loose and the so-called purists of the game made a villain out of this gentleman cricketer for spoiling the hallowed spirit of the game. Every similar dismissal in the future would now be described as 'Mankading'. As if wanting to erase his moral banishment from the game, dictated of course by the English 'lords' (pun intended), he wrote a book for us and titled it *How to Play Cricket,* which was a compilation of his articles published then in *Sportsweek*, explaining all the important aspects of the game in 25 chapters with illustrations. Interestingly, in a chapter called 'Running Between the Wickets', he emphasizes in bold type, 'Every cricketer MUST understand that the worst way of getting out in cricket is to be run out.' The ghost of 'Mankading' haunted this great Indian all-rounder for a long time, until he found solace and support in the words of the greatest cricketer of all time, Sir Donald Bradman, who in his autobiography titled *Farewell to Cricket,* stood firmly in support of Mankad:

> An early sensation came in Australia's innings when Brown was once more run out by Mankad, who, in the act of delivering the ball, held on to it and whipped the bails off with Brown well out of his crease...immediately in some quarters Mankad's sportsmanship was questioned...for the life of me I cannot understand why. The laws of cricket make it quite clear that the non-striker must keep within his ground until the ball has been delivered. If not, why is the provision there which enables the bowler to run him out?*

In 1976, Ramprakash Mehra, president of the BCCI and the Delhi District Cricket Association (DDCA), released the three books, *Cricket Delightful* by Mushtaq Ali, *Cricket Replayed* by Vijay Hazare and *How to Play Cricket* by Vinoo Mankad. Together, the three books started the series called *Rupa's World of Cricket.* Spinners in cricket are known to break the rhythm of a steady innings but off the field, our cricket publishing took another good turn with *One More Over,* the autobiography of Erapally Anantharao Srinivasa Prasanna or simply 'Pras'.

---

*Bradman, Don, *Farewell to Cricket: An Autobiography*, Rupa Publications, 1978.

Regarded as the world's best attacking spin bowler of his time, Prasanna wrote his autobiography in less than a week. Yes, the deceptive spin merchant took only seven days to write about his 15 years in international cricket. Working without a break, he turned in a wonderful manuscript. It was specimen of his relentless hard work. In the past, he had done just that to become a qualified engineer before he turned his science into an art, deceiving batsmen, mesmerizing the crowd, leaving everyone enchanted by his legerdemain.

Written in simple language, without embellishment or rancour, in *One More Over,* Prasanna recounts the highs and lows of a cricketing career spanning

The publishers, who have brought about a renaissance in sports literature, specially Cricket, through their many books of outstanding merit, have rightly turned the focus on the instructional aspect in *Cricket : The Indian Way*. I am sure, the book will be as much a hit as the great exponents of the game.

New Delhi — **RAM PRAKASH MEHRA**
President,
August 12, 1976 — **Board of Control for Cricket in India**

Ramprakash Mehra lauded the efforts of Rupa in a foreword written for one of our books, Cricket: The Indian Way

With President Fakhruddin Ali Ahmed in 1976. He was a great tennis and cricket fan. Here I am presenting him with a copy of Cricket: The Indian Way *published by Rupa in 1976.*

With Maharaja of Baroda, Fatehsinghrao Gaekwad releasing One More Over: An Autobiography *by E.A.S. Prasanna*

15 years and 49 Tests. Bringing out the autobiography of Calcutta's very own jamai babu (Prasanna's wife Sheima is a true-blue Bengali) was a great privilege. The book was an instant bestseller when it hit the stands on 1 January 1977 and went into several reprints.

The same year, we published a colourful account of one of Australia's most explosive cricketers, Ian Chappell. Titled *Chappelli: Life, Larrikins & Cricket*, it was an absorbing and brilliant account of the best captain Australian cricket had seen up until then. Known for his bluntness and controversial decisions, Chappell was the one who lifted the Australian Test team from mediocrity to brilliance. Chappell, the toughest and the most forthright of men, was also a captain who stood by his players. During the tour of England in 1975, the English press was baying for Jeff Thomson's blood, highlighting his homesickness issues in every article. The Australian manager decided to send Thomson home, but Chappell was not in agreement. He threatened to go home too if Thomson

Prasanna's One More Over *delivered several reprints!*

was put on a plane to Australia. His tough stance immediately defused the issue. We published Thomson's autobiography in India in 1980. Titled *Thommo,* it was his story as he told to the formidable British cricket journalist, David Frith. Thomson's parting words to his co-writer tell you everything about the man he was. David Frith wrote:

> He signed off like a man collecting his belongings at the prison exit: 'that's it Frithy. That's all you are getting. There ain't no more. If you wanna ring me, don't, cos I won't be home. I'll be out fishing mate…so if you've got any messages I'd suggest you put' em in a bottle, seal it and throw it in the sea. It might float up somehow to the Barrier Reef.*

Thankfully, the manuscript was completed without David Frith having any further questions for Thommo. He surely was a boy who never grew up, a

*Frith, David, *Thommo: Story of Jeff Thomson*, Rupa Publications, 1980.

(From left) Rajan Bala, a famous sports editor who published several books with us, talking to Sunil Gavaskar

refreshingly simple and uncomplicated man who loved bowling at a lightening speed, crashing into the cleansing waves of the Pacific or racing after wild pigs to build up his stamina and tone his muscles. His book was as electrifying as his fast bowling and did well, running into several reprints.

Publishing Don Bradman's *Farewell to Cricket* in 1978, which had been unavailable to Indian readers even after its publication in Australia 28 years earlier, will forever remain a badge of honour for me. This was followed by another book by Bradman, *The Art of Cricket*, which was suggested to me by veteran journalist Rajan Bala and which was hailed by newspapers and cricket experts as a 'classic'. It was an instructional book on the various facets of cricket, peppered with Bradman's wisdom. The ever so humble Bradman considered it his duty to put his theories about cricket on paper, drawing upon his years of experience. He said in the foreword that he was still learning about the game and quoted an interesting anecdote about an

What an innings it has been for Rupa's World of Cricket!

old English professional bowler who retired and took to umpiring. When asked what he had learned as an umpire, he replied, 'Just that a lot of wickets I took LBW when I was bowling were not out.' *The Art of Cricket* remains a perennial classic on the game.

Our cricket publishing juggernaut continued with *Whispering Death*, the autobiography of Michael Holding, whom Geoffrey Boycott called the Rolls Royce of bowling. We were proud to publish *Blasting for Runs* by Rohan Kanhai, wherein Kanhai narrated how the two great Test captains of his era, Peter May of England and A.H. Kardar of Pakistan, didn't know the rules of the game because they refused him a runner when he was hurt, nearly sparking a riot. A few more of the cricket books we published and had success with include: *Zed*, an autobiography of the Pakistani batsman Zaheer Abaas, *Spin Punch* by Dilip Doshi, *Lala Amarnath Life and Times: The Making of a Legend* by Rajinder Amarnath, *Arlott and Trueman on Cricket* edited by Gilbert Phelps, *The Art of Fast Bowling* by Dennis Lillee, *Complete Cricket*

The flamboyant cricketer of his times, Sandeep Patil did well with the pen too with his autobiography, Sandy Storm

Coaching Illustrated by Frank Tyson, *Cricket Punch* by Frank Worrell, *The West Indies: Fifty Years of Test Cricket* by Tony Cozier, *Sir Gary: A Biography* by Trevor Bailey and *Sandy Storm* by Sandeep Patil. But the greatest of them all was Sunil Gavaskar's autobiography, *Sunny Days.*

When Rupa published Sunny Days, *I never anticipated that the sun would never set on the title. I signed off on its first print run in 1976 and my son, Kapish, signed off on its thirty-first reprint edition in 2023.*

• Chapter 20 •

THE IDOL

'*Niche paan ki dukaan, upar gori ka makaan,*' was a song from the movie *Silsila* by Yash Chopra, starring Amitabh Bachchan and Shashi Kapoor. I adapted that song to fit someone I idolized. My version of the story went: *Niche paan ki dukaan, upar mere idol ka makaan!* This was because the Rupa office in Bombay was in Konark building, which also housed the office of the Little Master, Sunil Gavaskar.

When Rupa published *Sunny Days*, I never anticipated that the sun would never set on the title. I signed off on its first print run in 1976 and my son, Kapish, signed off on its thirty-first reprint edition in 2023. To date, it is the longest running sports autobiography we have published and, to my knowledge, no other cricket autobiography has been in print for that long. It hasn't been out of print in 46 years, and its longevity and sales numbers are quite likely a record for any cricket book published anywhere in the world.

Just like Gavaskar's time on the cricket pitch, *Sunny Days* is a delight and we found it enormously fulfilling to publish it. However, its journey began with a little confusion just as two new batsmen at the crease often are prone to misunderstandings that could lead to a run out.

Our confusion pertained to a meeting venue, which had been a wrong call on my part. But, thankfully, our innings went on. On 28 August 1976, my friend, the renowned Bombay-based media baron, Khalid Ansari, the owner of *Sportsweek* and *Mid-Day* (his father had started an Urdu daily, *Inquilab*), and Sharad Kotnis, who was the associate editor of *Sportsweek*, arranged an appointment with Gavaskar for me.

So, who was Gavaskar in 1976? To put things in perspective, in 1971, Gavaskar, in his debut Test series in West Indies, had scored 774 runs in eight innings—a spectacular feat. No other cricketer, Indian or international, had scored as many runs in his debut series. It was also the first time that India had won a series in the Caribbean, making Gavaskar a national hero. I was going to meet this national hero to sign him for his autobiography until I got the venue wrong.

We were to meet at the Taj at Apollo Bunder; I thought the venue was the coffee shop at the Taj while Gavaskar thought it was the Sea Lounge. Mobile phones were still 20 years away and it took us some time to sort out the confusion. Thankfully, when I finally rushed to the correct venue, Gavaskar was still waiting. Once the adrenaline rush subsided, I was able to focus on what he was saying. Famously, Gavaskar played with a straight bat, and there was no exception to this practice here either—he told me without dissembling that he'd had offers from A.H. Wheeler and Symonds. I appreciated his honesty and presented my offer. He would get a percentage of the book's sales royalty and there would be no advance. To my astonishment and relief, the rising star of the Indian cricket agreed to sign up with Rupa. He had but one condition—the book should be out on 16 December, just as India were to start its home Test series against England. This meant that I had three and a half months to transform the manuscript into a book. These were the times of rather primitive printing and communication technology (as compared to today)—no computerized typesetting, no latest digital versions of offset printing, no mobile phones, no WhatsApp, etc. But, if Rupa had to make its presence felt as a serious publisher of sports books, it had to accept the challenge. Ajit Wadekar's *My Cricketing Years* by Vikas Publishing House had just been published and was a bestseller already. The pressure to match the sales of *My Cricketing Years* was immense.

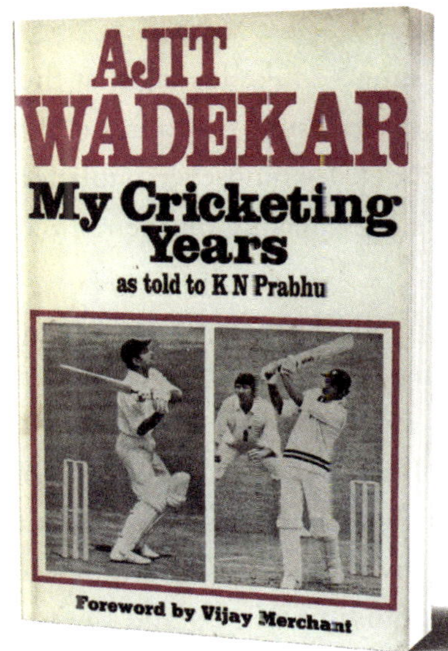

With the manuscript in my hand, I said goodbye to my idol, assuring him that in three months' time he would add 'author' to his biodata. I left the hotel and headed straight to the YMCA near Maratha Mandir, where I was staying. The sky was overcast and it soon started pouring. It rained incessantly till the streets were flooded and all the taxis seemed to have magically disappeared. And there I was, clutching the unprotected manuscript by Gavaskar—the only copy on the planet. Something had to be done quickly to prevent it from getting wet. A grocery store owner nearby came to the rescue. I quickly got a plastic bag from his shop and wrapped my prized possession in it. Holding the manuscript in one hand and my shoes in the other (I had taken them off so I could feel my way along the flooded street with my bare feet—the city was notorious for its open manholes into which unwary pedestrians could fall) I crept along and somehow reached the lobby of the YMCA with my precious cargo intact.

Having changed out of my wet clothes, I ordered a hot coffee from room service and settled down to read the manuscript. But before I began reading, I turned on the radio and heard the announcement that a singer many loved, Mukesh, had just passed away in New York. Memories of my tuneless singing of Mukesh's songs in the office canteen flooded my mind; I also recalled Gavaskar telling me how he had used a Mukesh song to spur on the spinner B.S. Chandrasekhar to great heights when he had been bowling in a cricket match in Calcutta. Apparently, no sooner had he sung a Mukesh song that the spinner bowled the batsman in his next ball. It was a strange sensation to be reading the manuscript of the finest cricket book I would ever publish while listening to the songs of the immortal singer playing on the radio.

Work began on the manuscript. R. Srinivasan, the sports editor of *The Times of India*, edited the manuscript for a paltry sum of ₹500. The manuscript was returned to me with no discernible changes, leaving me a little worried. I decided to ask the sports commentator Sardendu Sanyal to have a look at the manuscript. His price was princely though—₹2,000. But I decided to invest that money, and it paid off. The manuscript underwent a thorough round of editing and the final version was a decent improvement on the first draft. Next, the manuscript had to be manually typeset. I would go from Daryaganj to Dhavan printers at Mayapuri to get it typeset. Dhavan himself was a good proofreader and very often would point out errors and solecisms. I would then take the pages that had been typeset to the airport, so they could be dispatched to wherever Gavaskar was playing—Kanpur, Nagpur or Ahmedabad. He would have it sent back after reading the draft, and then the next batch would be dispatched, and so on. The hard work paid off and within a span of 121 days, a 350-page book was published—error free!

On 16 December 1976, we released *Sunny Days*, just a day before the Test series with England started at home. And what a beating the home team took. We lost the first Test, the second and the third. The fourth was won by India but so far, my author had been mild with the bat. Naturally, response to the book was lukewarm. The final rubber at Bombay was drawn but Gavaskar shone with the bat. A century against his name on the Wankhede Stadium scoreboard set the cash registers ringing for *Sunny Days*.

On the field, the cricketer was scripting history and in the stores, he and Rupa were smashing sales records. So, how did *Sunny Days* prove to be the monster hit

The crowd is waiting to buy its first copy of Sunny Days. *The story goes that in this crowd was a young Sourav Ganguly.*

it became? Gavaskar's profile notwithstanding, I believe it succeeded because it was a no-holds-barred account of the life of one of our greatest cricketers ever.

The Little Master tells us with wit and honesty the key details of his life. How the baby (Gavaskar) was switched at birth in the hospital ward with the infant of a fisherman's family, but was luckily restored to his rightful place by an eagle-eyed uncle; how he almost broke his mother's nose with a mighty hit; his cricket exploits in school and college; how he was, at times, booed by the crowd when he was playing domestic cricket, as his uncle happened to be a selector! And then, at the age of 21, at Port of Spain, how Gavaskar burst upon the international cricket scene with the sound of thunder.

The year 1971 was Gavaskar's year. Thereafter, the records kept piling up. By the end of the 1975–76 season, Gavaskar had played 147 first class matches, amassed 11,574 runs and 38 centuries. He had played in 24 matches and 8 Tests, with 2,123 runs and 8 centuries. He still had eight years to go for the

The batter turned author working on the proofs of his manuscript at my Model Town house in Delhi

great feats at the Kotla and the Chidambaram stadiums but, as the saying goes, in the beginning is the end. Fluently written, the self-effacing modesty of the author imparting a rare grace to the pages, *Sunny Days* is still perhaps the most honest sports autobiography to have come out from India.

I'm glad that Gavaskar and I are still around to see his great book selling 47 years after it was first published. I believe this is no accident. Simply put, the book is a masterpiece and I'm not the only one who believes this. Rahul Dravid at the Jaipur Literature Festival in 2013 said *Sunny Days* was the best in its genre.

We did everything we could to make *Sunny Days* a success, including resorting to unorthodox sales methods. At the time, our book was climbing the bestseller lists. A UK publisher called David & Charles also published a book on Gavaskar's records and statistics. It was a dull, unimaginative book, full of data and lacking in soul. It couldn't have dented the sales of *Sunny Days*, but I did not want anything to stop the success of the autobiography.

Kapil Dev displaying the copy of Idols *by Sunil Gavaskar on 28 October 1983, a day before he equalled Don Bradman's record 29th century. Now* Idols *has completed 40 years of its publication on 28 October 2023.*

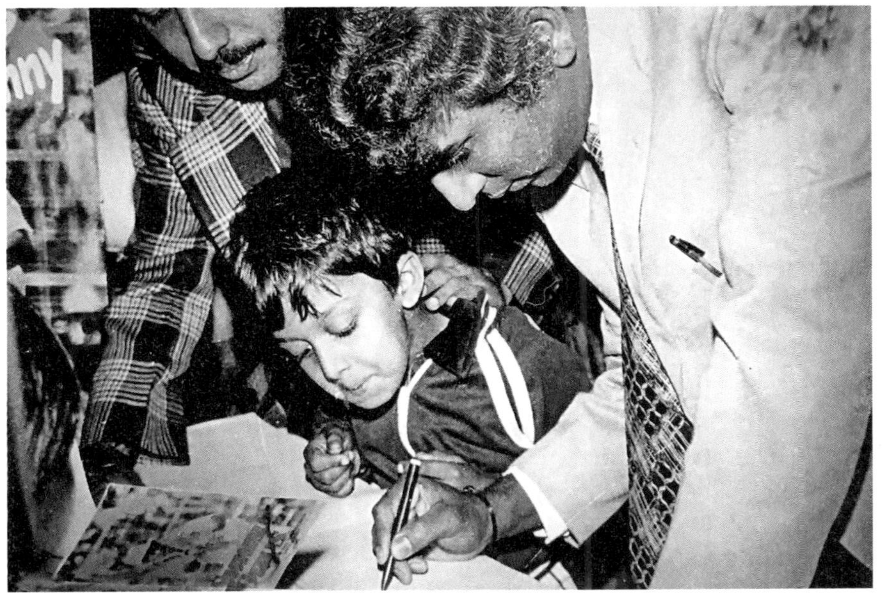

As the father signs his book, the young Rohan Gavaskar looks on curiously

At the launch of Idols, *the entire visiting West Indies cricket team graced the event, showcasing their support and presence*

Banter and laughter during the book launch of Idols. *(From left) Clive Llyod, Sunil Gavaskar and Bishen Singh Bedi.*

Twenty-five years of Sunny Days! *To mark the occasion, we displayed Gavaskar's handwritten manuscript and the champion was all admiration.*

The sun keeps shining on Sunny Days! *Felicitating my author at the twenty-fifth anniversary of his autobiography as his wife Marshneil looks on.*

At the launch of Idols *in Madras. A young Gautam Padmanabhan getting his author-signed copy.*

With Sharad Kotnis, who was the associate editor of Sportsweek *then.* Sportsweek *was run by my friend Khalid Ansari and the two of them introduced me to Gavaskar.*

My young nephew K.K. Mehra, son of S.K. Mehra, with Gavaskar

(From left) The young author with a younger Shekhar Gupta

Gavaskar (centre) at the launch of SMG: A Biography of Sunil Manohar Gavaskar, *authored by Devendra Prabhudesai (second from left)*

A piece of history! The manuscript of Sunny Days *written by Gavaskar in long hand*

confidence was boosted by the fast arrival of Imran Khan to who was to play for his country after a lapse of two years. His shin fracture had healed and he was back in the business of bowling fast. His very presence in the side must be a great morale booster for the players because like all top allrounders he has the ability to change the course of the match single handed. In Imran's case it is more so with his bowling but others like Kapil, Botham & Hadlee can do so with either their bowling or batting or both.

On the eve of the match we practised under the lights for the first time and found that though the lights were very good ~~the lights~~ those in Delhi were much better. Most eyes however were focused on Imran who was limbering up in the other net. He came in with his full run-up and bowled and though the speed looked marginally less than before ~~the~~ any doubts regarding his fitness were removed.

Imran is a splendid example to budding youngster fast bowlers. He really works hard doing several laps of the ground and then his own special brand of exercises. However the most notable part of his bowling, as also Kapil's, in the nets is that they

HOTEL TOPAZ
ANNIWATTE, KANDY.
SRI LANKA (CEYLON)

T'phone : 08-24150, 08-23062 Office
08-24172 Manager
581191 Colombo.

DATE:

3

on my right. And the call button also was not working. When later I asked the same steward for some duty free item on board he just looked through me.

Maybe the Indian team is spoilt by Air India and we expect the same standards from other airlines which perhaps is expecting too much. After all only one airline can treat you like Maharajahs isn't it?

When we landed we found that there was a media boycott because the Press & ~~the~~ TV were not allowed in the Customs Enclosure. Not that it made any difference. I've never understood why TV cameras should pan into a players suitcase as it is opened for the Customs examination. Surely that is a gross invasion of privacy and is hardly of any interest to viewers. Also with the current security problems it is absolutely essential that all cameras etc be away from sensitive areas ~~and~~ and the Customs enclosure is a sensitive area. After all a camera can identify Customs men in plain clothes which is not going to help them do their duties unobtrusively in the future.

There was thus no Press conference at the airport though I did give a TV interview at the airport. I enjoyed that though I felt sorry for Milind Wagle who is a friend for getting my back up by asking whether we expected to win. No team goes into a tournament to lose and although our form prior to the tournament was not encouraging we all knew that cricket is a game which can confound the greatest experts. Haresh Munwani, another person I like then asked if I thought it was a fluke. I answered tongue firmly in cheek that since this was the age of sequels to hit movies like Jaws I, Jaws II, Rocky II etc this win could be termed "fluke II." I had a heavily bandaged middle finger as well as a tape on my forehead where extra skin growth had been removed and inevitably there was a question as to what happened. That was the question I was waiting for. My answer "I had a fight with Kapil Dev." Of course everybody laughed. We had won so how could there be a fight but since we had lost ~~so~~ earlier it was believable that there could have been a fight. And the practice is to look for excuses other than cricketing ones to explain away India's defeats.

The crowd outside was nothing compared to the crowds that welcomed the team ~~after~~ on its arrival after winning the 1983 World Cup. It was just as well because we have always had either excessive praise or excessive abuse. Somewhere in between might be ideal but having been in

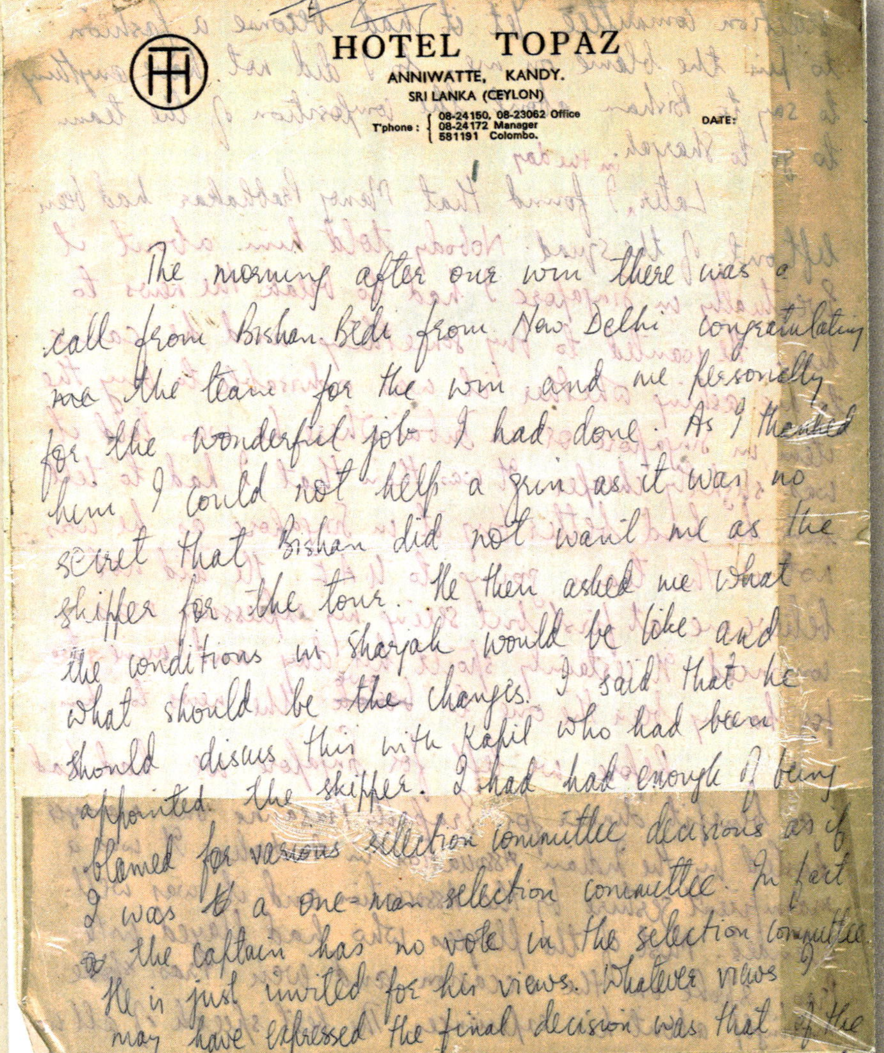
HOTEL TOPAZ
ANNIWATTE, KANDY.
SRI LANKA (CEYLON)
T'phone : 08-24150, 08-23062 Office
08-24172 Manager
581191 Colombo.
DATE:

The morning after our win there was a call from Bishan Bedi from New Delhi congratulating me the team for the win and me personally for the wonderful job I had done. As I thanked him I could not help a grin as it was no secret that Bishan did not want me as the skipper for the tour. He then asked me what the conditions in Sharjah would be like and what should be the changes. I said that he should discuss this with Kapil who had been appointed the skipper. I had had enough of being blamed for various selection committee decisions as if I was a one-man selection committee. In fact the captain has no vote in the selection committee. He is just invited for his views. Whatever views I may have expressed the final decision was that of the

Bishan Singh Bedi unveiling the Sunny Days *in Delhi at the Imperial Hotel on 16 December 1976*

So, I promptly bought all 300 copies of the David & Charles book that had been imported at ₹400 per copy. And *Sunny Days* sailed serenely on.

Gavaskar's fans were crazy about him. And, to his credit, he always made time during a Test match in Delhi to help us promote his book.

There were three bookshops at Connaught Place, Ramakrishna and Sons, Galgotia Book Shop and New Book Depot in B Block, and he would often autograph copies of the book there. During one such session, I noticed he was visibly fading, so I gently took the pen from him. But not for nothing was he Gavaskar—he could and would keep going, no matter how tired he was. When a fan clamoured for his signature, he smiled and said, 'Ask my publisher if I have his permission to do so.' I returned his pen and he went on. After the phenomenal success of *Sunny Days*, Gavaskar published another book with us, *Idols*. My budget was limited for this book and I was not able to hire a cover designer. So, using my own camera, I took a picture of Gavaskar on the field. I then requested him to write the words 'Idols' on a piece of paper. We

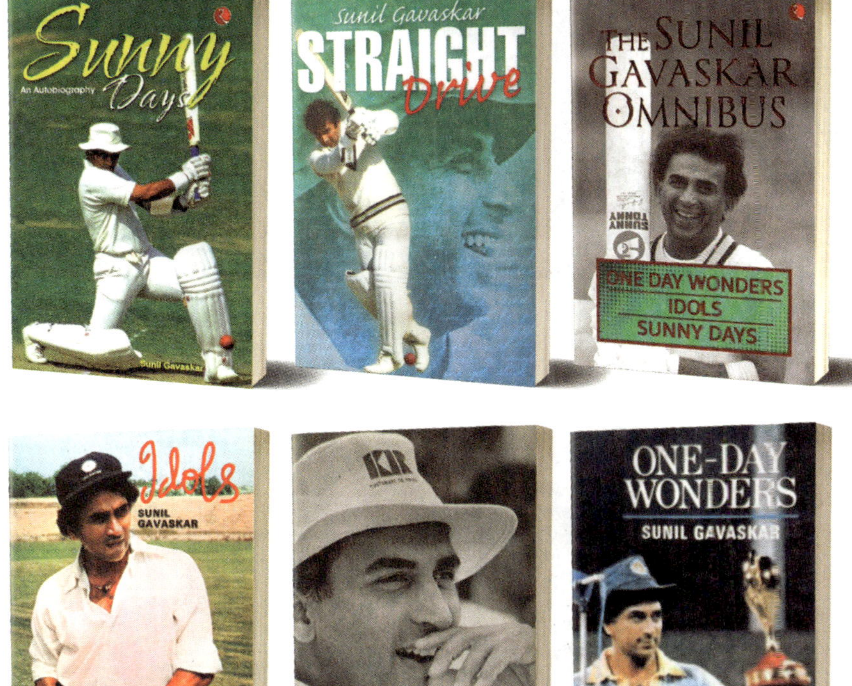

A long innings with Sunil Gavaskar...

put the photo and his handwritten title together and that became the cover for the book and remains so till date.

Idols was published in 1983, the year Gavaskar was slated to reach another milestone—his twenty-ninth century, equalling Sir Don Bradman's record. In the first Test at Kanpur against West Indies, he got out for a duck and 7. Naturally, he was upset about being in his in-law's city and not only missing a milestone but being brutally booed by the passionate Green Park crowd. Back in Delhi, we were preparing ourselves for the launch of *Idols*. On seeing

Dr Harish Seth, an old acquaintance of Gavaskar at the twenty-fifth anniversary of Sunny Days

Sunil Gavaskar with Rupa's Bombay team at the launch of SMG *by Devendra Prabhudesai*

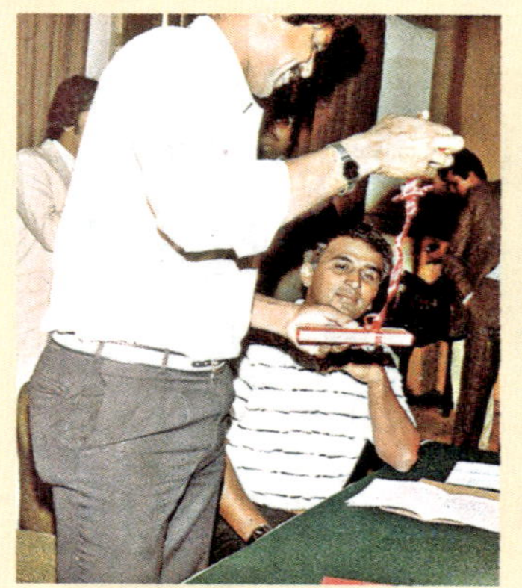

Kapil Dev releasing Idols

When the two idols shook hands; Sunil Gavaskar with Clive Llyod at the release of Idols

Ravi Chaturvedi turned Nostradamus and prophesied that Gavaskar will score a century the next day, and he did! Ravi seen here waving his hand.

Setting the tone before the launch of Idols

what had happened at Green Park, I immediately left for Kanpur and met him and his wife Marshneil at their hotel. Sunny was disillusioned with the whole Green Park crowd experience. To get him out of his sullen mood, we decided to go to his in-laws' place where soon, Sunny was comforting himself by polishing off pakoras and sipping hot chai. He was to reach Delhi after this for the second Test, and I offered to receive him at the railway station at Delhi, an offer he readily accepted. He was on the verge of reaching a milestone in his batting career and we at Rupa too were eyeing a milestone, launching his second book, *Idols*. Naturally, I wanted to be with my author as much as I could. The second Test was on 29 October 1983. A day before that, we launched *Idols* at a venue in Pragati Maidan. Attended by the entire Indian and the West Indies team, the event was a success. Gavaskar had an easy demeanour that evening—chatting, mingling and eating. The man was just having fun. He didn't let the demons of his earlier failure bog him down for long. Ravi Chaturvedi, the voice of cricket in those times, declared to him that he will hit a century the next day. I, too, told Kaminee that if he

(From left) Sunil Gavaskar, the editor of Sportsweek *and* Lifestyle *with Khalid Ansari. Rupa also published Khalid Ansari's memoir in 2022 titled* It's a Wonderful World.

scored a century, I would gift her a diamond necklace! She could only look at me in bewilderment. That day, the genius in the Little Master came to the fore. He hit Malcolm Marshall, the fearsome West Indian fast bowler, for a six in the very first over and after that, there was no stopping him. After that, the runs continued to flow from his bat, as did the books from his pen. *Idols* was followed by *Runs 'n Ruins* and *One Day Wonders*.

Over time, we became like family. I was invited to his son Rohan Gavaskar's wedding reception at the Taj Lands End in Bombay. It happened to be Gudi Padwa—the first day of Chaitra Navratri. I never travel during this period and did not know what to do. After much thought, I decided to take the afternoon flight to Bombay after my puja and return by the 10.00 p.m. flight. I asked my colleague Indira to pick me up from the airport and drive me down to the venue. The scheduled time of the reception was 7.00 p.m. and in Bombay, everything happens on time. I got there around 7.30 p.m. In the queue ahead of me were Jyotiraditya Scindia and Shobhana Bhartia.

Behind me were Amar Singh, Amitabh and Jaya Bachchan, and Subrata Roy of Sahara (who published his musings from inside the Tihar Jail with us). I was meeting Rohan after a long time.

On another occasion, in 2012, I bumped into Gavaskar one evening at Park Hotel in Delhi. We watched the Delhi–Bombay Indian Premier League (IPL) match being played in Delhi late into the night. I was supporting Delhi while he was cheering for Bombay. I enjoyed watching the match and in the end, his team won. Just as I was leaving, he asked me to publish a book by him on his sixtieth birthday. 'But why?' I asked.

'My father wishes it so,' he said. It was thus that we published *Straight Drive*, his fifth book. An advance copy of the book was taken by Gavaskar to Sai Baba for his blessing. It was then that I saw a spiritual side to this great cricketer.

In the course of my association and friendship with him, I have seen many facets of the man and have been impressed by his humility, simplicity and warmth. Our innings has been a long one, and I have cherished every moment of it. I was only 29 when I first met Gavaskar, who was then a rising star of Indian cricket. He gave me my greatest book ever, *Sunny Days* and made me a publisher. Kapish, meanwhile, is still waiting for the sixth book from the master, a sequel to *Sunny Days*, a definite sixer off a no ball!

Sucheta Kripalani and Acharya came together for a patriotic cause and spent the rest of their lives together

• Chapter 21 •

DADA AND BOUDI: J.B. KRIPALANI AND SUCHETA KRIPALANI

Fretting and fuming, I reported at Lucknow's Amausi airport some time in late 1970s after a hectic day of business appointments with buyers and distributors. The heat wave was at its peak in the plains of UP with temperatures soaring to 45 degrees. Somehow, I had managed to reach the airport on time, grasping my most precious possession—a flask filled with cold water. I had hardly settled into my seat when suddenly, a posse of policemen seemed to invade the airport. Clearly some VIP was around. I glanced up irritably and then my irritation subsided, for the VIP was someone I had long admired—Sucheta Kripalani née Majumdar. A pioneering woman politician, she had followed her heart and married a man 20 years older to her, Jivatram Bhagwandas Kripalani, popularly known Acharya Kripalani.

Sucheta Kripalani was born in Ambala, Haryana, to a Bengali family. Her father, S.N. Majumdar, despite being a government doctor during the British Raj, was a nationalist. His patriotic fervour was passed on to his daughter. Educated at Indraprastha College and St Stephen's College, Delhi, she went on to become a professor of Constitutional History at Banaras Hindu University. In 1938, she married Acharya Kripalani and became fully involved with the Indian National Congress. In due course, she became the country's first woman CM when she served as the CM of UP from 1963 to 1967.

At the airport, Mrs Kripalani was soon joined by her husband Acharya Kripalani. From 1912 to 1917, he had been a professor of English and History at Muzaffarpur College in Bihar. He first came into contact with Mahatma Gandhi in 1917, during the Champaran Satyagraha, and that proved to be a turning point in his life. For a short period, he taught at the Banaras Hindu University (1919–20) and from 1920 to 1927, he served as the principal of the Gujarat Vidyapeeth founded by Gandhiji. It was at Gujarat Vidyapeeth that he earned the sobriquet Acharya. When the Congress Party was deliberating as to who would become the first PM of the newly independent country, Acharya Kripalani earned the second highest vote after Sardar Patel. However, on Gandhiji's insistence, both Patel and Acharya Kripalani backed out to allow Pandit Nehru to become the first PM of India.

Given my Calcutta roots, I could only think of the husband and wife as my dada (elder brother) and *boudi* (sister-in-law). I noticed Dada was coughing in the dusty, hot airport and without a moment's hesitation, I handed him the flask with ice cold water that I was carrying. Acharya Kripalani drank deep from it and then, looking visibly less wilted from the heat, he asked me, '*Kya karte ho mere bhai* (What do you do, my brother)?' I immediately pulled out a business card and handed it to him. Dada smiled when he saw that Rupa had an office in Allahabad, a city that was frequented by many freedom fighters including him. Noticing his reaction, I was struck by the thought that here was someone who could write a great insider's account of the freedom movement. I politely asked him, '*Kya aap hamare liye ek kitaab likhenge* (Will you write a book for us)?' Dada confessed that he was already writing one. He promised to get in touch with me once he completed it.

Time flew by. To my distress, Boudi met an untimely end after a fatal attack of jaundice. This was an irreparable loss for Dada, as they had no children of their own. Fortunately, Giridhar Kripalani, his nephew; Mr Krishnamurthy, his secretary; and H.D. Sharma, a librarian at Teen Murti House, became pillars of support for him and saw him through this very difficult period. Although I was really keen to find out whether he had been able to complete

At the launch of My Times: An Autobiography by J.B. Kripalani. *(From left) Former PM Chandra Shekhar, Bhairon Singh Shekhawat and Prabhash Joshi. T.N. Chaturvedi can be seen at the lectern. Three other former PMs also attended the event: Inder Kumar Gujral, Atal Bihari Vajpayee and P.V. Narasimha Rao.*

his manuscript, this was not the time to get in touch. Then one day, my phone rang. On the line was Giridharji. 'Dada would like to see you,' he said. 'Please come tomorrow at 8.00 a.m. to his Mehrauli house.'

The next morning, I left my house at 6.30 a.m., as I wanted to be punctual for this important appointment. In those days, horrendous traffic snarl-ups were not so common, so I reached Dada's place well in time. I was received by Giridharji and Mr Krishnamurthy, both almost 20 years older than me. I was served a cup of tea and, a few minutes later, I was ushered into the presence of my hero. Dada was sitting on the floor, his back turned towards me and a huge pillow lay by his side. He seemed to be writing something and that image of Dada has been etched in my mind since then. Soon, he turned around and asked me to publish a pictorial biography of his late wife, Sucheta Kripalani. He informed me that he was writing his memoir and had already written 500 pages in long hand—single spaced. He said that he would hand the manuscript over to me as soon as it was completed,

Dada's autobiography, which was published years after his passing away

but first, the book on Boudi would have to be published. He added that I could write to him and send him the contract. I did so promptly and then heard nothing about it.

Several months later, matters took a very strange turn. A senior director of a rival publishing firm phoned me to ask why we hadn't yet published the pictorial biography of Sucheta Kripalani. Frankly, this was not just bizarre but also rather fishy. What was this man's interest in a book that I had been asked to publish? I realized that Dada hadn't yet returned the contract I had sent him. I investigated and discovered that Giridharji had kept the contract with him for months, not showing it to Dada. Soon after, matters grew further complicated when Dada fell ill and passed away. This came as a big shock to me. He had promised his memoir to me but now, with his death and a rival in the picture, what was to become of that assurance? I learned that Dada had completed the manuscript, but his nephew wanted the rival firm to publish it.

Krishnamurthy and H.D. Sharma were not in favour of this. Things became even more complicated when Giridharji died. Months passed. I began talking to H.D. Sharma. I asked T.N. Chaturvedi, an erudite reader and a Rajya Sabha MP (who later became governor of Karnataka and served as the Comptroller and Auditor General of India when the Bofors controversy arose) for his advice. My efforts began to pay off. I discovered that the manuscript had been deposited in the archives of the Sucheta Kripalani Memorial Trust. The Trust went to court and obtained permission to publish it, as there was no other claimant for it. The rival publisher had faded away by then, and given my own correspondence with Dada and his desire to have Rupa publish the book, we

Shri Krishnamurthy (second from left), secretary to Dada, at Rupa's Madras office

were given permission to go ahead. When the book was finally published, it ran into 1,000 pages in royal size. It was launched in the presence of four former PMs Inder Kumar Gujral, Atal Bihari Vajpayee, Chandra Shekhar and P.V. Narasimha Rao. Despite the dignitaries present at the launch, to my deep regret, the book sank without a trace. It wasn't reviewed in a single broadsheet and sales were abysmal. How shabbily we treat leaders who are truly heroic!

In the preface of his book, Dada had written, 'I would like my readers to correct my delineation of events, wherever they think it is not factual. If I am among the living after the publication of this book, none shall be happier than I to correct any mistakes that may have crept in my account. If I have needlessly annoyed anybody, I shall make suitable amends.'*

Alas! Dada never lived to see his book.

*Kripalani, J.B., *My Times: An Autobiography*, Rupa Publications, 2004.

The beginning of Presidential Years

• Chapter 22 •

R. VENKATARAMAN: HIS PRESIDENTIAL YEARS

On 12 January 2009, R. Venkataraman was admitted to the Army Research and Referral Hospital with complaints of urosepsis.* In a week's time, his condition deteriorated further when he was detected with low blood pressure and an E. coli infection. After fighting for his life for another week, he breathed his last on 27 January. When I heard the news of his demise, I was shattered. Memories of the time I had spent with the former first citizen flooded my mind.

R. Venkataraman was born in Rajamadam village in Tanjore district, Madras Presidency in 1910. A nationalist and a patriot, who was actively involved in the freedom struggle, Venkataraman participated in the Quit India Movement and was later appointed as a member of the constituent assembly and the provisional cabinet. He was elected to the Lok Sabha four times and served as the Union finance minister (1980–82) and minister of defence (1982–84). In 1984, he was elected the seventh vice president of India and in 1987, he became the eighth president of India, serving from 1987 to 1992.

One rainy afternoon in August 1986, I received a call from Vice President Venkataraman's office. He had a question and a request. This was the year that we were holding a Rupa–Penguin exhibition to celebrate our 50-year-long association at the AIFACS* Gallery. The Vice President was very keen to visit the exhibition and his office was curious to know if its dates could be extended beyond Sunday. Unfortunately, I couldn't comply with this request, but I was

*A toxic condition caused by the extravasation of urine into bodily tissues

*All India Fine Arts and Crafts Society Gallery

R. Venkataraman visited the Rupa's stall at World Book Fair when he was vice president. His keen interest in the book assured me that our paths would cross soon.

elated to know that the vice president of the country was a book aficionado. I hoped our paths would cross soon.

I didn't have long to wait. The Vice President came visiting the World Book Fair, spent quality time at the Rupa stall and bought a number of books. He was a special guest and as was customary, I refused to let him pay for the books. But R. Venkataraman persisted and paid for all the books he had bought. A humble man with strong middle-class values, he lived those values in every way. In fact, when he retired as the president of India and was allotted an official bungalow at 5 Tughlaq Road, he preferred to spend his last years in his home state Tamil Nadu. He was a man who never forgot his roots.

On 25 July 1992, the day Venkataraman was to retire and Dr Shankar Dayal Sharma was to be sworn in the incoming president of India, I wrote the outgoing president a letter suggesting he may consider writing his autobiography. A while later, I received a formal letter from Madras from Dr K. Venkatasubramanian, a former vice chancellor of Pondicherry University, who was now the former

There was a huge crowd outside the venue and R. Venkataraman had to be brought in from the back gate. Between the two of us can be seen a young Kapish.

Sunil Gavaskar flew in from Bombay to attend the launch of My Presidential Years. *On the extreme right is P. Murari who was secretary of R. Venkataraman.*

My Presidential Years *makes its debut. It was released by the former Chief Justice of India M.N. Venkatachaliah and former Lok Sabha Speaker Shivraj Patil on 25 July 1994, two years after his demitting office as President.*

president's personal secretary. The letter was an invitation to meet Venkataraman in Madras. I was very excited to meet him because no recent Indian president had published a memoir until then. Decades earlier, in 1946, Dr Rajendra Prasad had written an autobiography*, and Dr Radhakrishnan had published books on philosophy, religion and Indian history. Other than these, there had been nothing.

During our meetings, Venkataraman had very clear-cut demands: the royalty would be 20 per cent, and while an advance was not necessary, it would be welcome. The book would confine itself to his five years in office as president. The typed manuscript would be sent from Madras to Delhi and after it was edited, it would be sent back to him for his approval. Dr Venkatasubramanian would coordinate all this. In the course of our discussion, it transpired that several other publishers had been trying to acquire the book, with Penguin

*It was originally published in Hindi in 1946. The English version titled *Autobiography* was published by Penguin in 2010.

The Hindi edition of R. Venkataraman's autobiography, published by Vani Prakashan, was launched by former PM Chandra Shekhar

(From left) Veteran journalist Prabhash Joshi (1936–2009) seen here with Arun Maheshwari of Vani Prakashan at the launch of the Hindi edition of My Presidential Years

leading the pack. When I was told that we would be the book's publisher, I was honoured, delighted and wildly excited.

When *My Presidential Years* arrived, it was immediately clear that this was not a straightforward autobiography but rather a day-to-day record of his time in office. It could be best described as a sort of diary with notes that would need to be threaded together to form a narrative. It was decided that the book would be published on 25 July 1994, exactly two years after he had relinquished office as president. A lot of work would need to go into the manuscript to prepare it for publication. As the technology of that era did not facilitate easy and continuous communication, most of the work could only be done with him in person. As Venkataraman was largely based in Madras and I in Delhi, this meant I was in Madras quite frequently. Whenever he visited Delhi, I would go to Rashtrapati Bhavan to meet with him.* Our meetings, conducted over gulab jamuns and samosas served in bone china, became so frequent that the security guards stopped checking my car when it drew up before the majestic presidential palace.

Venkataraman was a seasoned politician and skilfully avoided courting controversy on a number of sensitive subjects like Kashmir and the PMs during his tenure. Despite his tact and circumspection, the book had its share of controversy. In the book, he wrote, 'Rajiv Gandhi used to consult me.' In fact, while referring to the Bofors controversy Venkataraman had said, 'Rajiv Gandhi came under a cloud of the *inexperience* of his advisers in parliamentary culture.' This line was picked up by the journalist Karan Thapar, and when he interviewed the former president on his book, Thapar zeroed in on the word 'inexperience' being used in relation to Rajiv. In fact, while referring to Bofors controversy, Venkataraman had said, 'Rajiv Gandhi came under a cloud of the *inexperience* of his advisers in parliamentary culture.' Venkataraman's reply to the journalist's probing was not very diplomatic and it created a stir

*He stayed at the Rashtrapati Bhavan annexe for two years after leaving office.

among the Congress politicians. As a result, most of them boycotted the launch of the book. The book was released by the former Chief Justice of India M.N. Venkatachaliah and the former Lok Sabha Speaker Shivraj Patil. Only two Congress leaders came for the launch—Dr Karan Singh and Mani Shankar Aiyar. I had also invited my idol Sunil Gavaskar to attend the function, and he was gracious enough to fly down from Bombay for the evening. What was in it for Gavaskar to attend the event? Nothing at all. He could have politely refused and I would have understood. But the true gentleman that he was, he respected the wishes of his publisher. My respect for him in particular and sportspersons in general increased manifold that day. When I saw Gavaskar at the launch, I instantly recalled an anecdote from my childhood. I had asked my father, 'Who do you think would be the best leader for a nation like India—a soldier, a teacher, a journalist or a businessman?' My father's reply had been, 'A sportsperson.' The reply had surprised me then, but I understood it now. The evening was a grand success and *My Presidential Years* hit the bestseller lists and was a mainstay on our list for years afterwards. It would also be the precursor to other books we would publish by presidents and vice presidents.

The evening after the launch, I invited the former president at my Model Town home for dinner, which he graciously accepted. We were delighted, unaware of the maze of protocols that awaited us. When I returned home from the launch, I was stopped by uniformed security personnel. Our home in Model Town had been turned into a fortress, bristling with men with guns. All I could do was persuade them to let me in, as I lived there and I was the host!

As the hour of the former president's arrival approached, I could see curious neighbours peeping from their windows and terraces to catch a glimpse of the VIP in their gully. I was relishing every moment of it. He arrived punctually at 7.30 p.m. We were all gathered in the drawing room when he expressed his desire to catch the 8.00 p.m. news on Doordarshan to watch the coverage of his book launch. This was a very ordinary request except that there was one problem. We had no TV in our drawing room. There

(From left) Atal Bihari Vajpayee, R. Venkataraman and Chandra Shekhar enjoying post-launch refreshments

was one TV in the house, and it was in our bedroom. Naturally, the former president could not be asked to watch TV in our bedroom, so the TV would have to be brought to him. Huffing and puffing, I dragged the instrument to the living room and we were all able to watch the news on Doordarshan. The public broadcaster had given the launch substantial coverage. This was because his political opponents had set up a protest meeting outside the FICCI Hall, where the book had been launched.

Food was ready and as is the practice in some households, it is always first served to the gods in our puja ghar. But here, the custom deviated from the divine to the canine! Before reaching the former president's plate, his men served the food to the dogs they had with them for security reasons. The canine survived and then the guest of honour could take his first morsel. The evening went off well, to my satisfaction. I was delighted that I'd been able to host the former president at my modest house. The next day, I received a bouquet and a letter written by Venkataraman thanking me and my wife for the wonderful evening.

Once the book had been published in the Indian market, it was time to go global. A launch was planned in London and New York for the UK and US editions of the book. For a man of his stature, it was necessary that sufficient buzz was created in the international market as well. Dr L.M. Singhvi was the Indian High Commissioner in London and Venkataraman, being a former president, had expected to be a guest of the Indian High Commission. However, the book had ruffled some feathers in the establishment back home, especially among the members of the Gandhi family, and as such, Dr Singhvi had to excuse himself from being the host. We received a response from his office that during Venkataraman's visit to London, the High Commissioner would not be in the city. The unstated message from India House was that it would be inappropriate for the former president to stay in the Indian High Commission when the High Commissioner was not there. I knew Dr Singhvi from my Calcutta days and had an excellent rapport with him. But this time, I didn't want to presume upon our friendship, so I accepted this excuse. Venkataraman then decided to stay at the St James' owned by the Taj Hotel group. It would cost him £750 per night to stay there, and he was going to pay out of his own pocket for the five nights he was staying there. I wasn't prepared for this. At the same time, paying for the whole stay would blow my publicity budget to bits. An idea came to me. I was friendly with Camellia Panjabi, then the marketing head of the Taj Group of Hotels. The 'Queen of Indian Curry' would frequently order books from us in bulk to place in various hotels. I got in touch with her and requested her to give me the best deal she could for my VIP guest. She instantly agreed to do her best.

I flew to London before Venkataraman's arrival and headed straight to the St James' hotel after I'd cleared immigration at Heathrow. When I got to the hotel, I asked the receptionist what it would cost me to put the former president in a suite. 'No suite, Sir. We have booked him into an apartment.' When I began to remonstrate, she probably realized that I was unfamiliar with

R. Venkataraman releasing former foreign secretary of UK, Sir Geoffrey Howe's autobiography, Conflict of Loyalty, *in Delhi*

the intricacies of five-star hotel culture and politely told me, 'Sir, an apartment is the best; a suite is too ordinary for such a dignitary.' There was nothing I could say in reply to this. When I asked what it would cost me, she said it would be £750 for all five days, including food. Camellia had outdone herself. I settled the bill in advance, much to the surprise of the receptionist and then requested her to give me a sheet of paper. I wrote a short note to my honoured guest, 'It is my privilege, Sir.'

The London book launch went well as did the one in New York but sadly, the autobiography of the ex-president of the largest democracy in the world attracted no international media attention. Fortunately, my author was more than satisfied with the international launches. In London, the book was released by Foreign Secretary Sir Geoffrey Howe. Years later, Venkataraman reciprocated the gesture when he released Sir Geoffrey's autobiography in Delhi, which was published by Macmillan and distributed by Rupa.

Venkataraman was a rare individual in whose personality, science, religion, economics and music fused to produce a remarkable man. He was a respected statesman, held in high esteem by politicians across the political spectrum including Atal Bihari Vajpayee, Chandra Shekhar, Madhu Dandavate, V.P. Singh and Narasimha Rao, to name a few. Venkataraman himself held Pandit Nehru, Indira Gandhi and C. Rajagopalachari in high esteem.

After his first book, he had plans to write a sequel. However, that was not destined to be. I mourned his passing both as a publisher and a friend.

The comrade who wrote about love, friendship and revolution, Mohit Sen aka Mohit kaka

• Chapter 23 •

MOHIT SEN: TRAVELLING WITH A COMMUNIST

An imposing five-storey building on Indrajit Gupta Marg near Connaught Place is an unmissable structure. It is the headquarters of the Communist Party of India (CPI), a party that was inspired by the Communist Party of China but has its own unique Indian identity. Ajoy Bhavan, as it is called, is a fascinating building and whenever I passed by it, I was intrigued by its fortress like façade. Why would the headquarters of a political party be constructed in a way that made it appear like it were perpetually ready to ward off attackers? The man who explained the look of Ajoy Bhavan to me was Mohit Sen, one of the CPI's notable leaders. Publishing this fierce communist's autobiography, *A Traveller and the Road,* was, in a way, a tribute to my childhood and adolescence in a city that was known for its traces of Chinese culture—Calcutta.

One of Kaminee's classmates in Allahabad University and our neighbour at our South Malaka house in Allahabad was Shantanu Mukherjee. He held important and sensitive positions in the UP Police, Research and Analysis Wing (R&AW) and the PM's security. While handling tough administrative duties, he kept the literature aficionado inside him alive; he could easily recall and quote from any classic. He was Mohit Sen's nephew and through him, I was introduced to this veteran communist. Sometime in 2002, Shantanu requested me to meet Mohit Sen, who was finishing his autobiography. 'The man has led a remarkable life, soaked in communism. You should go and visit him and see if his story is worth publishing,' he said. At first, I wasn't persuaded, I wasn't sure Sen's book would be a worthwhile commercial proposition. Eventually, with some reluctance, I went to meet Sen who was staying with P.C. Sen (his nephew)

Shantanu Mukherjee (extreme right), a senior Indian Police Service (IPS) officer who also was Mohit Sen's nephew. He had introduced me to the veteran communist.

in his house behind the Supreme Court in Tilak Lane. P.C. Sen had served as chairman of Indian Airlines and perhaps a book by him would attract more sales, I thought to myself. Nevertheless, within a few minutes of meeting with Mohit kaka, I was blown away by his sharp memory and incisive political wisdom. A man committed to democracy and civil liberties, he witnessed all the major events and trials the country had dealt with at the time—the freedom struggle, Partition, Chinese aggression, Emergency and the liberalization of the economy in the 1990s. An eye-witness to history in the making, it was clear that his book would be a remarkable record of an eventful period in the history of the nation. 'My wife insisted that I chronicle events in my life, even if my own life didn't deserve to be chronicled,' he said self-deprecatingly. 'Now that she is no more, I have to be faithful to her wishes. Would you help me finish this autobiography, Rajen babu?' Although I wanted to publish him, I wanted to do a fair amount of research and reading, so I could do justice to my evaluation of his book. It was a worthwhile exercise because it made me appreciate the extraordinary life Mohit kaka had led. For example, in order to understand land reforms in China, he had met Mao Zedong and Zhou Enlai. I came to know he abhorred the Stalinist interpretation of Marxism—which

Mohit Sen speaking at the launch of his book Traveller and the Road, *at IIC, New Delhi*

was violent and perverse—and how he was a vocal critic of the rigid organizational structure of the party. I learned of his proximity with Pandit Nehru and Indira Gandhi and why he supported Emergency. The more I read, the more I wanted to know.

The book was published in 2003, four years after his beloved wife Vanaja's death, to whom he dedicated the book by calling her a 'great-rooted blossomer'. His autobiography is a stirring account of his early years in Calcutta, student days and fascination with the Communist movement, his alma mater Cambridge University, how he entered politics and joined the CPI, his interactions with Pandit Nehru and Indira Gandhi, the Chinese aggression and his disenchantment with Stalin, the split in the Communist Party, the Bangladesh War and his support for Emergency. Even my questions about the fortress-like construction of Ajoy Bhavan were answered:

> It was from 1971 that I functioned as one of the central leaders of the CPI… Ajoy Bhawan was an imposing five-storey building with a basement. It was constructed by the famous architect Jhabvala, the husband of the still more famous novelist and writer, Ruth Jhabvala. It was very well constructed with plenty of air and space within but well-protected so that stones and other missiles could not reach the windows-somewhat like a modern fortress. The idea was that it should be easy to defend in case it is attacked by mobs organized by the Bharatiya Janata Party–Rashtriya Swayamsevak Sangh (BJP–RSS). Many years ago, at the time of the Chinese aggression, a mob had attacked our Asaf Ali Road office and managed to enter the first floor and burn some files and chairs. We were

> then attacked for being 'Russian dogs' though of course the aggressors were the Chinese and the CPI had condemned the aggression.*

His regard for Indira Gandhi came through in a poignant passage about the aftermath of her assassination:

> I cannot forget an incident that took place only a few weeks after 31 October 1984. I was going in a taxi and I seemed to recognize the driver. But he was clean shaven, had cut his hair short and wore no turban. I had memories of him having been a Sikh... I said I hoped he had not been humiliated in the riots. He said that that was not at all the case. When he learnt that her Sikh bodyguards had killed Indira Gandhi he felt such anger and shame that he had turned against the religion of the killers that was also his own and had cut his hair and shaved off his beard. Many of his former friends ostracised him but there were others who sympathized. Indira Gandhi's death left no one unaffected.

The book was filled with such insights and observations on the politics of the time.

The book was not a popular bestseller, but it attracted a great deal of attention in the media and in intellectual circles, particularly in Delhi. It was launched in the capital by Dr Manmohan Singh—a beautiful irony, the high priest of India's economic liberalization launching a book by a die-hard communist. But this was what Mohit Kaka was all about—he was a man who crossed political boundaries effortlessly and whose life and achievements were admired by all. I remember talking to P.V. Narasimha Rao at the launch. I told him that Mohit kaka had been excited that he was attending the launch. 'Mohit Sen is a legend. I am a nobody in front of him,' quipped Rao.

After the Delhi launch, we had planned another book launch in Hyderabad where

---

*Sen, Mohit, *A Traveller and the Road: The Journey of an Indian Communist*, Rupa Publications, 2003.

The high priest of India's economic liberalization Dr Manmohan Singh released a book written by a die-hard communist. A beautiful irony! Also in the picture, Professor Bipin Chandra and Mohit Sen.

Mohit kaka stayed. I was looking forward to this launch for one more reason; I wanted to peek into his world of books, his library which everyone who knew Mohit kaka kept talking of. Alas! This intellectual rendezvous never happened; a news ticker on 3 May 2003 declared the passing away of veteran communist Mohit Sen.

A tall figure reduced to just a tiny band after his death. But then, in the words of unassuming Mohit kaka himself:

> The road stretches temptingly. We shall not be there long enough to know who will travel along it to the end. But some will...communists we have been of different kinds. There will be other kinds in the future but communists there will be. More open than we were, less arrogant and going along with many others...history would do it in its own way. It is enough that we're given the chance to be part of its greatest forward movement.

Keep walking comrade, is all I would say.

Aviator, industrialist, institution builder, philanthropist, a legend. The many lives of J.R.D. Tata.

• Chapter 24 •

TATA: THE TAJ OF INDIA

One winter morning in 2003, an email arrived in my inbox. Its subject line gave me goosebumps that the chill in the air had nothing at all to do with. It read: 'Proposal to Publish J.R.D. Tata's Work'. With nervous anticipation, I scanned the contents of the mail which had been sent from Bombay House, the headquarters of Tata. The conglomerate was seeking a publisher to bring out a commemorative volume on the life and works of J.R.D. Tata, coinciding with his centenary year in 2004.

Jehangir Ratanji Dadabhoy Tata was, of course, the legendary industrialist who had taken India's greatest ever industrial house to unheard-of heights during his long years at the helm. Born in Paris, a man who loved 'France and flying', J.R.D. had returned to India at his father's insistence to join the family business. He launched Tata Airlines (the company that became Air India) and, eventually, a host of other Tata companies. When J.R.D. officially retired in 1991 from the Tata Group, I had written to his office, expressing interest in publishing his autobiography. We had received a reply saying that he was unwell and in Geneva and that we could discuss the matter when he returned to Bombay. Sadly, he did not recover from his illness. And now, after his demise, came this email.

Overwhelmed and sensing a big opportunity, I immediately called my son Kapish, who was in Bombay at that time. Although he had been a college student, I had sent him to Bombay with A.K. Singh to get a sense of our business there. I asked him to get in touch with the Tatas and understand what they were looking from us as the publisher of the book. Kapish made an appointment with the people in charge of the project at Bombay House the very next day.

He returned to Delhi with more questions than answers. Apparently, the Tata representatives wanted the 'best book' possible on J.R.D. without defining what that might be. Perhaps, they were themselves overwhelmed by the scale and complexity of J.R.D.'s writings and needed guidance on how to turn them into a great book. As other publishers were in the fray, I had to move fast.

I flew down to Bombay immediately after securing an appointment at Bombay House. Kapish had created a favourable impression and I was hoping to seal the deal. As I made my way to the imposing building, my mind went back to 1954, when the Rupa Bombay office had been set up in the Oak Lane area. Twenty years later, in 1974, when we moved to a place near Bombay House, I had waited in front of J.R.D.'s office to get a glimpse of my hero. That evening, I had seen him, dressed immaculately in a grey suit, coming out of the building and entering a waiting Mercedes car. He had been a picture of poise and dignity. It had been a fan-boy moment for me and now, here I was trying to get to publish him.

J.R.D. shared a special bond with Pandit Nehru and Indira Gandhi

The meeting lasted for more than an hour. Sharply dressed gentlemen from the Tata team quizzed me at length about my plans for the book. At some point, they were joined by a freelance editor who had done some work for Rupa and that helped my case. It also helped that R.M. Lala, a Tata director who had written biographies of J.R.D. and the Tatas, was not associated with the project at that point (although he did write a brilliant short life sketch of J.R.D. which was included in the book). His association at that point would have worked in favour of one of our rivals, as they had published most of Lala's books.

After a month of deliberations and meetings, the Tata group signed Rupa on as their publisher. The manuscript was a collection of J.R.D.'s letters and speeches. His correspondence with Gandhiji, C. Rajagopalachari, Pandit Nehru, Sardar Patel, Jayaprakash Narayan, Indira Gandhi, Rajiv Gandhi, and other such luminaries was an absolute treasure trove. One letter from Pandit Nehru, inviting him to his daughter Indira's wedding, stood out for its sheer charm. Nehru wrote

> My dear Jehangir,
> Within the next few days, you will get an invitation which probably you will not be able to read, as it will be in Hindi and Urdu. So I hasten to tell you that this is about Indira's marriage which is fixed for March 26 in Allahabad. It is perhaps too much to expect a very busy captain of industry in these strenuous times to attend to such functions. But of course if you and Thelly could come we would be happy.
> Yours sincerely,
>
> Jawaharlal Nehru*

And then the onerous task of editing began. There were 40,000 letters of J.R.D. in the Tata Central Archives in Pune. Sugata Raychaudhuri, a freelance editor who had once worked with us and was now settled in Pune, took on the task of pruning that pile of correspondence to prepare a two-volume set of books,

*Tata, J.R.D., *J.R.D. Tata Set (Letters & Keynote)*, Rupa Publications, 1995.

F.C. Kohli, a contemporary of J.R.D. and the doyen of IT revolution in the country. He was also the chairman of TCS and can be seen here with our editor Sanjana, who worked on the Tata book.

each with a couple of thousand pages. Every meaningful conversation that J.R.D. had, and there were plenty, was reproduced in the books. They were to be bound in leather for Tata clients. A hardbound edition would be created for libraries, a paperback edition for general readers as well as a low-priced edition for students. I wanted to use illustrations and poems that J.R.D. had created and composed in a private diary, but that did not pan out, as I wasn't allowed to take the diary out of the archive.

All this was done very rapidly, as the books were to be published in less than three months. Coupled with the logistical problems, I was also running out of money. So I had to prevail upon paper suppliers and printers to extend credit to me to produce the books on time and make them of the highest quality. Fortunately, everything came together as needed, and the books were dispatched on schedule on a Tata truck!

The two-volume set of books, which was published in record time to meet the centenary celebration of J.R.D. Each book ran into a thousand-odd pages

There is a curious coda to this story. For some reason, the otherwise classy representatives of the Tata Group seemed to have forgotten to invite their publisher to the launch of the book at the Taj Hotel in Bombay on 29 July 2004. Perhaps, it was so because the launch was a very private and exclusive event to which even the media wasn't invited. Nevertheless, it was an odd oversight. I remember standing in the lobby of the Taj with John Clement, a friend and former director of Collins, watching guests make their way to the ballroom where the event was being held. John had come to Bombay and I had just finished a lunch meeting with him at the Sea Lounge, Taj.

'Why don't you go inside?' John asked.

'Because I am not invited,' I replied.

'But aren't you the publisher?'

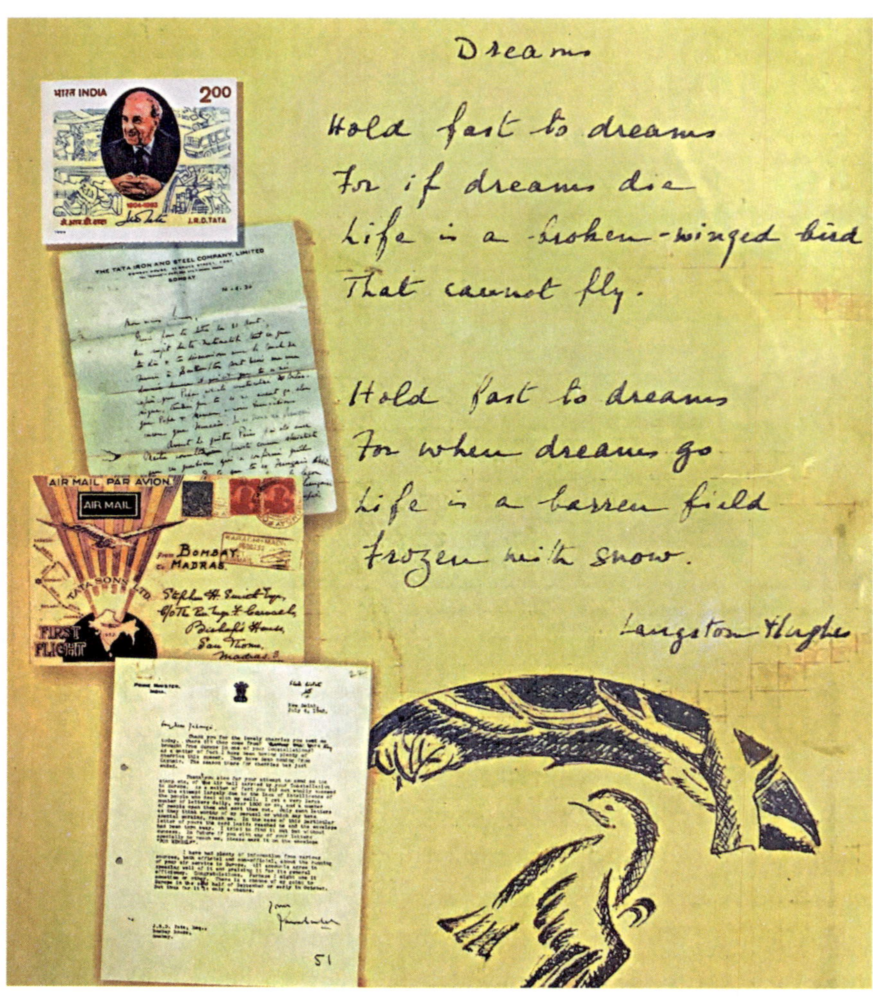

A man of steel was also a man of verse. Glimpses of one of the many poems that J.R.D. penned.

'Yes, my friend. But my job ends here,' I said with a smile.

I was in the lobby of Taj President, another Taj hotel where John and I were staying, until the event ended and the guests began to depart with the copies of the book that Rupa had published. I watched them pass by with mixed emotions. I was extremely proud to have published the legendary

Two legends! Sunil Gavaskar presenting his Indian cap to J.R.D. Tata

industrialist, but I was humbled by the fact that I had to remain anonymous on the day the book had been published. In the end, the fact that J.R.D. himself was famously humble and shied away from the limelight gave me comfort. When the Indian government was considering him for the Bharat Ratna, and sounded him out about accepting it, he replied: 'Why me? I don't deserve it. The Bharat Ratna is usually given to people who are dead or it is given to politicians. I am not prepared to oblige the government on the former and I am not the latter.'*

*'Jehangir Ratanji Dadabhoy Tata', *Tata*, https://tinyurl.com/y8fw7k28. Accessed on 25 July 2023.

Advaniji has been my friend and comrade-in-arms for ove fifty years. He has never compromised on his core belief ir nationalism, and yet has displayed flexibility in political responses whenever it was demanded by the situation. He has an open mind that always absorbs new ideas from diverse sources. I am certain that My Country, My Life wi. be read widely, and with keen interest, by people from diverse backgrounds. For mirrored in it is the remarkabl journey of a sensitive human being and an outstanding leader whose best, I hope and pray, is yet to come.'

From the *Foreword* by ATAL BIHARI VAJPAYEE
Prime Minister of India (1998-2004)

L.K. Advani's autobiography was the story of a nation itself with several political twists and turns

• Chapter 25 •

L.K. ADVANI: STORY WITHIN A STORY

In public life, we tend to meet many people but don't get to really know them. I have been fortunate to know one such high profile achiever: Lal Krishna Advani.

In August 2007, senior politician Jaswant Singh asked me if we'd be interested in publishing L.K. Advani's, book. Without a moment's hesitation, I said 'yes'—which publisher worth his salt would pass up the opportunity to publish one of the most towering figures on the Indian political scene, a man who had witnessed practically every twist and turn in the country's politics for several decades?

Kapish and I visited the great man at his residence to discuss the book. We were soon joined by L.K. Advani's wife Kamlaji, daughter Pratibha and political secretary Sudheendra Kulkarni.

What appealed to me the most about Advaniji was that he is a family man. His wife has been his inspiration. He wanted his family—especially Pratibha, Kamlaji, his son Jayant and daughter-in-law Geetika—to be involved in every aspect of the book. I was very pleased to have met Kamlaji; she reminded me of my own mother. A short while after the meeting, Advaniji handed over two chapters to me and said with typical humility, 'Please have this reviewed and let me know if Rupa would be interested in publishing this. I am in no hurry.'

The two chapters were subtly different. The first was on Deendayal Upadhyaya, a senior Jana Sangh leader. It also talked about the Jana Sangh, its formation, its activism, workers and goals. This chapter revealed the inner functioning and devotion of the Sangh workers; the other chapter was more political. The writer in L.K. Advani was clear in his mind—he wanted to devote space to both his political life and the Jana Sangh, the organization he was part of.

Soon after we had read the chapters, Kapish visited his residence with a contract and the production of the book was underway. Sudheendra Kulkarni, who was deputed to handle the project on behalf of the author, would meet us every day to exchange notes. This task was not easy, as the book covered in great detail all the major and minor events in Advaniji's long political career. We had to be meticulous about fact-checking and proofing because even a small factual inaccuracy would have been a huge embarrassment for a man who had spent more than seven decades of his life in the public sphere. His story, once out, would be under intense scrutiny and as publishers, we were aware of this.

Even as I was completely stretched by the demands of sending Advaniji's monumental book to press, another joyous event was added to my list of duties. Kapish was getting married to a wonderful girl, Asheena, whom I would thenceforth call my 'bitiya', and the wedding was to be organized. The two events took place back to back. 1 March 2008 was the day for Kapish to tie the knot. The launch of the book was scheduled for 17 March, which later got postponed by a day. The two events needed to be managed in parallel, but I wasn't fazed for an instance; instead I was totally overjoyed.

Kapish's wedding took place a few days before the launch of the book, and it's an event I will remember all my life. There was a small humorous sidelight to the occasion: I was stopped by security from attending my own son's reception, as the entire area had been cordoned off! 'But I am the father of the groom,' I said plaintively. 'Sorry Sir, protocol. Sir Shri Advaniji is arriving.' I nodded in agreement. What else could have I done?

The launch of Advaniji's book was naturally a major event. The former president of India Dr A.P.J. Abdul Kalam released the book. On the podium, beside

Advaniji, in all his humility, sent us two chapters and asked us if we would be interested in publishing his autobiography. At the time, he was one of the top political leaders in the country.

the publisher, were Bhairon Singh Shekhawat, Cho Ramaswamy, Advaniji along with his wife, Jaswant Singh and Mohan Bhagwat. Every inch of the Siri Fort Auditorium was occupied by luminaries—eight CMs, former and present cabinet ministers, the lieutenant governor of Delhi, industrialists, such as Ambanis, Mittals and Ruias, film personalities, like Sanjay Dutt, Hema Malini, Vinod Khanna, Shatrughan Sinha, among others and bureaucrats and important BJP leaders. The only noteworthy person who was absent was Vajpayee since he was unwell.

The road to the venue was jammed with vehicles. In fact, Jaswant Singh had to walk for almost one kilometre to reach the venue. In his inimitable style, Dr Kalam apologized for the traffic snarls—he attributed this to Advaniji's popularity and described the clogged traffic as an 'Advanijam'. The event had

(From left) Myself, Cho Ramaswamy, Kamlaji, L.K. Advani, A.P.J. Abdul Kalam, Bhairon Singh Shekhawat, Mohan Bhagwat and Jaswant Singh at the launch of My Country, My Life

A well attended event. Outside the hall, where the book was released.

L.K. Advani's daughter Pratibha was involved in every aspect of the making of the book

The then CM of Gujarat, Narendra Modi, with Rajnath Singh

(From left) Shashi Ruia of the Essar Group with Anil Ambani and the Mittal brothers Rajan and Sunil Mittal of Bharati Enterprises at the launch

The MDH Masala king, Mahashay Dharampal Gulati, with the matinee idol, Sanjay Dutt

(From left) Kumar Mangalam Birla and George Fernandes. From the industrialist to socialist, all came for the grand Advani event

several speakers. I delivered my welcome speech in Hindi. Post the launch, we had organized a get together for 1,500 people with an exclusive arrangement for about 30 dignitaries in a secure area. The VIP presence can be overwhelming, and I was a little nervous regarding the arrangements. To my surprise, a beaming CM walked up to me and said, 'Mehraji, don't worry. I will take care of your guests.' I was blown away by the modesty of this CM of Gujarat, Narendra Modi.

Immediately after this, the Bombay book launch took place. Advaniji wanted this to happen at the earliest, as his daughter Pratibha was to leave for the US soon after. The launch in Bombay took place at two venues—the Crossword Bookstores, where the author was to interact with readers and later, a more formal launch at the Rangasharda Auditorium in Bandra.

As soon as the Crossword event, which was besieged by readers, ended and we left for the gala event at Rangasharda Auditorium, our car was stopped by security personnel. As Advaniji had the highest level of security, his car would need to leave first. However, I was determined to get to the launch venue before him. Being the publisher, I wanted to greet him and the guests upon their arrival. Without further thought, I got out of the car and, holding my wife's hand, jumped into a taxi and asked to be driven to Bandra. My nervousness kept increasing as the taxi crawled along. Adding to the tension was the fact that I had not visited Siddhivinayak Temple—a ritual I undertook every time I was in Bombay. When we finally got to the venue, I was astonished to find that Advaniji—who was renowned for his punctuality—had not yet arrived. Just then, I saw his cavalcade draw up to the entrance. When I went forward to greet him, he said in an apologetic manner, 'Mehraji, I stopped my car midway to visit Siddhivinayak Temple and therefore I'm late.'

The launch went off well. Just as in Delhi, the hall was packed with celebrities. Amitabh Bachchan, Aishwarya Rai Bachchan, Dharmendra, Manoj Kumar, Dara Singh, along with a host of other Bollywood stars, industrialists and other noteworthy figures were present.

The launch event was followed by dinner at a nearby hotel near the Worli Sea Face, where hundreds of people from every walk of life got to meet the man who had touched their lives in myriad ways.

Advaniji, as I have mentioned, was noted for his humility and for the kindness he bestowed on everyone he dealt with. During the Holi festivities in 2008, when everyone was immersed in the colours of Holi, Advaniji wanted to present copies of the book to the then PM Dr Manmohan Singh and Sonia Gandhi. He phoned me and asked if some copies could be sent to his residence. Accordingly, I deputed one of the people who worked

Like Delhi, the Bombay launch, too, was a grand success

with me, Sudama, to go to our Daryaganj office, pick up some copies and take them to Advaniji's residence, so he could sign and present them to their intended recipients. When Sudama returned, he looked so happy that I asked whether he'd had his fill of Holi bhaang.

'No, sahib, something bigger happened. Advaniji served me laddoos with his own hands today!'

A monumental undertaking. The 11-volume set of Encyclopedia of Hinduism, running into 7,800 pages.

• Chapter 26 •

ENCYCLOPEDIA OF HINDUISM

'Your undertaking is rightly called the "Project of the Third Millennium".' This is a monumental undertaking. It is indeed a Jnana Yajna. Hence, all those who have offered their time, talent and scholarship as ahuti for the success of this yajna deserve our heartiest applause and felicitations,' so said Atal Bihari Vajpayee about the *Encyclopedia of Hinduism* project when he was the PM of India in 1998. The words were spoken at an event held in New York by the Indian Historical Research Foundation (IHRF).

The project had a long gestation period. It originated in a meeting that took place in 1987 in Monroeville, Pennsylvania, at a Hindu–Jain temple. A few anguished priests and spiritual thinkers were huddled in deep conversation about the diluted form of Hinduism that was being presented in schools, universities and colleges throughout the West, particularly the US, and the dearth of authentic books that probed deep into one of the world's great religions. Worried NRI parents attending the weekly sermons at the temple were bringing in reports about how their children had misconceptions and misinformation about their religion. Their American friends were well-versed with the Bible, but their own kids were clueless about Hinduism. Swami Chidanand Saraswatiji, the founder of this Hindu–Jain temple and the head of the Parmarth Niketan Ashram in Rishikesh, came up with the idea of producing an encyclopaedia of Hinduism, a task that had never been attempted before. A body, the IHRF, was established for the specific purpose of bringing out a multivolume encyclopaedia of Hinduism on the situation.

Sitting in my Daryaganj office, I was wholly unaware of all this. Then, 20 years later, in 2007, I was suddenly tasked with publishing the book by L.K. Advaniji, whose memoir we were working on at the time. One day, Advaniji summoned me and suggested that I visit the Parmarth Niketan Ashram in Rishikesh. 'Mehraji, there is a proposal to publish an Encyclopedia on Hinduism. Please visit this ashram. Sudheendraji will give you details,' he said. There were other publishers in the running but Sudheendraji's demeanour conveyed to me that we were the front runners.

On 1 January 2008, Kaminee and I travelled to the ashram in Rishikesh to meet the monk behind the monumental manuscript. The ashram was so inaccessible that we had to travel by car and then by boat to get there. The boat fare was ₹10 per passenger and the boatman refused to set off until he had the vessel's entire complement of 20 people. Although I was prepared to pay whatever it cost to hire the boat, the boatman would not listen. And so we waited. Half an hour later, after the boat filled up, we set off. The boatman, to my annoyance, was excessively chatty. As we were disembarking, the boatman said in passing, 'Sahib, your work will be done.' As we approached the ashram, any irritation occasioned by the boatman melted away because the ashram was stunning to behold, its beauty enhanced by its wild and remote surroundings.

I was shown into the presence of Sadhvi Bhagawati Saraswati, secretary to Swamiji, the head of the ashram. I was astonished to be grilled by the Sadhvi. I was under the impression that our visit to the ashram was a mere formality after Advaniji's recommendation. But here I was, being thoroughly interrogated. My patience was tested further when I was told I couldn't meet Swamiji right away, as he was meditating, following which he would be in *maun* (silent meditation). Subsequently, he would be performing the aarti. After a while, Swamiji made a brief entrance, asked whether we were being looked after, told us to join the ashramites for dinner at 6.00 p.m. and then disappeared. I was perplexed—he hadn't uttered a single word about the book. Nevertheless,

(From left) The current National Security Advisor (NSA) Ajit Doval, Kavita Sharma, Swami Atmapriyananda, the then head of Ramkrishna Math in Calcutta, Professor Kapil Kapur, Dr Lokesh Chandra and Sadhvi Bhagawati Saraswati

I decided to control my impatience. It transpired later that I was being tested as for my patience and 'suitability' for the project. The encyclopedia had been more than 15 years in the making and the board of trustees wanted to be sure that whoever took it on would be the right fit. I would like to assume that I passed the test because Rupa was formally declared the publisher of the encyclopedia. In the preface, the board of trustees proclaimed Rupa to be the right publisher for the encyclopedia:

> After many years of negotiations and discussions with various publishers, IHRF decided—for many reasons—to entrust the publication of this monumental work to Rupa & Co., as the Board felt they could do full justice to both the letter and the spirit of Hinduism. A publication of EH [sic] requires much more than flawless copy-editing and page layout. It also requires a profound understanding of and great appreciations for the depth and breadth of this ancient yet timeless wisdom. It requires editors who are both adept at proofreading and sentence structure, as well as who

Advaniji marvelling at the expanse of the work done by Rupa in bringing out the 11 volumes of the Encyclopedia of Hinduism in 2010

truly comprehend the essence of the text they are editing. The Board was confident that Rupa's experience with Indian texts, their academic and personal sensitivity to and appreciation for the subject matter, and their devotion to Hinduism would be assets to the project. The entire team at Rupa have committed themselves fully, with piety, devotion and tireless resolve, to this project. Rather than publishing an academic text, we are building a temple together—a temple of knowledge, a temple of history, a temple of insight and inspiration.

Once we were chosen, the enormity of the challenge facing us became apparent. For a project of this length and breadth, spanning countries and continents, and spread over a period of two decades, we were dealing with big numbers. The

L.K. Advani stands alongside the team that dedicated three years to crafting the magnum opus, the 11-volume Encyclopedia of Hinduism

project involved hundreds of scholars, authors and editors working in different time zones, with millions of entries to be fact-checked and verified. Rupa hired 26 editors for this enormous work (divided into 12 volumes), each assigned a specific number of entries. Every editor was required to finish a particular number of entries every day, which were then cross-checked by a peer. Finally, the entries were tabulated and placed in a folder, to be checked again with a fresh pair of eyes. Although all our editors were meticulous with their work, none of them knew Sanskrit and there was no way in which we could cross-check the diacritical marks, symbols, etc. The only way to ensure accuracy was to have an expert who could check the Sanskrit renditions of words and phrases. Fortunately, we were able to find someone who could take on that role—Dr Kapil Kapoor, Professor of English and Sanskrit Studies, who had recently retired as rector from Jawaharlal

Prof Rajneesh Mishra, Santosh Shukla and Dr Kapil Kapoor formed our pillar of strength for this gigantic project

Nehru University. Kamal Mallik, the publisher of East West Publishing Company, had published Dr Kapoor's work and provided a glowing reference. Dr Kapoor was a godsend. He came with his own team—academics from various universities—who constituted an editorial board to review the material. Once he came on board, the project took off.

The complexity of the project demanded a meticulous process. The entries in the encyclopedia were conceptualized and created by hundreds of local experts on Hinduism in numerous languages from several cities—Madras, Bangalore, Pune, Ahmedabad and Banaras. These entries were gathered and collated by satellite offices of the IHRF. Most of the entries were handwritten and it was the job of the satellite offices to have them translated and typed up. Most of the work was done using typewriters, since computers were not readily available in those days. The entries were then put through three levels of rigorous editing—content editing to check facts and academic accuracy; copy editing for language; and review editing to ensure consistency and narrative flow. The satellite offices would then send the entries to Dr Kapoor's office who would undertake the same process at his end before the material arrived at the desks of Rupa editors.

From the time we were given the green light in 2008, it took three years for the book to be published. It was a tremendous book, one which gave the general reader as well as scholars a comprehensive idea of an ancient way of life and a deep understanding of the facts, theories, systems, practices, institutions, beliefs, texts, thinkers, and much more.

The work was priced at ₹21,000 for each set (21 is an auspicious number in Hinduism). But not all was auspicious for me. Bringing together so many editors and scholars, coordinating with different people at multiple levels, investing money for the best production quality and not getting the return for all the hard work put in, took a toll on my health. I was admitted to the hospital soon after the project was completed—but I survived to tell the tale.

Jaswant Singh (right) was widely respected across political spectrum. Seen here with George Fernandes.

• Chapter 27 •

JASWANT SINGH: THE CALL OF HONOUR

It started with a friend from England, who was also in the publishing business, asking me one day: 'Would you be interested in publishing a book written by a famous Indian politician with a military background?' It was an easy answer, 'Yes, of course.' The only hitch was that this English friend of mine had forgotten the name of the author! However, it was not too difficult to ferret out the name of the famous Indian politician with a military background who could also write. In a week's time, the prospective author was traced: Jaswant Singh confirmed that he was, in fact, writing a book called *Defending India* and that he was at an advanced stage of signing the contract with Palgrave Macmillan. However, he promised to keep Rupa in mind for his next book. This happened sooner than expected. One of our authors, Arun Shourie, during a visit to our office, mentioned that Jaswant Singh was working on a new book. Kapish and I met Jaswant Singh at his residence sometime in 2005. In my view, what clinched the deal for us was Kapish mentioning that he had just finished reading a book by Strobe Talbott, a close friend of our prospective author.

Jaswant Singh proved to be a model author. He wrote eloquently, had profound knowledge of his subject, met his deadlines and was courtesy personified in all his dealings with us.

When *A Call to Honour* was finally ready, Jaswant Singh meticulously outlined his plan for the launch. The event was well attended, and the book received a great deal of media attention—we had a bestseller on our hands right away. We published a couple of more books by him, including a Hindi edition of one of his books.

A Call to Honour *was received warmly by the readers. Sir Mark Tully (left) with the author.*

Sometime in 2007–08, Jaswant Singh called me to discuss his new book. Apparently, it had to do with Jinnah and Partition (the book was eventually called *Jinnah: India–Partition–Independence*). This came as a surprise, given that Jaswant Singh was among the top brass of the BJP and a former foreign and defence minister with a miliary background. Considering the events a couple of years earlier—when L.K. Advani had praised Jinnah while visiting Pakistan and had to resign from his position as party president after the public outcry against his statement—I assumed Jaswant Singh would be cautious about his choice of subject. But he seemed unfazed about any adverse reaction that the book might elicit.

As the book took shape, he did show some trepidation but more on my account than his. When he asked me on a couple of occasions, 'Mr Mehra, are you sure you will publish it?' my answer was always in the affirmative.

The book was finally released in 2009 and the launch was fixed for 17 August—Rupa's founding day. Jaswant Singh invited a galaxy of speakers, including Ram

(From left) Namwar Singh, Jaswant Singh, Lord Meghnad Desai, M.J. Akbar and Sir Mark Tully at the launch of Jinnah: India–Partition Independence

Jethmalani, M.J. Akbar, B.G. Verghese and Hameed Haroon, the editor of *Dawn*, Pakistan. The book was launched at Teen Murti Bhavan and it could not have been more atmospheric to launch a book on Jinnah at the official residence of India's first PM, Jawaharlal Nehru. Although the gathering was huge and distinguished, his party people were conspicuous by their absence. At the launch, several speakers felt it was wrong to hold Jinnah solely responsible for Partition—both Pandit Nehru and Sardar Patel would need to shoulder some of the blame. This made the news and ramped up the controversy surrounding the book.

Next day, the BJP leaders, including Jaswant Singh, were due to start a conclave in Shimla. As the BJP luminaries arrived, the media interrogated them for their views on Jaswant Singh's book, especially his favourable views on Jinnah. Within hours, the ire of his party men spilled over into concrete action. Then Party President Rajnath Singh informed Jaswant Singh that he had been expelled from the party for endorsing Jinnah. As soon as I heard of this, I called

Whispers from the power corridor: Did we have an inkling that the book would generate controversy?

Jaswant Singh but no one answered the phone. On his way back from Shimla, he returned my call and asked if we could meet. He sounded like a person wounded by his own men. By evening, the Gujarat government prohibited the sale and distribution of the book. This heightened the controversy. On being asked for my views, I said that I would make a comment after studying the Gujarat notification on the banning of the book. Next day, Jaswant Singh arrived and we met on 21 August at his residence. He looked sad and troubled.

The Delhi World Book Fair was taking place at the same time and I invited him to our stall. He was a huge draw. My phone kept ringing. Arnab Goswami, the TV anchor, asked me for a live chat along with a minister and spokesperson for the Gujarat government. During the chat, I said point blank to the minister and spokesperson for the Gujarat government: 'Two wrongs do not make one right.' Goswami loved the way the debate was shaping up and peppered the minister and me with many questions. I opposed the ban as did many senior

The book became a big success. The author can be seen here with Mahesh Bhatt at the Bombay launch.

members of the party. Jaswant Singh, Ved Marwah, governor of Manipur and former police commissioner of Delhi, senior bureaucrat T.N. Chaturvedi and a host of others called me the next day to congratulate me on my stance.

A public interest litigation (PIL) was filed in the Gujarat High Court. On 27 August, both Jaswant Singh and Rupa moved the Supreme Court before a division bench. Fali S. Nariman and Soli Sorabjee appeared for us before the division bench of the court of the Hon'ble Altamas Kabir. It was an interesting moment. Many lawyers were carrying a copy of *Jinnah*. A notice was served to the Gujarat government to reply within two days. On the plea that people in Gujarat were not able to read the book, the bench politely remarked that it, in fact, may rather be outselling itself in Gujarat at this moment. The press had already reported that a large number of copies were reaching Ahmedabad and Baroda (now Vadodara), via Bombay. Two days went by and still there was no reply filed by Gujarat government to the Supreme Court's notice. The bench gave them seven more days.

Jaswant Singh seen here with Jagmohan (left) and T.N. Chaturvedi (centre)

In the meantime, politics was also in play and many lawyers from Gujarat invited both Jaswant Singh and me to speak on various platforms. I refused to get into the politics of the controversy. I was interested in only fighting the ban and exercising my right to do business and defending people's rights to read whatever they liked. I also made a statement on the record expressing my anguish on the silence of Advaniji on the issue. He was, after all, a Rupa author and a votary for freedom of expression.

The ball was in the judiciary's court now. Before the next hearing in the Supreme Court, the Gujarat High Court lifted the ban on the book. The same night, Goswami called me again for a live chat. On the other side was the same minister who had been on the panel with me earlier. Our argument was just as heated as before. I strongly defended the book. Later, Jaswant Singh called me to congratulate me for standing up for the book.

The book became a major bestseller. NDTV did a story that stated, 'Thick tomes of history normally don't sell like hot cakes but Jaswant Singh has beaten Amartya

Sen and Nandan Nilekani to the top spot of the bestseller list.' The story further quoted a prominent bookseller saying that the book had a 'Harry Potter touch'.

We also launched the book in Bombay, where Mahesh Bhatt made a remarkable speech along with advocate Raian Karanjawala. In Hyderabad, M.J. Akbar and Aminuddin Khan spoke; the function was organized by Sarita Reddy of the Reddy family. At each venue, the book's popularity continued to rise.

Predictably, there was also a huge demand for the book from across the Radcliffe Line. Jaswant Singh visited Pakistan to promote the book. Though I was also granted a visa by Pakistan, I didn't go—I didn't want to get involved in the politics of the controversy, especially beyond the border. I again missed visiting the city of my ancestors—Peshawar.

When I think of the book today, I remember Jaswant Singh's words to senior television journalist, Rajdeep Sardesai, on one of his shows, 'If thinking, reading, writing, debating, discussing, disagreeing on any issue or on any written material is taboo, it will be a very sad India, it will be a very dark India.'

Jaswant Singh continued to have a turbulent time within his party till his sunset years in the party and life. Having been denied a party ticket in the 2014 Lok Sabha elections, he contested against the party's official candidate and was expelled. He lost the elections but his fighting spirit remained intact.

In his life, Jaswant Singh had effortlessly imbibed the two different worlds of tradition and modernity. The women in his household practised purdah in the traditional Rajasthani style. He was a god-fearing man who used to worship every day and sip his scotch whiskey every evening. Sadly, he fell in his bathroom, slipped into a coma and on 27 September 2020, this fierce soldier–scholar breathed his last.

Graceful, captivating, elegant—the ethereal beauty of Maharani Gayatri Devi

• Chapter 28 •

MAHARANI GAYATRI DEVI: FAIRY TALES DO COME TRUE

Once upon a time, there lived a princess. The world beat a path to her palace and she was feted as one of the 10 most beautiful women in the world. Princess Gayatri Devi of Cooch Behar, who became Maharani Gayatri Devi, Rajmata of Jaipur, after her marriage, made headlines throughout her life.

An avid equestrienne, the princess was an excellent rider and an able polo player. She first came to my attention when I read about her in the newspaper. One day, when her husband, the dashing Maharaja Jai Singh or Sawai Man Singh II, a scratch polo player, was on the field, his stunning wife ran onto the field and kissed him—an action that was dutifully recorded by *The Statesman*.

The third Maharani of Jaipur through her marriage to His Highness Maharaja Sawai Man Singh II (Jai Singh), Gayatri Devi was born into a Bengali Hindu family. Her father, Prince Jitendra Narayan of Cooch Behar, West Bengal, was the younger brother of the yuvraja (crown prince). Her mother was a Maratha princess—Indira Raje of Baroda—the only daughter of Maharaja Sayajirao Gaekwad III. Princess Indira Raje was extremely beautiful and a legendary socialite in her own right.

My granduncle was a great admirer of Gayatri Devi. He would often talk of her beauty, confidence and generosity. She remained one of those people I admired from afar until one day, Naveen Patnaik—the CM of Orissa for two decades, our published author and a friend—told me sometime in 1994 that the Maharani had expressed a desire to meet me. When I met with Naveen at his 3, Aurangzeb Road* residence, he informed me that the Maharani wanted to update the autobiography she had authored with Shanta Rameshwar Rao.

Soon enough, a meeting was arranged and my colleague Jayant Bose, my wife and I drove down to Jaipur to meet the Maharani. We were extremely nervous at the prospect of meeting the iconic royal. A long-time friend of my wife, Sudha Ramchandani, whose brother-in-law had once been ADC to the Maharaja of Jaipur, was acquainted with the Maharani and had briefed me thoroughly about her likes and dislikes. To make matters a little complicated, Jayant began to feel unwell. When the Maharani arrived, punctually at the appointed hour, draped in a green georgette sari, I was awed by her beauty, presence and grace. Just then, Jayant whispered in my ear that he was feeling really sick. I asked him to return to the hotel and explained his absence to the Maharani. She graciously enquired if there was anything she could do to help. After Jayant had left and we had exchanged the customary pleasantries, we got down to work at a beautifully carved tea table that had an astoundingly beautiful silver tea service on it.

The Maharani was very clear about her expectations and within minutes, all the terms and conditions regarding the publication of the book had been finalized. She had put me at ease by now and I began talking to her about her political career. She had swept a resounding victory in the 1962 Lok Sabha elections, polling 192,909 votes of the 246,516 cast in her constituency. Former US President J.F. Kennedy had once introduced her as 'the woman with most staggering majority that anyone has ever earned in an election'.† The achievement was even endorsed by the Guinness World Records. However, her political career came to an end after she ran afoul of Indira Gandhi's government, who accused her of breaking tax laws. Gayatri Devi had to serve five months in jail during the infamous Emergency. However she wasn't

---

*Aurangzeb Road was renamed A.P.J. Abdul Kalam Road in 2015.

†'Obituary: Gayatri Devi', *Hindustan Times*, 29 July 2009, https://tinyurl.com/2uhzxc65. Accessed on 25 July 2023.

Pictures of Maharani Gayatri Devi from A Princess Remembers, *which we published to much acclaim*

Maharani Gayatri Devi being presented a memento on the release of her autobiography in Jaipur

Grace and elegance personified: Gayatri Devi signing her book at the launch event in Jai Mahal Palace, Jaipur

one to hold a grudge. When asked to express her views on Indira Gandhi, she said, 'People do make mistakes; I forget and forgive.' She went on to speak about her love of thoroughbreds—a passion that she shared with her husband. When the meeting ended, I went back to my hotel on a high. This was publishing at its best.

After a couple of months, the book was out. I left for Jaipur with my sales team. We left Delhi at 6.00 a.m. in three cars filled with piles of the book. Two cars left from the Daryaganj office; I left from my house with my driver, Mahavir. At the time, the National Highway 8, connecting Delhi and Jaipur, was a nightmare, a highway in name only. Trucks, buses, tractors, trolleys, bullock carts and everything and anything that could move plied on it. Traffic rules were unheard of. Eighteen kilometres from a place called Kukas, an insanely overloaded bus headed straight towards us. It was being driven full tilt on the wrong side of the road. Panicking and desperate to avoid a collision, I wrenched the steering wheel to the left—the car went off the highway with a bang, the door on the driver's side opened and I was thrown on to the service road parallel to the highway. Apart from some scratches and bruises, I was okay but Mahavir was lying motionless on his side of the car.

Dreading the worst, I hobbled across to him and was relieved to find that he was still breathing and seemed unhurt—he had fainted from the shock of the accident. The left side of the car was completely smashed. Soon, some villagers came to our rescue; they sprinkled water on Mahavir, and he came to his senses. The rogue bus driver was nowhere to be seen. The onlookers gradually dispersed, and Mahavir and I decided we'd somehow drive our damaged vehicle to the spot where my team and I had arranged to meet. As there were no mobile phones in those days, there was no way we could inform my colleagues or my wife about the accident. Everyone was shocked when they saw my battered car drive up. But there was no time for long-winded explanations, since we were already late, and needed to make haste to meet the Maharani at 11.00 a.m. When I handed her the copies of the

The extent of the accident I got into en route Jaipur can be imagined from my damaged car

book, all the trauma of the past few hours vanished. She was delighted to see the book. She invited us to stay for lunch, but I needed to get back to Delhi to organize the dispatch of the book. Touching her feet, I excused myself and the team and headed back to Delhi.

By the time I reached hòme, it was late. I parked my car in the portico of the house and had a quick dinner. I woke up at around 10.00 in the morning to the sound of wailing. Several members of the household were weeping because they had noticed the damaged car and the fact that Mahavir was missing. When my wife, whom I had told about our narrow escape, asked me: 'Where is Mahavir?' I replied, 'He must be at home.' But Mahavir was not at home. When the household staff had checked the damaged car and found no trace of Mahavir, they had jumped to conclusions and informed the driver's family that he was dead. A massive commotion ensued. I immediately rang up a colleague and asked him to find out where Mahavir was. Finally, he phoned back saying that the taxi Mahavir had been travelling in had broken down, which caused the delay in him getting home.

Gayatri Devi with journalist Tavleen Singh

Sudha Ramchandani (left), my wife's long time friend, was an important communication link between Maharani Gayatri Devi and me

Compared to these rather dramatic events around the publication of the book, the launch was uneventful. The Maharani didn't want a grand, public function but just 25 to 30 people at a private event. Consequently, we had a gathering with some select guests on the lawns of the Jai Mahal Palace—a quiet cocktail party. Gayatri Devi arrived punctually at 7.30 p.m. and the event kicked off. She mingled graciously with everyone present with no press in attendance. She had her customary two sundowners, a ritual that was sacred for her. When I requested her to autograph a copy for a guest who had to leave early to catch a flight, she declined my request politely, 'Please allow me to finish my drink,' she said. I had heard stories of her shooting a panther when she had only been 11, and I wisely decided not to remonstrate with her. Once she finished her drink, she signed every book that needed to be autographed. She remarked, 'I like to autograph my book more than savouring my drink. But I like to take up just one task at a time.' We would often see her at Rupa functions in Jaipur and she never failed to impress me with her grace, elegance and lack of airs.

The last time I got in touch with her was in London. An aide had phoned to say that the Maharani wanted five copies of her book to be delivered to her in London. As I was travelling to the city, I decided to hand them over in person at her Cadogan Square residence. As soon as I left, it started pouring on what had been a sunny day until then. I hadn't reckoned the weather in London and had forgotten to carry an umbrella. By the time I reached the Maharani's residence, I was sopping wet. When I rang the doorbell of her flat, the member of her household staff who opened the door must have assumed I was a courier boy and was astonished when I said I wanted to meet the Maharani. 'She is taking a bath,' he said, and politely indicated that I should leave. When I got back to my hotel, at around 4.00 p.m. I got a call from the Maharani. 'Thank you for taking

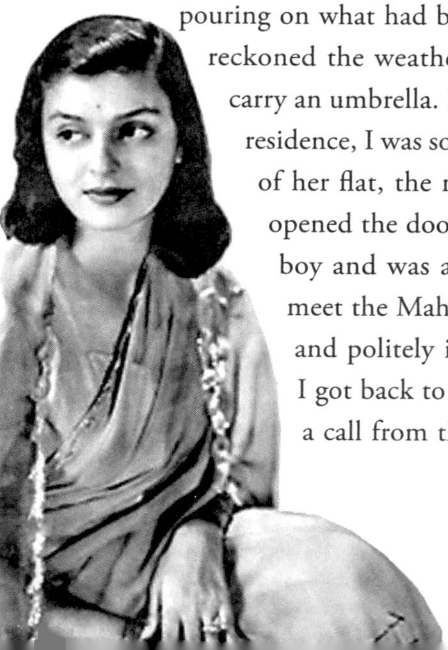

WikiCommons

Man Singh II and Gayatri Devi

the trouble to bring the copies. I needed them badly. I know you are on a business visit but much the same, please do drop in any day after 4.00 p.m. as and when you are free,' she said. She read my small note at the back of my visiting card and cared to call back! Unfortunately, my schedule was quite packed on that trip that I couldn't call on her. So I took a 'raincheck' and said we would meet when she was back in India.

Sadly, that was our last phone call, for she fell ill in London, was brought back to Jaipur and admitted to Durlabhji hospital. She never recovered and passed away on 29 July 2009.

MANUSCRIPTS TO MASTERPIECES

A Collaborative Journey with Authors

Salman Khurshid

Bijoylaxmi Hota

Sunita Dwivedi

Yatindra Mishra with Muzaffar Ali

C.P. Belliappa with his wife

Sunil Gavaskar signing an author copy for another bestselling author Ravi Subramanian

Arif Mohammad Khan's book is still a masterpiece on issues facing Islam

(From left) Anuradha Mathur, author of Deccan Traverses *with Girish Kanad at the launch*

Roopinder Singh

Tarun Vijaya

Rita Bhimani

(From left) Anuradha Mahindra with Indira Mahindra, our author

Dr Manmohan Singh releasing a two-volume memoir of Hirubhai M. Patel as Amrita Patel, his daughter, looks on

(From left) George Fernandes and Nitish Kumar releasing The Indian Railways Strike of 1974: A Study of Power and Organised Labour *by Stephen Sherlock (centre)*

Prakash Singh (left) with former Vice President Venkaiah Naidu at the release of his book, The Struggle for Police Reforms in India: Ruler's Police to People's Police

T.S.R. Subramanian, former cabinet secretary and the author of Journeys Through Babudom and Netaland: Governance in India *speaking at an event in Lucknow*

'Reading my poems in English is like seeing them in a new dress; well stitched, well starched and ironed very carefully'

• Chapter 29 •

GULZAR: THE MAN IN WHITE

दिल ढूँढता है फिर वही फुर्सत के रात दिन...

Dil dhhondta hai phir wahi fursat ke raat din...

The heart looks for the same leisurely nights and days...

Now that I play a less active role in the business and have some time to contemplate life, the brilliance of Gulzar's poetry often permeates my mind. Sampooran Singh Kalra aka Gulzar can make the most ordinary things look extraordinary. Gulzar was born in pre-Partition India, in 1934, in Dina tehsil of Jhelum district (now Pakistan). He was born into a Sikh family to Sardar Makhan Singh Kalra and Sujan Kaur. Gulzar's poetry and lyrics tap into the wellsprings of Hindi, Punjabi and Urdu culture. Before achieving renown as a poet and becoming one of the greatest lyricists Bollywood has ever known, Sampooran Singh Kalra worked in Bombay as a car mechanic in an automobile garage called Vichare Motors. His job was mixing colours, painting and beautifying damaged cars. Even as a car mechanic, he strived for the beauty later reflected in his words. It was the celebrated film-maker Bimal Roy who gave this turbaned car mechanic a chance to write a song for his film *Bandini,* starring Ashok Kumar and Nutan. This sardar then penned, '*Mora gora ang lai le, mohe shyam rang dai de.*' And Gulzar was born.

In 1993, one of our editors, Sanjay Shekhar, wanted to acquire books by Gulzar sahib. Thus began a memorable and lasting relationship between the bard and the publisher. We started with two books: *Silences*, a book of poems, and *Ravi*

Silences was released at the midnight of 31 December 1994 at the Juhu Beach. (From left) Gulzar, Om Puri and our editor Sanjay Shekhar.

Paar and Other Stories, a collection of short stories. *Silences* was a collection of his poems translated in English, a literary rarity. When the editor of *Silences*, Sanjana Roy Chowdhury, and I presented a cloth-bound edition of the book to Gulzar at the Taj Palace hotel in Delhi, the bard grabbed the book like a child does his newly acquired toy. In the preface to the book, he had beautifully summed up what an English translation of his poems meant to him:

> Reading my poems in English is like seeing them in a new dress; well stitched, well starched and ironed very carefully. When I used to read my poems in Urdu, they used to sound like me. In English, they sound like my teachers. I used to like them. Now I am impressed by them.*

Quintessential Gulzar!

---

*Gulzar, *Silences,* Rina Singh (trans.), Rupa Publications, 1994, New Delhi.

Ravi Paar was a montage of stories, weaved with myriad emotions, tailor-made by Gulzar to fit the occasion called life. Many more followed As the years passed, Gulzar sahib became a part of the Rupa fraternity. Be it a book launch, a book fair or an exclusive city exhibition, he would grace the event. On how he chose the name Gulzar, the poet says in one of his books *Pukhraj* published by us in 2002:

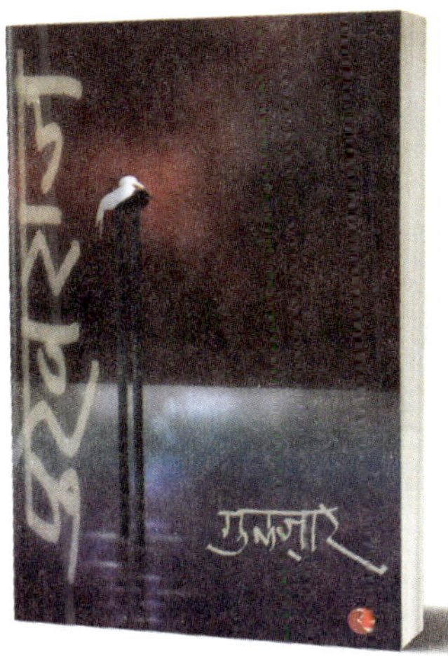

नाम सोचा ही ना था, है की नही
अमा कह के बुला लिया एक ने
ऐ जी कह के बुला लिया दूजे ने
अबे ओ! यार लोग कहते हैं
जो भी यूं जिस किसी के जी आया
उसने वैसे ही बस पुकार लिया
तुमने इक मोड़ पर अचानक जब
मुझको 'गुलजार' कह के दी आवाज
एक सीपी से खुल गया मोती
मुझको इक मानी मिल गया जैसे
आह, यह नाम खूबसूरत है
फिर मुझे नाम से बुलाओ तो

Naam socha hi na tha, hai ki nahin
'amaa' kehke bula liya ek ne
'Ai ji' kehke bula liya duje ne
'abe o' yaar log kehte hain
Jo bhi yun jis kisi ke ji aaya
Usne vaise hi bas pukaar liya
Tumne ik mod par achanak jab
Mujhko 'Gulzar' kehke di awaaz
Ek seepi se khul gaya moti
Mujhko ik maani mil gaye jaise
Ah, ye naam khoobsoorat hai
*Phir mujhe naam se bulao to!**

---

*Ibid.

Gulzar's daughter, Meghna, reciting verses from her father's book before the event

Never thought of a name, whether it's there or not.
Someone said 'Ama',
The other referred to me as 'Aey ji',
Friends call me 'Abey o',
Whoever felt whatever inside,
They just called me by the names of their choice.
And when all of a sudden,
You called me 'Gulzar',
A pearl came out of its shell.
As if I had an identity.
Oh! This name is beautiful.
So call me by this name then!

Gulzar sahib became an integral part of Rupa fraternity

Gulzar being felicitated by Dr Murli Manohar Joshi at one of our events

Raising a toast to Meghna Gulzar's Because He Is

The word wizard with the bookseller. Gulzar with Anuj Bahri of Bahrisons Booksellers.

Over time, Gulzar sahib became family. We would occasionally meet at each other's house and soon, the four walls of our rooms would convert into an adda of stories, laughter and life. At Kapish's wedding, he was present on every important occasion, at the marriage ceremony in Karnal and the reception in Delhi. I would often visit him in Bombay at his Pali Hill home, where I remember partaking delicious home-cooked poha and fragrant tea, dipped in the poetry of the man himself.

His family includes his ever-so-talented daughter Meghna, his son-in-law Govind and his grandson Samay. They make a wonderful, wholesome family. Meghna, now an acclaimed film director, put together an emotional and intimate biography of her father, whom she endearingly calls Papi. Meghna begins the book, titled *Because He Is*, with the following lines, which set the tone for the pages to follow:

I know I'm protected
Because his arms cradle me.
I know I walk the right path
because his little finger leads me.
He dabbles with celluloid
So I know I can see,
I can write
Because his ink flows in me.
I know I can
Because he believes.
I know I am
Because he is…

Because He Is was launched in 2004 at Crossword Bookstores in Bombay. The occasion was graced by Jagjit Singhji and his wife, Chitra Singh, two of Gulzar's favourite singers. The daughter penned the life of her father, as if returning in abundance what she received in instalments from her father as a child. Gulzar wrote books for his Bosky (as he fondly called her) and presented it on each of her birthdays till she turned 13.

The literary adda organized by Rupa which Gulzar often attended. (From left) Gulzar, Kamleshwar, Alok Bhalla and myself.

We published Mirza Ghalib, *which was a screenplay of his famous serial on Ghalib. (From left) Gulzar with Naseeruddin Shah at the launch of the book.*

(From left) Meghna with her husband Govind and Nandita Puri

Gulzar with Subhash Arora of Tekson Book Shop behind him

Rupa cherishes and will forever remember the Gulzar books that we published

Gulzar is a child of undivided Punjab. He was all of 11 when he witnessed the horrors of Partition after moving to Delhi. A para in *Because He Is* narrating what this child witnessed is blood curdling:

> Then they actually witnessed the horrors—corpses strewn on the streets on which they played, rioters and looters wreaking havoc, bodies being set on fire with anything that was found—tables, chairs, beds… My father remembers a man called Samandar Singh dragging another boy, a Muslim, who used to lead their prayers at school. When asked where he was going, Samandar Singh replied in Punjabi, 'to cut him to pieces!' After a while, Papi saw him return with a bloody sword in his hand.

Any child would turn insane and fanatic witnessing such horrors, but Gulzar channelled his nightmares into words. His poetry is etched with the scars of Partition. His pain finds a lyrical form in some of his poetries. Somehow, initially, I was not able to look beyond his exterior. However, I have always felt that here is a man who has been christened with pain. But

किताबें झांकती हैं बन्द अलमारी के शीशों से
बड़ी हसरत से तकती हैं
महीनों अब मुलाक़ातें नही होतीं
जो शामें इन की सोहबत में कटा करती थीं,
अब अक्सर
गुज़र जाती हैं 'कमप्यूटर' के पर्दों पर
बड़ी बेचैन रहती हैं किताबें....
इन्हें अब नींद में चलने की आदत हो गई है
बड़ी हसरत से तकती हैं,

जो क़दरें वो सुनाती थीं।
कि जिन के 'सैल' कभी मरते नहीं थे
वो क़दरें अब नज़र आती नहीं घर में
जो रिश्ते वो सुनाती थीं
वह सारे उधड़े उधड़े हैं
कोई सफ़हा पलटता हूँ तो इक सिसकी निकलती है
कई लफ़्ज़ों के माने गिर पड़े हैं
बिना पत्तों के सुखे टुण्ड लगते हैं वो सब अल्फ़ाज़

Gulzar's poignant lamentation on the state of books and reading in todays times

I have never asked him about his inner turmoil, the vacuum that seems to be inside him. He wears white and beneath it lies a poetic pain, a sense of loneliness. But Gulzar, at least, knows his place and in his own words, 'The mirror in my house recognizes my face!'

Over and above the strong bond of our friendship is the genius of his poetry, which has given me so many deep and lasting insights into life.

With his simple, witty and inimitable writing style, Ruskin Bond is one of India's most beloved writers

• Chapter 30 •

RUSKIN BOND: THE AUTHOR ON THE HILL

He is our 'bond' with 'The Woman on Platform No. 8', 'The Girl on the Train', 'The Boy from the Hills', 'The Kitemaker' and so many more memorable characters. Oddly enough, Ruskin Bond, the man whose words have touched millions, is often at a loss for words when asked to speak on stage. I learnt this early on in our association and would do my best to restrict his book launches to one-on-one interactions, at which he was superb.

Ruskin was first published by Rupa at the insistence of Nirupam Chatterjee. When Nirupam da approached him, Ruskin gave us two of his greatest works to publish—*Angry River* and *The Blue Umbrella*, which have never been out of print since their publication in 1992.

Ruskin has lived in Mussoorie, and later in its outlying suburb Landour, since 1962. When he moved there, the population of Mussoorie was thinning, as the boarding schools in the area were declining and the expat population, primarily British and American missionaries, was departing. Bond initially moved to Landour from Delhi for the 'peace and quiet' to be found there. Things are rather different now in Mussoorie, which is often described as 'Delhi's Chandni Chowk on a hill'. However, Landour Cantonment, where Ruskin lives, is much calmer.

Ruskin has been a lifelong bachelor, but over the decades, an extended foster family has grown up around him. Many years ago, when I first visited his home, I found him sitting on a cot with a squealing toddler in his lap. Ruskin was unperturbed by the noisome infant and calmly continued to converse with

Ruskin at his desk in his home in Mussoorie

me. Over the years, the family that he once sheltered and protected now has been sheltering and protecting him as his fame has grown.

As a writer in his late eighties, he is as productive as ever. He gets most of the ideas for his stories while gazing out of his window at the forested slopes of the Lower Central Himalayas, the Pauri Hills and the Doon Valley. These sylvan surroundings and the experiences of his life, especially his childhood and adolescence, have been woven into his most memorable stories.

Over the course of a writing career spanning 50 years, he has written over 100 short stories, essays, novels and more than 30 books for children. During the early years of his career as a writer, his earnings were meagre. He suffered many hardships, but he never gave up. With his simple, witty and inimitable writing style, he is one of India's most beloved writers.

The Room on the Roof was his first novel, written when he was 17. It was immediately acclaimed when it was published and went on to receive the John Llewellyn Rhys Prize in 1957. *Vagrants in the Valley* was also written in his teens, and it picked up from where *The Room on the Roof* left off. These two novellas were published in one volume by Penguin India in 1993 as was a remarkable collection of his short fiction, titled *The Night Train at Deoli*. Other brilliant books from this period included the non-fiction anthologies *Rain in the Mountains, Delhi Is Not Far* and *The Best of Ruskin Bond*.

In 1992, Ruskin received the Sahitya Akademi Award for English writing in India for *Our Trees Still Grow in Dehra*. On his autobiography, *Scenes from a Writer's Life,* published in 1997, V.S. Naipaul commented in *The Literary Review*,

> I have read nothing like that from India or anywhere else. It's very simple. Everything is underplayed, and the truths of the book come rather slowly at you. He is writing about solitude, tremendous solitude. He himself doesn't say it. He leaves it all to you to pick up. I haven't read another book about solitude from India. In a way, from this great subcontinent so full of people, to write a book about solitude is quite an achievement.*

Although Ruskin published many of his books with Penguin, I was able to persuade him to write several children's books for us. Over time, we became one of his main publishers. This led to me visiting him every month. I would drive down to Dehradun and take a cab to Landour. When it would be time for me to return, Ruskin would often accompany me to Delhi and spend a few days at my place, during which time we would organize author events and a variety of promotions for his books.

On one such occasion, I decided to cook for him and made omelettes for

*Dhondy, Farrukh, 'An Interview with V S Naipaul', *Literary Review*, August 2001, https://tinyurl.com/hxymdh56. Accessed on 25 July 2023.

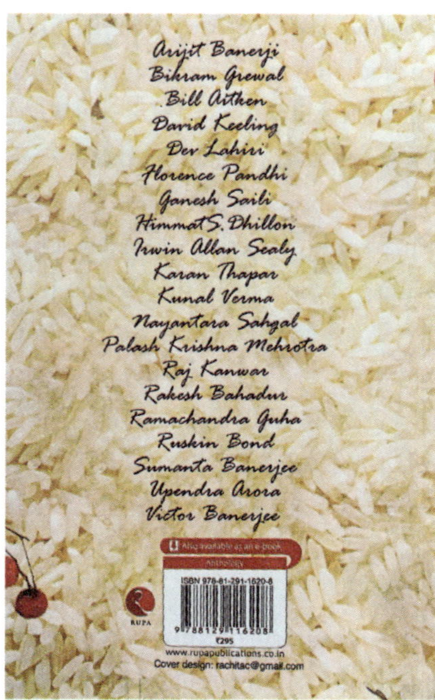

Once Upon a Time in the Doon *was a tribute to the Doon valley paid by eminent people who had lived in the valley*

breakfast, as I was aware of his fondness for eggs.

'*Kaisa laga* (Do you like it)?' I asked.

He didn't answer immediately and then said, 'To be honest, this is tomato omelette, not an omelette omelette.'

'*Maine anda to daala tha* (I did add eggs to it),' I muttered under my breath. To be honest, though, the dish did look more red than yellow! Since then, I left the preparation of meals to my cook.

Ruskin's children's books were a big hit, and we promoted them heavily in schools. Ruskin visited schools to promote the books and before each visit, nearly 500 copies used to be pre-sold. We also arranged for him to judge various writing

Vishal Bhardwaj, who made the movie The Blue Umbrella, *releasing Ruskin Bond's anthology of stories* The Mini Bus

competitions for companies like Max and ITC—the fees he received augmented his income at a time when he hadn't succeeded commercially. After a hectic day spent in promotions, Ruskin would come home to rest and relax and down a glass or two of Scotch. Kapish used to become our bartender and made drinks for Ruskin and me. Over time, a long-lasting bond developed between Ruskin and Kapish, and he went on to publish several children's books with Kapish.

Soon, celluloid beckoned Ruskin. Vishal Bhardwaj, the versatile film director, acquired the rights to *The Blue Umbrella*. When the film was released, it won a national award in the children's film category. Much later, when he made another film based on Ruskin's novella, *Saat Khoon Maaf* with Priyanka Chopra as the heroine, Bhardwaj managed to get the shy and taciturn Ruskin to do a cameo as a Catholic priest. To tease him, I'd mention his association with

Bond's Baraat! In such fashion did Ruskin Bond arrive at the Bombay Festival

Gulzar receiving Ruskin Bond at the event

Life, celebrations, friends: Tom Alter, Ruskin Bond, Gulzar and myself cherishing the moment

(From left) Deepak Shah, Nitin Shah and Ruskin Bond at the Sapna Book House in Jayanagar

Ruskin flanked by Sunil Arora (left) of Cambridge Book Depot and his friend (right)

Ruskin Bond receiving the Publishers' Award, on behalf of Rupa, by Upendra Arora of Natraj Publishers at Hotel Madhuban, Dehradun

Dining in literary bliss at Cheetal Grand, in Khatauli, Uttar Pradesh; where great food is savored with Ruskin Bond tales

(From left) Pankaj Arora of our sales team with Shariq Rana, the owner of Cheetal Grand and a great admirer of Ruskin Bond

A Thank-you Verse

A wonderful family called Mehra
Has a home and a garden in Dehra,
They grow roses and lilies,
Cucumbers and chillies,
No garden in Dehra is fairer!

~ Ruskin Bond
18/8/19

Landour, Mussoorie
18/10/19

Dear Mr. Mehra,

At this Diwali I take the opportunity to thank you and all your wonderful family for the kindness and consideration you have shown me over the years. May all of you prosper and be happy through the coming years.

Ruskin Bond

The man of letters keeps sending us these very warm and personal letters

Ruskin Bond with Sandeep Arora of English Book Depot (left) and our author Ganesh Saili (right)

Priyanka Chopra, and it would never fail to elicit a blush.

I'd like to conclude this chapter with an anecdote about an anthology that Ruskin edited about the Dehradun region, *Once Upon a Time in the Doon.* The book had a lot of distinguished contributors including Bikram Grewal, Bill Aitken, Florence Pandhi, Allan Sealy, Dev Lahiri, Shanti Verma, Karan Thapar, Nayantara Sehgal, Ramachandra Guha and Victor Banerjee to name a few. The book was launched by another well-known inhabitant of the Doon valley, Prannoy Roy of NDTV. As the launch got underway, the quiet of the hill station was shattered by the blare of sirens—it turned out that the CM of Uttarakhand Shri B.C. Khanduri had decided to attend the launch. No sooner had he stepped out of his car than another siren sounded nearby; another VIP, the state's former CM N.D. Tiwari had also arrived for the launch. As he was being escorted to his seat, I was made aware of a problem—since we hadn't expected these VIPs, we only had one bouquet, which had already been presented to our chief guest Prannoy Roy. However, some quick thinking resulted in that bouquet being passed from Prannoy to the CM and then to the former CM.

(From the top) The same bouquet kept changing hands, from Prannoy Roy, to B.C. Khanduri and then to N.D. Tiwari at the launch of Once Upon a Time in the Doon

In the by lanes of Daryaganj, visiting our office with A.K. Singh (centre) and Sugeeta Roychaudhary (right)

Everyone pretended that this was entirely normal; it was a situation tailor-made for a Ruskin Bond story.

As part of our promotional tour for *Once Upon a Time in the Doon*, we flew Ruskin to Kathmandu, where he was mobbed at every book store, every event and every shop we visited. We even took him on an Everest flight to see the mighty Himalayas. Two front seats were taken and when the pilot manoeuvred through turbulence, I could see Ruskin clenching his fists in nervousness. An adorable, childlike gesture from the grand old dad of Indian stories!

To honour one of India's greatest storytellers and one of our most esteemed authors over the years, Rupa has presented him with two awards—the N.D. Mehra Memorial Award, instituted in the memory of my late father, and the Author's Recognition Award. These are small tokens of appreciation for his genius.

Manik da swirled his brush on a blank canvass and created Rupa's previous logo. His fee had been a few Rupa books!

• Chapter 31 •

MANIK DA (SATYAJIT RAY): THE 'DADA' OF STORYTELLING

In the '70s, the world was looking at Indira Gandhi in admiration for her handling of a host of problems—a war with Pakistan, an influx of refugees from the genocidal attacks of the Pakistani army on its eastern part that would soon become the independent nation of Bangladesh, bullying by Richard Nixon in the US and Harold Wilson in the UK, and much else besides. Mrs Gandhi met each of these challenges with resolve, courage and ingenuity and came out on top. It was the ideal moment to publish a book about her. Clinching the opportunity, Peter Owen in London decided to publish her very first biography. Its author Ela Sen even managed to convince the PM to cooperate on a biography. Once it was written, Peter Owen was to be its publisher outside India and we were to publish it here.

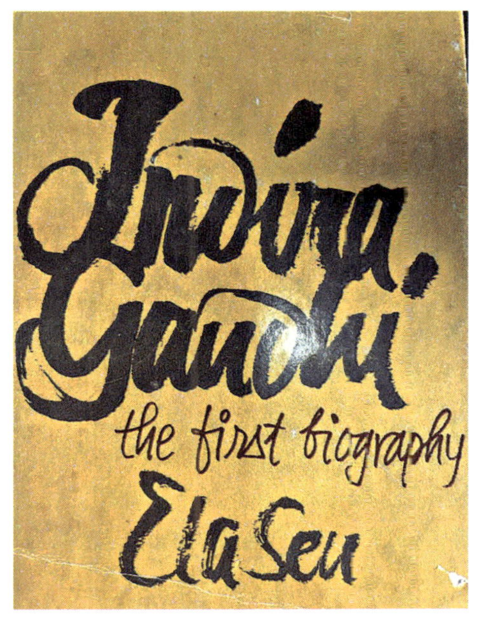

Indira Gandhi's first biography, published by Rupa, with its cover designed by none other than Satyajit Ray

Ela Sen was a friend of Satyajit Ray and when he heard that Rupa was publishing Mrs Gandhi's biography in India, he told my granduncle, D. Mehra, that he would like to design the cover. As I have mentioned earlier in the book, many members of the Calcutta film fraternity, especially

Manik da was a magician, with both camera and pen. Here he is with Pandit Ravi Sankar during the music recording of Pather Panchali.

habitués of the Indian Coffee House, were friendly with D. Mehra, as they were frequent visitors to our office and showroom. Many of them would request us to open early or close late, so they could fit their visits to Rupa between their shooting schedules. Ray was a frequent visitor. He would usually arrive late in the evening. Soumitra Chatterjee used to come in the morning hours while Utpal Dutt would pop in during lunch breaks. It was quite extraordinary to have Soumitra Chatterjee in the morning, Utpal Dutt in the afternoon and Ray in the evening at our office. Rubbing shoulders with such brilliant cinematic stars was amazing.

Ray was known as Manik da to friends and close associates, but I called him Kaka babu. One day, when I was visiting Calcutta, D. Mehra asked me to go to Ray's house and pick up the cover for Mrs Gandhi's biography, if it was ready. So, I went to his house and was fortunate enough to find him sitting in an armchair reading a book. When I told him the purpose of my visit, he looked startled—he had completely forgotten about his offer to design the cover for the book. However, unperturbed,

Satyajit Ray with my father N.D. Mehra at the Rupa office. The bonhomie, respect and courstey between them is clearly visible.

he lit a cigar, ordered two cups of coffee and biscuits from the household staff and then began pacing around his large living room. Hardly had the coffee arrived, than Ray suddenly darted across to an easel in a corner of the room. Picking up two paint brushes, he dipped one into a bright yellow pigment and painted the canvas yellow. On it, he painted in green with elegant calligraphy—Indira Gandhi–Ela Sen. And that was pretty much the entire cover design. He asked me to pick it up the next morning at 11.00. By this time, his cigar had burnt out. As I was leaving, he asked me if the new Alistair MacLean title had arrived. The next day, armed with a copy of the new MacLean, I collected the rather unusual cover.

Talking of Ray's genius for design, he also designed Rupa's first logo, which adorned every one of our books until well into the twenty-first century. And his fee for this labour had been a few Rupa books!

A glittering novelist and a master of perpetual storytelling, Salman Rushdie has had a long association with Rupa

• Chapter 32 •

SALMAN RUSHDIE: MAKING THE WEST MEET THE EAST

Since the horrific attack on him in the US in 2022, Salman Rushdie is back in the news. Rather than highlighting his literary genius, the reports are all about the *fatwa* that has blighted his life. It's something that greatly saddens me.

My association with and admiration for Salman as a writer dates back to the early '80s. One day, during this time, I received a rather unusual Christmas gift from my friend Peter Hensen of Collins. It was unusual because Peter would usually just send a Christmas card. When I opened the package, I found a substantial hardbound book entitled *Midnight's Children*. Its author was Salman Rushdie, an Indian-born, London-based advertising professional. He, in fact, had left his job in advertising to write this book. When I finally put the book down, having read it almost continuously over a few days, I was amazed by its style and content. It was about a boy who is born at the stroke of the midnight on 15 August 1947; as a result, the newborn child's destiny was linked with the destiny of the newly independent nation. It is a fantastic piece of magic realism in which the history of a nation is beautifully embedded into the life and times of its main character, Saleem Sinai. The book was published in paperback by Picador, and I immediately acquired the rights to exclusively distribute the book in India. *Midnight's Children* won the Booker Prize that year and the rest, as the cliché goes, is history.

After *Midnight's Children* came *Shame,* which was a political satire on Pakistan. Pan-Picador licensed its publishing rights to us in India. Kaminee and I went to London in 1983 to seal the deal with Picador's publisher, Sonny Mehta. Sonny gave Salman a call and the author turned up within 10 minutes, clad in a kurta and pyjama.

Salman Rushdie with Khushwant Singh at the launch of Shame *at IIC, New Delhi*

Back in India, I arranged a book discussion on *Shame* and *Midnight's Children* at the IIC with Rushdie in attendance. Khushwant Singh chaired the meet and Ravi Dayal was the keynote speaker. There was a stampede to meet the author at this and a host of other events. Salman was elated by the reception he received wherever he went in the country.

A few years later, Penguin India received the manuscript of *The Satanic Verses.* Khushwant Singh, the literary adviser to the firm, and Zamir Ansari, who was in charge of sales and marketing, were both apprehensive about the reception of the book, as there were passages potentially offensive to orthodox Muslims. In fact, Khushwant Singh advised Penguin India against publishing the book in India. Zamir, then, sent me the manuscript. As I didn't feel qualified to comment on whether or not it could be considered offensive, I sent it to a couple of Muslim friends, scholars and intellectuals, whose opinions I respected. They didn't think there was anything wrong with the book, and we imported

During his visit to India, the distinguished writer Salman Rushdie made an appearance at K.D. Singh's bookshop, with Singh standing right by his side

500 copies of *The Satanic Verses*. The book didn't take off immediately—we did not sell even 30 copies on day one.

Then, Syed Shahabuddin, an MP from Bihar and the editor of the monthly magazine *Muslim India,* lodged a complaint about the contents of the book and appealed the then PM Rajiv Gandhi to ban it immediately. Shahabuddin had not read the book and neither had Home Minister Buta Singh who would have to act on the matter. On 5 October, around 5.00 p.m., my dear friend Tejeshwar Singh, the news reader from Doordarshan and publisher of Sage Publications, called me and said, 'Be careful, the book might get banned.' At 9.00 p.m., the very same day on Doordarshan news, Tejeshwar Singh announced, '*The Satanic Verses* by Salman Rushdie has been banned in India.'

Our country was the first to ban the book. I had stocks left with me and as per the banning orders, which interestingly came from the Ministry of Finance, the

Of bookworms and book nerds: Salman Rushdie with Balraj Bahri Malhotra, founder of Delhi's iconic bookshop Bahrisons at IIC

book could not be imported under Section 11 of the Customs Act. Technically, I could still sell it and liquidate my current stock. The next morning, I put the rest of the books in the boot of my Ambassador car, fearing that they might be damaged by fanatics if displayed in the showroom. Sham Lal, the editor of *The Times of India*, telephoned me for a copy. Soon, others followed. My phone line wouldn't stop ringing. A list of buyers was compiled and my driver went around the city delivering copies of the book to customers.

By evening, 400 copies were sold. According to the initial arrangement I had with the original publisher, we'd agreed to import 10,000 copies of the paperback edition. I had to now say no.

Soon after, Ayatollah Khomeini issued a fatwa against Salman and overnight, the situation worsened to the extent that Salman had to go into hiding, fearing for his life. But his courage and fortitude were noteworthy. A lesser author's creative

My long time friend, Hassan Suroor who is an advocate of liberal Islam and who advised me on issues related with Islam

instincts would have been paralysed, but Salman was made of sterner stuff—while contending with death threats and hatred, he wrote a delightful book *Haroun and the Sea of Stories* for his son Zafar. The book was an absolute delight.

His next novel was *The Moor's Last Sigh*—a witty family saga set in India and peppered with spicy satire and his unique magical touch. Shortlisted for the Booker that year, *The Sunday Times* called it 'Salman Rushdie's greatest novel'. However, the controversy over *The Satanic Verses* cast a long shadow and affected this book as well, with the Shiv Sena and a few others objecting to passages in it. I was caught up in the dilemma that publishers are sometimes enmeshed in. Should we publish and defend the author's right to be heard or give in to the political pressure? I decided we would import and sell the book in India.

The book, however, was detained by customs, and we knocked at the doors of the Delhi High Court. The judge took up the matter in seven days. Another

Raju Barman with Salman Rushdie at Rupa office. The Presidency College can be seen from the window behind.

21 days went by before the final hearing, which eventually gave the book a green signal. The World Book Fair was about to begin. I was informed by the Customs Department that since the book had been detained, we would have to pay demurrage for the number of days it had been with them. I was clear that I would not be paying a single penny to Customs and I again went to court, where the fine was waived. *The Moor's Last Sigh* was finally 'unbanned' from the Indian market and became a fairly successful book. I was delighted to make the book available as was the author. Salman has written about it in detail in his memoir, *Joseph Anton*.

Salman and controversy seem to have a magnetic relationship, though I must say, never intentional. To commemorate 50 years of the country's independence, Salman jointly edited a voluminous 600-page book, *The Vintage Book of Indian Writing*, with Elizabeth West. It was an anthology of the best Indian writing in the half-a-century since Independence. With writings of literary luminaries from the country, this book promised to be a bestseller. Rupa was distributing the book in the Indian market but surprisingly, the initial response was lukewarm. As the book gradually became available to the Indian intelligentsia and reading class, a line from Salman's introduction to the book rubbed Indian translators and regional language writers the wrong way. Salman had written:

> ...prose writing—both fiction and non-fiction—created in this period by Indian writers working in English, is proving to be a stronger and more important body of work than most of what has been produced in the 16 'official languages' of India, the so-called 'vernacular languages', during the same time.*

These lines set the cat among the pigeons. Everyone wanted to have their copy and see what the English language writer had written for his vernacular brethren. It was good news for what had been till then a slow-moving book!

Salman has an ancestral house in Civil Lines in Delhi. His father Anis Ahmed who first took the surname Rushdie had sold the property to a businessman and a former Congress leader Bhiku Ram Jain in 1970. Salman's sister and brother-in-law wanted to visit their ancestral property and I was able to organize a visit for them, with Salman loitering around the place smiling gleefully like a child. It pained me to see the attack on Salman in 2022. He was knifed by a fanatic in August that year for writing *The Satanic Verses* in 1988. He lay in a hospital for days, paying the price for championing free expression in a world getting increasingly radicalized. Salman, I am told, has lost sight in the eye as a result.

---

*Rushdie, Salman, and Elizabeth West, *The Vintage Book of Indian Writing*, Vintage, UK, 1997.

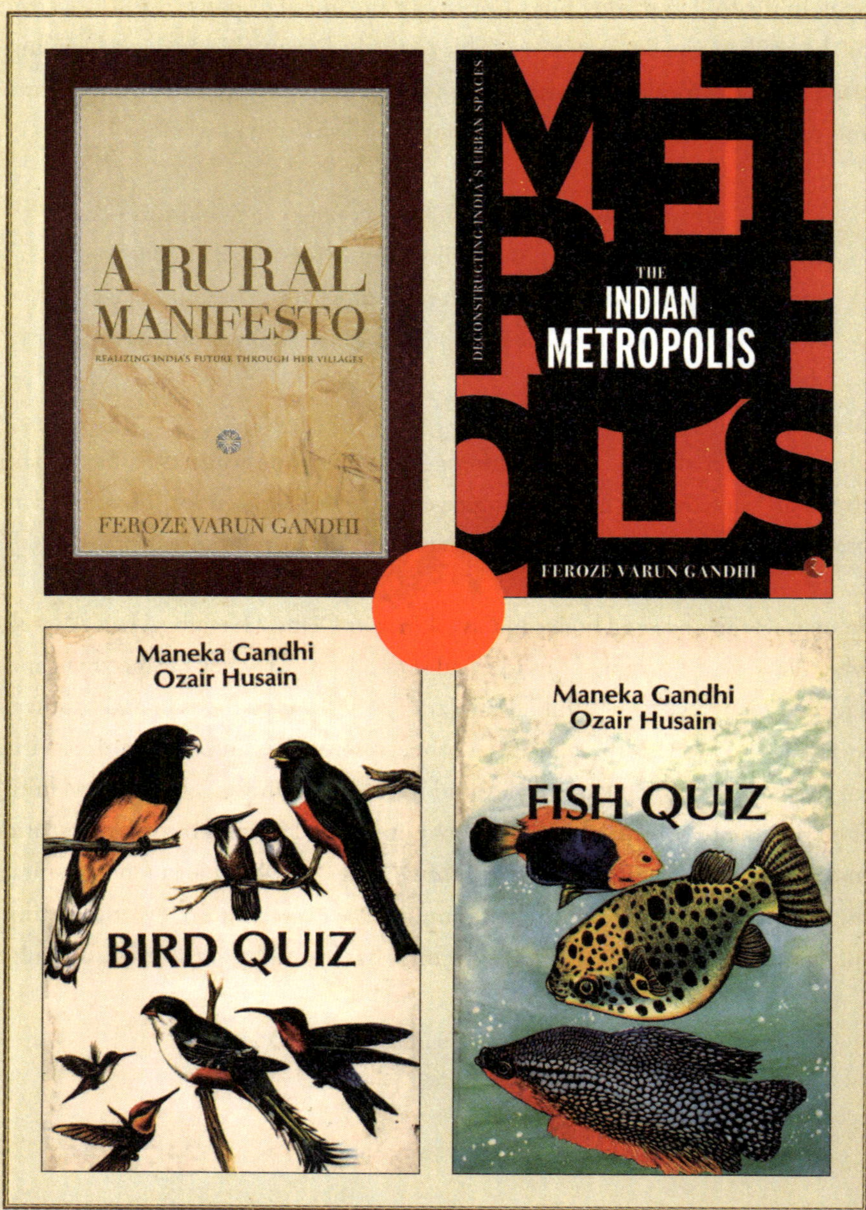

Rupa takes pride in the fact that we have published both mother and son

• Chapter 33 •

MANEKA AND VARUN: THE OTHER GANDHIS

Some people love books. Some people love animals. Very few have an equal passion for both. Maneka Gandhi is one such person. I was introduced to her by my friend, the legendary bookseller K.D. Singh, who was close to Maneka at the time. She was turned out of the PM's residence by her mother-in-law, Indira Gandhi, when differences flared up between the two after the death of Maneka's husband Sanjay Gandhi. It was K.D. who accompanied Maneka from the PM residence to her mother's place, a brave job indeed.

Maneka and K.D. would often visit our Pataudi House showroom to buy books. Over time, our connection strengthened, and one day, she invited me to visit her at home in New Friends Colony. I drove down to her place around 10.00 in the morning. When I got out of the car, to my dismay, I was surrounded by around 20 odd stray dogs—Maneka routinely rescued strays from the streets. I was rather nervous when they converged on me, baring their teeth and barking. I was on the verge of leaving when Maneka emerged and pacified them.

I was settled in her study and noticed two little puppies beneath my chair, playing with several sheets of paper. When Maneka saw what I was looking at, she said casually, 'Ah, this is the manuscript I've written for a publisher. The proposal didn't work for them and so I have discarded it.' My curiosity was piqued and I retrieved some of the pages from under the puppies. As I glanced through them, I was impressed by what I was reading—up until then, I hadn't been aware of Maneka's talent as a writer. Unhesitatingly, I asked her to write

Maneka Gandhi at the launch of her book The Complete Book of Muslim and Parsi Names *with her son Varun Gandhi*

for us—a book on animals. *1000 Animal Quiz* was her first book for us. The book was a success and was reprinted many times.

Her next book had a unique title, *Brahma's Hair*—a collection of pieces on Indian plants. Things were going well with our publication plans until we ran into trouble over the cover. Maneka had engaged a freelance designer to come up with a cover. She loved it but I knew it wouldn't work. Neither of us would give in, and we were in a fix. I thought of a common friend, Pritish Nandy, a writer, journalist and MP, who I hoped could act as a mediator. Pritish is an extremely helpful person and he proved to be so on this occasion as well. He arranged for a new cover to be designed that both parties were happy with, refused any payment and salvaged the project for me.

Varun's first book with us The Otherness of Self *was published in 2000*

Rajnath Singh came to grace the occassion and encourage the budding author and aspiring politician

(From left) Amar Singh, Rajat Sharma, Arun Jaitley, Varun Gandhi and Lalit Suri at the launch of Varun's book at IIC

Since this standoff has been resolved, our relationship with Maneka has been very satisfactory. Rupa has published several of her books on animals and birds. They are all quiz books that have sold well and gone into several reprints.

Some years later, Maneka's son, Feroze Varun Gandhi, wrote a collection of poems, *The Otherness of Self,* which we published and it was well received. Varun had, by then, entered politics and was elected to the Lok Sabha from Pilibhit, UP. In 2009, he was embroiled in a controversy for allegedly making communally inflammatory speeches. He was arrested and sent to jail. When he was in prison, I sent him books to read. After his release, Varun thanked me for the gesture. Our professional relationship continues to flourish. In 2018, we published his enormous study on rural India, *A Rural Manifesto: Realizing India's Future Through Her Villages*. Running into almost 850 pages, Varun's critical commentary on rural economy and society and the rural–urban chasm in policymaking is remarkable. He followed it up with another 800-page tome *The Indian Metropolis,* which talks about challenges faced by our cities and what

From poems to policies, Varun Gandhi has grown tremendously as a serious author. His three books with us were published in 2000, 2018 and 2023.

can be done—at the policy and the individual level—to make them liveable. I look forward to publishing more of his books—he is a serious writer who is well worth publishing and promoting.

Camellia Panjabi, a pioneer in the hotel industry

• Chapter 34 •

CAMELLIA PANJABI: THE QUEEN OF INDIAN FOOD

Camellia Panjabi is the author of one of the world's bestselling books on curries, *50 Great Curries of India.* It has sold over 800,000 copies and has been described as the definitive guide to Indian cooking. Born in Bombay, Camellia studied Economics at Cambridge and went on to become the marketing director of Taj Hotels, India's most prestigious hotel group. With a lifelong passion for food, Camellia helped create several restaurants for these premier hotels, featuring little-known regional dishes. Camellia opened the Bombay Brasserie in London in 1982, introducing regional Indian cooking to the UK for the first time and changing the way Indian cuisine was perceived here. In 2001, she joined her family's restaurant company, Masala World, owners of Chutney Mary, Veeraswamy, Masala Zone and Amaya.

Kyle Cathie Ltd, a UK-based publisher, sent us a telex (as was common in those days) asking whether we would be interested in publishing the Indian edition of *50 Great Curries of India.* Even though I had never met Camellia, the proposal was of interest to me, since I was aware of her stellar reputation in the hospitality industry. I also happened to have a very favourable opinion of her, as she often bought copies of books in bulk from publishers to stock in the various hotels of the Taj Group. Considering these factors, I took Kyle Cathie up on their offer and agreed to publish Camellia's book in India.

This book changed the way Indian cuisine is perceived in the UK.

I first met Camellia at Taj Mansingh in Delhi and was impressed by her humility and the way she carried herself. Her marketing ideas for her book were exceptional and contributed a lot to its spectacular success.

She was a stickler for detail and had an incredible eye for design and presentation. One evening, we had arranged to meet in the lobby of the Hotel President by Taj Vivanta, where I was staying during a visit in Bombay. When I got out of the lift, I noticed Camellia looking closely at an enormous vase of flowers in the lobby. Even as I watched, she summoned a hotel employee to change the placement of the vase by half an inch. The employee did not know who she was but Camellia was an authoritative presence. She complied with the request, although it was, in reality, a command. Camellia was finally satisfied with the positioning of the vase, and I walked up to her and told her how impressed I was by her commitment to excellence. She gave me a wry smile and we spent the rest of the evening talking about everything she was doing to improve the standards of the hotels in the company.

Camellia was a pioneer in the hotel industry. Today, not only the Taj but also luxury hotels across India, offer idli, dosa and vada with sambar for breakfast. This was one of the things Camellia was responsible for introducing. Till the mid-'70s, toast and butter and eggs were the only things available for breakfast. She continues to innovate at her restaurants in London, which routinely win top honours in the industry.

Natwar Singh's interest and knowledge in a range of topics reflect in all his books

• Chapter 35 •

ONE LIFE IS 'SURELY' NOT ENOUGH: NATWAR SINGH

'A retired husband is often a wife's full time job,' read a social media forward on my phone. This made me smile because I knew there was some truth to it, especially for me after I had dialled down my involvement in the business after some health issues. Kapish has been largely responsible for running the company although I did make myself available to help with strategic decisions.

Then, one day in 2013, Kapish left a package on my desk. I didn't open it immediately and it was only after I received a phone call from the former Congress leader and writer, K. Natwar Singh, asking whether I had gone through the contents of the package he had sent me that I opened it and found a potential bestseller waiting for me.

It was Natwar Singh's autobiography! He had been 16-years-old and glued to his father's radio set when Nehru had announced India's tryst with destiny at midnight. Less than a year later, the same boy had heard Nehru's 'the light has gone out…' address to the nation on the passing away of Gandhiji and had been mesmerized by the statesman's 'memorable and eloquent words'. Natwar Singh was an indispensable part of the political institution called the Nehru–Gandhi family, a career diplomat who was Indira Gandhi's confidante, an erudite scholar and a sounding board on matters of international politics for all the three Gandhis—Indira, Rajiv and Sonia—and someone who would regularly recommend books to Rahul Gandhi. At the time I received the manuscript, he had become a peripheral figure within the Congress Party and the government owing to his name

Natwar Singh told me, 'Mehra sahib, there is so much still to write that I don't even know if one life is enough.' And we had our title. (From left) Saeed Naqvi, Prof Dipankar Gupta, Soli Sorabjee, Natwar Singh and Prof. Mushirul Hassan at the launch of the book.

cropping up in the Volcker Report as a 'non-contractual' beneficiary of the UN's Oil-for-Food programme for Iraq.

I finished reading his manuscript in less than 24 hours. It was an enthralling, informative read and I decided to publish the book. It was decided that we would have it out on 16 May 2014, his birthday.

I had met Natwar Singh years before this during one of our book launch events. A diplomat by profession and scholar by temperament, he had an enviable collection of books from across the world in his library. I knew this and casually asked him about the three books I was interested in—*The Wisdom of China*, *The Wisdom of India* and *Death Be Not Proud*. Natwar Singh was amused by my interest in rare books and remarked that I could borrow them from him. He also said: 'You are one of the very few well-read publishers I have come across.' Our mutual interest in books across the literary spectrum led to a long-lasting association.

Soon after getting to know him this way, he began publishing with Rupa. We started with *E.M. Forster: A Tribute*, an anthology edited and introduced by K. Natwar Singh that was published in 2002. It had contributions from writers like Ahmed Ali, Mulk Raj Anand, Narayana Menon, Raja Rao and Santha Rama Rau. Natwar Singh dedicated this book to his daughter Ritu, whose birth, in 1969, made Indira Gandhi confess to Natwar Singh in an emotional letter that 'my heart has always yearned for a daughter', and whose untimely death at the age of 30 shook Natwar Singh and his family.

Natwar Singh's second book with us was *Heart to Heart,* a collection of his writings, published in 2004, about famous personalities, like Gandhiji, Tagore, Churchill, and his recollections of his interactions with quite a few of them. From listening to whispers in the corridors of power to avoiding diplomatic mishaps; from interacting with Nobel laureates to encounters with the Dalai Lama, this book was a masterly collection of literary portraits. Just as his previous book with us, this book too was dedicated to Ritu.

One Life Is Not Enough *was a hit from the word go and the finest intellectual minds discussed the book at the launch.*

For years, his name remained smeared on account of the Volcker Report controversy. The publication of the book helped with Natwar Singh's rehabilitation in the public eye.

After this book, there was a long gap of 10 years until his autobiography landed on my table. This was not an easy book to edit. Its sweep was immense. Starting with his early days in politics, it covered subjects like the Volcker Report controversy, which ultimately led to his resignation as Minister of External Affairs by the end of 2005, his Indian Foreign Service career, his stint at the United Nations, working with Indira Gandhi during Emergency, his days with Rajiv Gandhi, his observations on the demise of the USSR, his equation with Sonia Gandhi and the Congress and much else besides this. Although the manuscript was incredibly rich and dense with insights, stories and observations, it was extremely long and needed a lot of work to set its brilliance free. I was reminded of Michelangelo's observation, 'I saw the angel in the marble and carved until I set him free.' Months of rigorous editing followed. At one point, there was a serious difference of opinion between the editor and the author, and I had to intervene to break the deadlock. The conference room in our office was booked every day for the whole day, the manuscript was projected on the TV screen, and the author, editor and I went over each sentence, determining whether it would need to be retained, revised or excised. When the book was finally ready for publication, the country was in the midst of the 2014 General Election and we decided to postpone the publication until the news cycle calmed down.

When the election results were announced, it was clear that a major shift had occurred in the political landscape. The Narendra Modi-led BJP had displaced the Congress-led coalition. The timing was perfect for Natwar Singh's no-holds-barred autobiography, as he finally broke free and spoke his mind on all sorts of controversies that had taken place when the Congress was in power. We were ready to send the manuscript to press; only the preface from the author was awaited. And then, Natwar Singh disappeared. His phone started going unanswered, his secretary's responses to our calls ranged from 'he's in the bathroom' to 'not feeling well', 'gone for a walk', 'not in the city', 'will come back after some time', 'will call back', and so on and so forth. We

(From left) Dr Namwar Singh and Natwar Singh at the launch of the Hindi edition of Mangal Pandey *by Amaresh Mishra at 30 January Marg. Natwar Singh attended the event an evening before he was expelled from the party.*

also sent a messenger to his house but he was told that there was no one inside, although the lights were on.

Thoroughly demotivated by Natwar Singh's behaviour, I decided to cancel the publication. I asked Kapish to personally take the edited manuscript to Natwar Singh's Jorbagh house. Kapish did so and left the manuscript with his secretary who was still framing excuses for his boss's absence. As he was returning to the office, Kapish received a phone call from our author. 'Sorry, I was not in the right frame of mind to continue with the book. You will have the preface soon and then you can send the book to press.' When the preface finally arrived, it solved the mystery of its author's disappearance.

> As I was finishing this book I had a surprise visit from Sonia Gandhi and her charming daughter on 7 May 2014. It was an extraordinary encounter. Even bizarre. They were apprehensive about my autobiography touching raw nerves.
>
> On Sunday, 6 May, Priyanka called me to ask if she could meet me. I agreed and invited her to my house. Attractive and with an engaging personality, she shares her mother's sartorial elegance. Unlike her mother and brother, she is a natural communicator; the exactness of her expression is an asset. She is, as far as I know, free from the chattering fidgetiness so common among ladies of south Delhi... initially she was a bit subdued, even hesitant, but she soon came to the point. Her mother had sent her to meet me. She recalled the interview I had given to *The Economic Times* on 28 April about my autobiography. Would I be writing about the events that took place in May 2004 before the swearing-in of the UPA government? I said I intended to. No one could edit my book. I would not skirt the truth, nor would I hit below the belt...just then Sonia Gandhi walked in. 'What a surprise!' I said. Her overtly friendly and gushing greeting bewildered me. It was so out of character. It was a giveaway. Swallowing her pride, she came to her 'closest' friend to surrender her quiver. It took her eight and a half years to do so.

His autobiography ruffled a few political feathers and created a storm.

When I read it, this preface confirmed two things. One, that the book would be an instant hit and, two, we might have some sleepless nights fielding calls from the media and certain powerful politicians. How right I was! This is our occupational hazard; publishers, at times, have to live with these political pressures.

Even before anyone saw the book, it started making headlines. It made some people conscious of their not-so-glorious past. We decided to go full throttle when it came to pre-release publicity for the book. Kapish had booked a room at the Claridges exclusively for the author's interaction with the media. He, along with his team of young marketeers—Vasundhara Raj Baigra, Geetu Martolia and Rizwan Khan—ensured that all requests for media interviews would be accommodated. I was present at the venue with the octogenarian author to ensure that everything went smoothly. Media

What every author dreams of! Natwar Singh was thronged for his signed copies at the event. Ram Jethmalani can be seen here sitting next to the author.

interest in the book was so immense that the interviews took three days to complete. The day would begin at 10.00 in the morning and go on till 7.00 in the evening. Natwar Singh would finish each hectic day with a glass of red wine, unwinding and preparing for the next day with the media. He and I would dissect the events of the day and try to anticipate what would happen on the morrow.

A hilarious incident happened during our last evening there. Natwar Singh had gone back home, satisfied with the way Rupa's marketing team had handled publicity. I decided to treat them all to dinner. I ordered drinks for Vasundhara, who was leading the marketing team, her young colleague Rizwan, and myself. No sooner had I placed the order than the waiter politely said that he couldn't serve liquor to Rizwan, as he seemed to be under the age of 25. His looks were not deceptive but I said to my young colleague that while the hotel was prohibited by law from serving him liquor, the law did not say he was underage when it came to having a drink. I passed on my glass of wine to him, and everyone was thereafter full of good cheer. It was a happy augury for the impending release of the book. When it was finally released, the book was a hit from the get go. The eminent lawyer Soli Sorabjee released the book and legal luminaries like Ram Jethmalani and Fali S. Nariman were on the discussion panel at the launch event. In many ways, the publication of the book rebuilt Natwar Singh's public image. For years, his name had been smeared on account of the Volcker Report controversy, but now he was back.

The book launch heralded a new Natwar Singh, energized and enthused. As I looked at him glowing with pride, my mind wandered back to an incident during the eventful editorial process. When we were discussing the title of the book, he said, 'Mehra sahib, there is still so much to write that I don't even know if one life is enough to pen it all down in an autobiography.' I immediately remarked, '*One Life Is Not Enough*', and we had our title.

There was a time when we sold one copy of Chetan Bhagat every 31 seconds!

• Chapter 36 •

CHETAN BHAGAT: MILLION COPIES SOLD

कुछ बात है कि हस्ती मिटती नहीं हमारी,
सदियों रहा है दुश्मन, दौर-ए-ज़माँ हमारा ।

Kuch baat hai ki hasti mitati nahi hamari,
Sadiyon raha hai dushman daur-e-zaman hamara.

My persona doesn't fade away, somehow,
For centuries, the world has been against me.

کچھ بات ہے کہ ہستی مٹتی نہیں ہماری
صدیوں رہا ہے دشمن دور زماں ہمارا

This verse by Iqbal was very much on my mind when HarperCollins parted ways with us in 2002—an episode mentioned earlier in the book. My state of mind at that time was similar to what I had felt years earlier, when, soon after my father's sudden death, a Penguin export manager had decided to terminate our 56-year-long relationship coldly and with minimal courtesy. These setbacks necessitated a change in the company's strategy—we needed to reduce our dependence on foreign publishers and work to strengthen our own list. I have written about this at length in the book but have saved the story of our most successful author for the final pages of the section.

Sometime in 2004, we received an email from someone called Chetan Bhagat. He was an unpublished author and wanted Rupa to have a look at his manuscript. As

I attend to all my emails myself, we wrote, 'Please send in your full manuscript for internal evaluation.' Chetan was living in Hong Kong at the time—almost two-and-a-half hours ahead of India's time zone. By evening, my inbox had a new manuscript titled *Five Point Someone*.

I had a quick glance at the manuscript—the story of a student and his two friends at IIT Delhi, told with a light and humorous touch. Rupa had already had success with *The Inscrutable Americans* by Anurag Mathur, which was similar in some ways, and we felt this could also work in the market. I printed out the manuscript and took it home to read. As soon as I began reading, I was engrossed and finished the book in one sitting. I felt I might be on to something big but just to be on the safe side, I sent the manuscript to two able critics, who were not on the Rupa payroll, Amrita Kumar and Bijaya Kumar. Here's what they said:

> Critic 1: In conclusion, this book may be about a bunch of five pointers, but it deserves 9 points plus nevertheless, even without grade inflation! With the right kind of copy-editing and marketing, it will certainly prove to be another *The Inscrutable Americans* for Rupa.

> Critic 2: I stayed up all night to read this manuscript in one sitting and am sure anyone who gets to read it will do the same. It has the potential to become a bestseller. Its chief quality is humour, a rare enough quality among Indian writers of fiction, but what really makes this book special is that under the humour lies deep perception. This is a writer of intelligence, who has made no attempt to appear intelligent and herein lies the charm of the book. Not only would every IIT student want to keep this novel by his bedside but anyone who wishes to recapture the tensions, tragedies and joys of their student days—which is virtually everyone.

(From left) Shinie Antony, who recommended Chetan Bhagat's manuscript to us, with Deepti Talwar, the editor who worked on Chetan's book, and myself

> The author has got the three personalities, the student lingo, the campus romance, the professors and the family backgrounds just right.

Deepti Talwar, the fiction editor at Rupa at the time, read it and loved it. Shinie Antony, a dear friend from Bangalore, who went on to become a Rupa author a few years later, also loved and recommended the book for publication. *There definitely is something big here,* I told myself. An agreement was soon to be signed with Chetan now. I was scheduled to travel to meet Ruskin when Chetan had to sign the agreement. I left my signed copy at my Daryaganj office and informed Chetan over email about it. On my way back after meeting Ruskin, I stopped my car at Roorkee and rushed to the nearby STD booth to check whether Chetan had come to office to sign the agreement. Vijay Sharma, one of my colleagues, confirmed that he had; Vijay's voice was the sweetest sound for me at the time.

The House of Bestsellers: Chetan Bhagat seen here with Anurag Mathur

It was decided that the book would be released in October 2004, around the festival time. In the meantime, Chetan flew thrice to Delhi from Hong Kong and met us. During our very first meeting, I found Chetan to be a decent person, modest and down to earth. He never asked for an advance or for an increased royalty. He loved the cover design as soon as it was sent to him—he was proving to be an easy author to work with. When it came to fixing the price of the book, which is usually the prerogative of the publisher, we wanted to know Chetan's mind on the matter. Chetan wanted the book to be priced at ₹150 but I stuck to ₹95. After a prolonged discussion, he saw my point of view. The price of *Five Point Someone* was fixed at ₹95.

The book was launched at the IIC on 14 October 2004. There wasn't a large audience. Kapish had just graduated from college and was eager to handle the launch. Kapish and Deepti shared the dais with Chetan. I requested our bestselling author, Anurag Mathur, to formally launch the book. Anurag gracefully did the honours.

The popular meets the greatest–what a Bond!

After this low-key event, we waited for the real test of the book's mettle—the response from readers. Within 48 hours of the book hitting the market, the first print run of 4,000 copies was sold out! Much of the initial impetus for sales was on account of the author's diligence in promoting the book. Chetan had informed IITians (both present and former students) about this book in a very systematic way. Many of them bought multiple copies and its popularity spread through word of mouth. All of this was taking place before the social media revolution—*Five Point Someone* became the talk of the town.

Soon after the launch, I visited Madras and met the owners of Landmark, the formidable couple Hemu Ramaiah and Jaishankar Subramaniam. Both had their fingers on the pulse of the market and knew their books. They predicted that *Five Point Someone*, which they had read, would become a huge bestseller. Jaishankar, in particular, applauded our pricing strategy. He

Raj Chengappa (second from left) the chief editor at India Today *presenting The Publishers' Recognition Award to Chetan Bhagat*

had a sharp business sense and this endorsement meant a hell of a lot to us.* The book topped the bestsellers list and was translated into 15 languages, including Chinese, Vietnamese, Japanese, Korean, many European languages, and a number of Indian languages. Thus, Chetan Bhagat, the 'paperback prince', was born.

Two years after the publication of *Five Point Someone*, in May 2006, Chetan came out with his second book *One Night at the Call Centre*. As soon as the manuscript arrived in mid-January, there was a mad tussle between Kapish and me as to who would read the manuscript first (when it comes to business, we keep each other on our toes)! Both of us called Chetan to congratulate him. *One Night at the Call Centre* had a first print run of 1 lakh copies, 25 times more than his first book. But the price was still fixed at ₹95. It was released by Raj Chengappa, then managing editor of *India Today*, a dear friend and our author.

---

*Jaishankar was in the restaurant business while his wife, Hemu, looked after Landmark.

Chetan was keen on *Five Point Someone* being adapted into a movie. I requested Gulzar sahib to fix a meeting with Shaad Ali, whose recent movie *Bunty Aur Babli* had been a huge success. Chetan and I met in the study of Gulzar sahib's Pali Hill residence, where the poet would sit immersed in his piles of books, papers, letters and notes. Unfortunately, the meeting did not yield much result. Chetan was disappointed but not hurt. Despite the initial setback, *One Night at the Call Centre* was eventually made into a film titled *Hello* starring Salman Khan and Katrina Kaif. Then came *Three Idiots* based on *Five Point Someone* and it became an instant blockbuster, though a controversy revolving around giving Chetan adequate credit vitiated the atmosphere between him and the producer of the film, Vidhu Vinod Chopra.

There was no stopping Chetan after that. He was planning to move back to India and settle in Bombay. Despite a hectic schedule, he managed to finish his third book *The Three Mistakes of My Life.* It was based in Gujarat and the story revolved around cricket and communalism, against the backdrop of the Gujarat riots. This also was adapted into a film titled *Kai Po Che,* which saw the debut of another young talent Sushant Singh Rajput.

Kapish had handled the sales and marketing of Chetan's two earlier books *Five Point Someone* and *One Night at the Call Centre,* and for the third book, he tied up with the Big Bazaar Group. Their first order was for one lakh copies. The print order was getting higher and higher. Preeti Vyas, who was handling

Chetan's wife Anusha Bhagat is a Tamilian and he is a Punjabi. The couple can be seen here reciting pages from their own life!

the marketing and sales of Big Bazaar back then, invited me for the multiple launches of the book in Hyderabad, Bangalore and Ahmedabad. I was, therefore, able to see for myself what a huge draw Chetan had become. The youthful crowds at each venue were immense. Chetan would sit for two to three hours at each venue and sign 700–800 copies of his book while being mobbed by thousands of fans. He was unstoppable now. After the Ahmedabad launch, all of us were tired to our bones. Preeti had a brainwave. She decided we should go out for dinner to an open-air restaurant; fresh air would soothe our tired muscles. Chetan, his wife, Preeti and I drove to this eatery, ordered food and by the time the hungry souls were served, we all went off to sleep on the cots nearby! Success-induced slumber is a dream we all chase, isn't it?

Chetan's next book broke all the publishing records he had set. Chetan's wife is a Tamilian and he is Punjabi. Theirs had been a love marriage. He

Rupa BOOK NEWS
Vol. 44. No. 01 MONTH OF PUBLICATION 15 DECEMBER 2009 Rs. 2/-

2 STATES HELPS UNITE TWO HEARTS

Chetan Bhagat's novels have always left an undying impression on the reader's mind. The simple manner and humorous tone in which he addresses the otherwise grave issues, make people realise how plain and sweet our life is.

Well, this time his latest novel has helped in uniting two lovers. The proof of the same was received by Mr Bhagat in the form of a wedding invitation from Mr S.K. Sharma, a Punjabi father firmly against marrying off his beloved daughter Meghna with Lt. Nandakumar (a Keralite) until he read *2 States: the story of my marriage*. Ananya and Krish's story persuaded him to unite Meghna and Lt. Nanda. He says, 'Your book has acted as balm to my deliberately, delayed decision. I now have no regrets.' He plans to gift *2 States: the story of my marriage* to his guests at the wedding. Now that is called an impact! We wish Meghna and Lt. Nandakumar, a happy married life! And of course, kudos to Mr Bhagat!

'Chetan Bhagat, a bestselling brand doesn't need reviews ...2 States has an excel-sheet precision, balancing, young love, parental pressures, youth aspirations, elementary social commentary, one-liners, self-improvements tips, new-age speak, and the mandatory mush, sex, toil and tears.'

— India Today

'However, this latest novel [2 States: The Story Of My Marriage] reminds one of Vikram Seth's A Suitable Boy. Both are on marriages.'

— Hindustan Times

'A Winning plot... Chetan Bhagat altered the literary landscape with his bestselling books.'

— Graphiti

'Bestselling author Chetan Bhagat ...spread the good cheer this Diwali through his latest book, which is return to the more humour-oriented style of his first book.'

— The Times of India

When the book united two hearts!

wove a story titled *Two States* in which a Tamilian Brahmin and a Delhite Punjabi family are brought together due to the protagonists' love story. With tongue-in-cheek humour and just the right amount of melodrama, this book was a recipe for success. The first print run was 5 lakh copies was printed at five different printing centres to meet the deadline of the release. Life imitated art after the book's release. A father wrote to me that after reading *Two States*, he allowed his Punjabi daughter to marry her Malayali boyfriend!

Time passed and Chetan became a household name. His books connected with the vast majority of young, aspirational Indians. He was speaking to his readers in a language they understood, and the stories he told plugged into their emotions and everyday lives.

When his fifth novel, *Revolution 2020,* was published in October 2011, it set an Indian record for a trade publication in English, with an initial print run of a million copies. Seven printing presses worked simultaneously to print the book. Despite being priced at ₹140 this time, readers were not dissuaded from buying the book—it flew off the shelves. History was again repeating itself and *Revolution 2020* started selling in huge numbers. The novel's theme of small-town coaching centres resonated with readers. It was set in Banaras, and I had to make multiple visits to the holy city, making me holier by the day!

WikiCommons

In the following months, the country was plunged into a variety of scandals and crises—the 2G Scam, Coalgate, corruption in organizing the Commonwealth Games, etc., to the chagrin of the nation's youth. We decided to bring out a book that analysed what the country was going through. And thus, *What Young India Wants*, a compilation of Chetan's articles, was born. The book was released in August 2012 and it

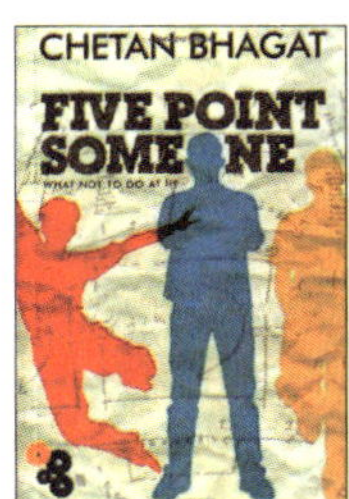

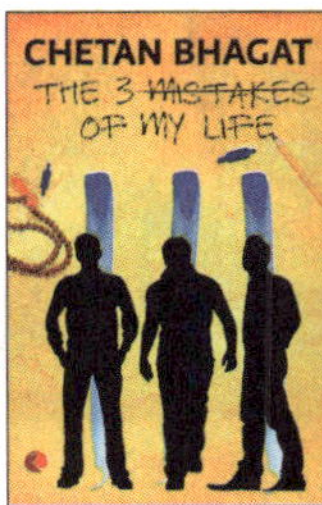

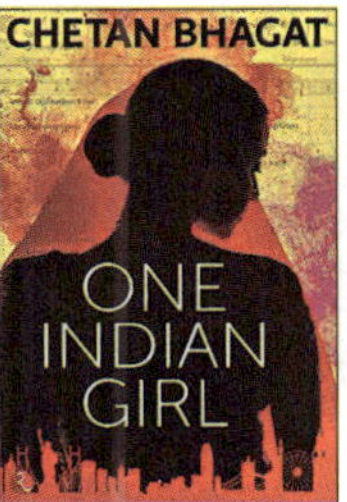

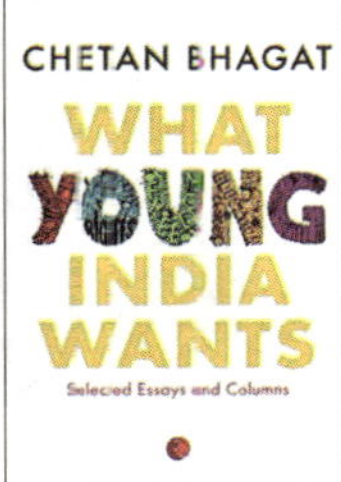

Phenomenal success of each of his books built the brand that Chetan is today

captured the attention of the country's youth. Chetan's words were resonating with the readers and with every book, he was getting bigger. He now lived in a Pali Hill bungalow owned earlier by Waheeda Rehman and surrounded by film personalities, like Gulzar, Dilip Kumar, Javed Akhtar, etc. Chetan was living his dream and it felt good to be a part of his journey. During my visits to his Bombay home, I ensured that I at least met two to three celebrities, convincing them to write books for us. Once a publisher always a publisher!

What is the essence of Chetan's writing? Why is he so popular, why is he loved and disparaged, what is so special about his work? Pritish Nandy captured the reasons for his popularity in his review of *Revolution 2020* in *India Today*. He wrote:

> If you enjoy reading Dickens or Jane Austen for pleasure, don't even bother picking up this book. Chetan Bhagat is not for you. He is for all those who stopped reading English literature the moment they stepped out of school.

The author who altered the literary landscape of the country

> [...]
> Then why do millions of young people read Bhagat, follow him on Twitter? Why does *Time* magazine rate him among the 100 most influential people in the world? [...] The answer is actually very simple. Bhagat has successfully deconstructed the idea of literature, and demystified it as well. In the great tradition of Indian pulp fiction.
> [...]
>
> You could well conclude that he is desecrating literature as we know it. Or you could simply sit back and have fun reading what he writes with such amazing conviction and commercial success. You can also marvel at the kind of readership he is bringing to Indian fiction in English. No, these are no longer old-fashioned lovers of literature like you and I. These are real people looking for a quick, fun read that does not test your intelligence but artfully tells you a story that you can easily identify with.*

Anurag Mathur, Chetan Bhagat and many young and popular fiction writers of

*Nandy, Pritish, 'A Look into "Revolution 2020": Love, Corruption, Ambition by Chetan Bhagat', *India Today*, 31 October 2011, https://tinyurl.com/3ph3urua. Accessed on 25 July 2023.

that period put Hinglish, the language of India's aspiring class, on the world map. On the literary side, we already had authors like Upamanyu Chatterjee, Vikram Seth and Aniruddha Bahal to name a few. All in all, it was a perfect combination.

And then one day, Chetan decided to part ways with us by signing a book deal with another publisher, which makes the following lines by the Pakistani poet Ahmed Faraz resonate with me today:

उस को जुदा हुए भी जमाना बहुत हुआ,
अब क्या कहें ये किस्सा पुराना बहुत हुआ ।

Us ko juda hue bhi zamana bahut hua,
Ab kya kahen ye qissa purana bahut hua.

It's been a long time since he parted,
There's nothing more to say, this story is too old.

اوہ تہب ہنامز یھب ےئوہ ادج وک سا
اوہ تہب انارپ ہصق ہی ںیہک ایک با

One can only imagine Nirupam da's plight while editing the pregnancy book

• Chapter 37 •

ENCOUNTERS WITH MEMORABLE AUTHORS

V.S. NAIPAUL

The year 1968–69, which was my first year in the book trade, witnessed the publication of *An Area of Darkness* by V.S. Naipaul, the first book in his much-acclaimed Indian trilogy. Sir Vidiadhar Surajprasad Naipaul was born in West Indies on 17 August 1932 to parents of Indian origin, before he emigrated to the UK. For the longest time, André Deutsch was his British publisher for hardbacks while the paperback editions were published by Penguin. *An Area of Darkness* was very critical of India and it ruffled a few bureaucratic feathers here. As a result, the Government of India detained the book at Customs. Sir Allen Lane was the chairman of Penguin at that time and he wrote a letter to then Finance Minister and Deputy PM Morarji Desai, who intervened and the book was released. This attracted a lot of media attention and contributed to its success in India.

V.S. Naipaul was a frequent visitor to India and was proud of his Indian roots. Over the decades, he published many exceptional literary works and won virtually every major literary award that he was eligible for, including the Booker Prize in 1971 and Nobel Prize for Literature in 2001. During the NDA rule of 1999–2003, he was honoured by PM Vajpayee. He, along with Dr Amartya Sen, were made permanent guests of India.

I longed to meet V.S. Naipaul. My wish came true when he inaugurated the World Book Fair in New Delhi in 2004. He paid a visit to our stall accompanied by Sonny Mehta, the publisher of Random House. V.S. Naipaul

V.S. Naipaul (far left) presenting the Jnanpith Award to our author Indira Goswami (third from left) who wrote an enchanting book The Shadow of Kamakhya *for Rupa. Also seen in the picture is the noted jurist Dr L.M. Singhvi (second from left) along with the owner of* The Times of India, *Indu Jain (far right).*

knew how aggressively Rupa had promoted and sold his books in the Indian market and thanked us for the efforts. It was an overwhelming moment for all of us present. He picked up a set of *The Mahabharata* by Ramesh Menon which was published by us. He browsed through it, and told me that, in his opinion, it seemed to be one of the most modern renderings of the epic to be had—something he'd been waiting for. It felt like winning the Kurukshetra of publishing!

SIDNEY SHELDON

The master of pulp fiction paid a visit to India sometime in 1980s as a guest of a royal family in Gujarat. Rupa had published a number of his books in the Indian market by acquiring rights from Pan. When he was in India, Sheldon was flabbergasted to find a pirated edition bearing his name for sale on the footpath. Making matters worse was the fact that he hadn't written the book. In anguish and anxiety, he made a public statement saying how disappointed he was. The next day, newspapers carried the sensational news with the tone: 'Sheldon was on a visit to India, noticed a book that was never written by him.' It was a story that immediately grabbed eyeballs. It was an embarrassment to all of us in the Indian publishing fraternity. It highlighted the glaring loopholes in the system and how easily the genuine reader could be duped by these fakes. It was a matter of grave concern for us at Rupa, as we were his publishers in India.

Sidney Sheldon, the master of pulp fiction

The afternoon the story broke, I got a call from the US embassy informing me that Mr Sheldon wanted to meet me over dinner that night in a house at Amrita Shergill Marg. When I entered the house, I was greeted by Mr Sheldon's lady escort, an Indian. The escort informed Mr Sheldon of my arrival; he was busy with a meeting but had asked that I be shown into the room where the meeting was taking place.

Once inside the room, I recognized G.P. Sippy, the film producer, Amitabh Bachchan, the actor and Sunil Sethi of NDTV's *Just Books* TV show. There were a few other people whom I couldn't recognize, but they seemed to be from the entertainment business. Mr Sheldon introduced me to each of the guests and then took me aside to say he would like to meet with me privately in just a few minutes after he was done with his meeting. Sunil Sethi and I chatted as we waited for him. The bestselling author joined us in a short while and said he was appalled by the unauthorized use of his name and the blatant piracy that was taking place. The man was concerned for me as well since piracy was cannibalizing our sales. I assured him that we were doing all we could to stop this illegal activity. The next day, I received a photo from the US embassy which showed a smiling Sidney Sheldon alongside me. I was glad I'd been able to mollify his concerns about his books in India.

KUNWAR NARAYAN

A legendary Hindi poet and writer whom I was lucky to meet and get acquainted with in the '80s and '90s was Kunwar Narayan. He would visit Rupa's office and his visits would often become literary events as he would be joined by eminent figures of the literary world—editors like Raghuvir Sahay of *Dinmaan*, writers such as Nirmal Verma, the famous Hindi writer, Gagan Gill (who later married Nirmal Verma), Vinod Bhardwaj, a Hindi film critic and art critic, Prayag Shukla, a poet and senior Hindi editor, Mangalesh Dabral of *Jansatta*, Namvar Singh of *Rashtriya Sahara* and Sham Lal of *The Times of India* among others. These gatherings reminded me of my days in Calcutta when the intelligentsia would meet at the Rupa office.

Kunwar Narayan had a great liking for Rupa books.

Every one of Kunwar Narayan's visits would be an educative one, as he would talk for hours about the major literary works in Hindi at the time and why they should be made available to a wider English-speaking audience. He made me read two books in Hindi *Kali-Katha via Bypass* by Alka Saraogi and

(From left) Vinod Bhardwaj, Nirmal Verma and Prayag Shukla would frequent Rupa's office

Alka Saraogi at the launch of her book Kali-Katha via Bypass

The cover of Yaadnama, *a delightful memoir of a Hindi writer where he praises an English publisher, Rupa*

चर्चित उपन्यास *द टिन ड्रम* पर फ़िल्म मैंने उसी यात्रा में देखी थी। शीर्षक उसी पर था।

ख़ैर।

मैंने नौकरी की शुरुआत तो *टाइम्स ऑफ़ इंडिया* की नई इमारत से की थी पर जल्दी ही मैनेजमेंट ने बेरहमी से हमें दरियागंज की पुरानी जर्जर इमारत में पहुँचा दिया। *दिनमान* उनके लिए *धर्मयुग* की तरह कमाऊ पूत नहीं था।

लेकिन दरियागंज जाकर हमारा रूपा एंड कंपनी की किताबों की दुनिया में जाना बहुत आसान हो गया। प्रयाग जी कलकत्ता के थे और कॉलेज स्ट्रीट की रूपा एंड कंपनी ऐतिहासिक थी। डी. मेहरा ने उसे स्थापित किया था और 1936 में वह पेंग्विन के प्रसिद्ध पेपरबैक भारत लाए थे। सत्तर के दशक के बाद रूपा वाले अंग्रेज़ी के बड़े प्रकाशक के रूप में दिल्ली में सक्रिय हो गए और सुनील गावस्कर, गुलज़ार और चेतन भगत की दुनिया में ख़ूब सफल हुए। ये लेखक बहुत बिकते थे।

हमें वेतन तब कैश मिलता था, जो ज़्यादा नहीं था। शुरू में मुझे 525 रुपये मिलते थे और प्रयाग जी का वेतन भी कुछ ही ज़्यादा रहा होगा। पर हर महीने वेतन मिलते ही हम रूपा पहुँच जाते थे और सौ रुपये की किताबें तो ख़रीद लेते ही थे। तब चैप्लिन की आत्मकथा दस रुपये में मिलती थी। रूपा में आप नेरुदा, चैप्लिन, जॉर्ज लुकाच, गुंटर ग्रास सब कुछ ख़रीद सकते थे और दस प्रतिशत डिस्काउंट के साथ।

डॉ. मेहरा के पोते राजन मेहरा हमारे दोस्त बन गए थे। एक बार उन्होंने मुझे बताया जब *टाइम्स ऑफ़ इंडिया* के एडिटर शाम लाल यहाँ आते हैं, तो किसी किताब को वह उठा भी लें, तो समझिए वह ज़रूर बिकेगी। बाद में कुँवर नारायण जब दिल्ली आते थे, तो हमारे साथ वह भी वहाँ जाने के लिए बेचैन रहते थे।

रूपा तब हमारी यूनिवर्सिटी थी। राजन मेहरा हमउम्र थे, वह अच्छे

दोस्त भी बन गए।

जब भी मौक़ा मिलता था तो हम रूपा पहुँच जाते थे। रूपा का लोगो सत्यजित रॉय ने कुछ मुफ़्त की किताबों के बदले में बनाया था।

ज़ाहिर है वो ज़माना और था।

अस्सी के दशक के अंत में हर जगह हम यह बात सुनने लगे कि *दिनमान* बंद होने जा रहा है। हम अपने भविष्य को लेकर चिंतित हो गए। राजन मेहरा ए.एच. वीलर में अपनी अंग्रेज़ी की किताबें डिस्काउंट के बाद पैसा लेकर भेजते थे। उन्होंने हिंदी में भी पेपरबैक छापने की योजना बनाई और मैं सलाहकार संपादक था। महेश दर्पण ने हिंदी की प्रेम कहानियों का संग्रह संपादित किया, अभय कुमार दुबे ने कुश्ती पर किताब लिखी, मेरी किताब नया सिनेमा का संशोधित संस्करण छपा, कार्टूनिस्ट काक का एक संग्रह मैंने एडिट किया। मृणाल पांडे ने *हिंदुस्तान टाइम्स* में काक की किताब की समीक्षा भी लिखी थी।

मेरे कहने पर मित्र रवींद्र त्रिपाठी ने रूपा में कुछ समय काम भी किया। वह जब छुट्टी पर थे, तो मंगलेश डबराल की सलाह पर कृष्ण कल्पित ने भी कुछ समय काम किया था।

हिंद पॉकेट बुक्स ने वीलर से रूपा के टर्म्स माँगे तो राजन मेहरा ने हिंदी की योजना बंद करना बेहतर समझा।

राजन मेहरा ने एक दिन मुझे बताया हम लोग हिंदी में सेक्स पर समझदार क़िस्म की किताब छापना चाहते हैं। ऐसी किताबों पर हिंदी प्रकाशक कोई रॉयल्टी नहीं देते रहे हैं। *दिनमान* बंद होने ही जा रहा था, मैंने कहा नियमित रॉयल्टी दें, तो मैं यह किताब लिख सकता हूँ। रूपा एंड कंपनी तो रॉयल्टी के लिए मशहूर थी।

राजन भी उत्साहित हो गए। दुनिया भर की अंग्रेज़ी की किताबें मुझे मँगाकर भेज दीं। मैं हिंदी लेखक मनमथ नाथ गुप्त से कुछ अलग लिखना चाहता था।

मनोविज्ञान का मैं छात्र था, सोचा एक चैप्टर फ़ैंटसी पर ज़रूर

13

Pages from Vinod Bhardwaj's Yaadnama, *in which he says that Rupa was like a university for those in literary circles*

Kalpana, a collection of literary pieces on Banaras edited by Prayag Shukla. I was so enchanted by *Kali-Katha* that I got it translated and published in English. We published English translations of some of Kunwar Narayan's poetry collections to critical acclaim. I remember his association with Rupa with gratitude and affection.

R.K. NARAYAN

Which reader from the subcontinent who has read *Malgudi Days* doesn't wish to visit that town? If only one could! R.K. Narayan's imagination was so powerful that he, inevitably, was the second recipient of the Yatra Award (after Intizar Hussain), which I had constituted in the memory of my late father.

Conferring this award on him was an honour for Rupa. I wrote a letter to R.K. Narayan in 1994 informing him of our decision. Dileep Padgaonkar,

R.K. Narayan was the second recipient of Yatra Awards. We flew in to Madras to honour him. When I asked if he has any advice for me, he said, 'Just keep publishing books.'

the editor of *The Times of India* had already spoken to R.K. Narayan about this.

When R.K. Narayan received the letter, he gave me a ring. Politely, he laid down two conditions before he could accept the award—first, there would be no public function and, second, it would be received by him at his granddaughter's residence in Madras.

I flew down to Madras and in the presence of N. Ravi of *The Hindu* and a few friends, the award was bestowed on R.K. Narayan. Frankly, I felt honoured to be honouring him. At the end of the ceremony, at which I literally sat at his feet, I asked him if he had any advice for me. 'Just keep publishing books,' he said.

IVAN ILLICH

One day in 1976, I received two phone calls regarding the same thing. One was from J.P. Naik, who was the head of Indian Institute of Public Administration (IIPA), and the other was from Professor Nurul Hassan, the education minister in the Indira Gandhi government. Both asked whether we had copies of *Deschooling Society* by Ivan Illich, the Austrian theologian and philosopher. Luckily, we had a couple of copies in stock.

Ivan Illich's books often challenged the accepted norms and establishments

The following day, J.P. Naik invited me to his office at IP Estate which was not far from our office. He asked us to import a good quantity of this book and said he would buy all of them. We were soon informed that Ivan Illich was going to be the guest speaker at a programme organized by the IIPA in India. We acquired the reprint rights to his path-breaking and provocative books *Medical Nemesis* and *Energy and Equity*. *Medical Nemesis* opens with the famous line, 'The medical establishment has become a major threat to health.' He can safely be said to have, if not coined, popularized the word 'iatrogenesis'—meaning the harm done by doctors. Being a priest, philosopher and theologian, he believed in the traditional method of healing, and considered pain and suffering to be part of human life. A high priest of counter culture during the '60s and '70s, Ivan was dismissed by medical establishment as an aberration. Similarly, in *Energy and Equity*, he commented on whether humans actually need the amount of energy they consume, which is beyond their natural right. His writings spoke of what needed to be done in the fields of literature, transportation, education, and so on. Illich's words were wise and prophetic and of particular relevance to India but naturally, no one in government paid the slightest attention to them, more's the pity. I don't recall any conversation with him except that because he was 7-feet tall, I had to crane my neck to converse with him. I really was 'looking up' to my author!

NUTAN PANDIT

Although Rupa was publishing some good literary and commercial fiction, and strong non-fiction, I was keen to publish commercial non-fiction—self-help books and the likes of which would be targeted at a mass readership. I was very taken with Faber's *Every Woman's Guide to Health,* which was a successful title. However, I felt that there was scope for a similar book geared to the Indian reality. As luck would have it, two manuscripts were sent to me; one on childbirth and the other on cookery. I decided that HarperCollins India should publish the cookbook and Rupa the one on childbirth. Interestingly, one was by the daughter of the late Hansraj Gupta and the other was by his daughter-in-law. Hansraj Gupta was a highly respected social worker; his contribution to girls' education in Delhi had been immense. He was also the first mayor of Delhi.

Najma Heptullah releasing the Pregnancy: The Complete Childbirth Book *by Nutan Pandit (sitting extreme right)*

(From left) Nirupam Da, the editor of the book with Nutan Pandit and her husband

The author of *Pregnancy* and Gupta's daughter, Nutan Pandit had provided a great deal of information in her book, but it needed to be restructured and revised by a good editor. I asked my mentor and editor Nirupam da if he would take on the job, but he declined saying pregnancy was an area he couldn't handle—he asked me to pass it on to the female editors at Rupa. None of my female editors were married and seemed unsure about editing the book. Consequently, progress on it was excruciatingly slow. Finally, in desperation, I asked Nirupam da to clean up the language and structure and not worry about the technical and medical information in the work. Nirupam da sportingly took up the challenge. He worked from home, and he and his wife, Ruby, who was a professor of English literature at Delhi University, would often have the most delightful conversations on all sorts of things—theirs was a great relationship. One evening, when I had gone over to their place for tea and samosas (Nirupam da made delicious samosas), Ruby walked in and said loudly, 'What sort of a man has my husband become? All he can discuss with me these days is childbirth as if he himself is going to deliver.' Nirupam da shot back, 'Why not give it a try?' It was under these circumstances that *Pregnancy* by Nutan Pandit was published in 1991. The author remained eternally grateful to her eccentric editor and the book ruled the bestseller charts for 30 years and continues to sell till date, both in hardcover and paperback.

ERIC NEWBY

The great travel writer Eric Newby and his wife Wanda would visit India every alternate year and stay at Hotel Imperial, Janpath. Eric was an accomplished illustrator and many of the caricatures done by him were framed and adorned the walls of the old coffee shop in the hotel for many years. Eric was one of the world's most intrepid travellers and had been to some of the planet's most wild and inhospitable places. But even he hadn't quite reckoned with the Diwali mayhem that used to unleash every year in Delhi. One such year, Eric, Wanda and Peter Hensen of Collins celebrated Diwali at my place. As night fell, the neighbourhood exploded with the sound, light and smell of crackers. Rockets whizzed through the sky and a few of them landed in neighbouring homes. Eric, experienced traveller though he was, grew increasingly nervous and very soon, after the din and chaos began, asked to be dropped back to the hotel. When he passed away in 2006, *The New York Times* mentioned in its obituary that the great travel writer had mentioned that some of his journeys had gone horribly wrong much to his delight—for some reason, they left out his Diwali visit to Model Town in Delhi!

Eric Newby spent more than half his life travelling and writing

RAMESH MENON

Ravi Dayal, the doyen of Indian publishing, published *The Hunt for K* by Ramesh Menon in 1992. The book recieved tremendous attention. Several years later, Ravi Dayal telephoned me to say that he was bringing down his publishing list. He wanted Rupa to publish the future books of Ramesh Menon. A recommendation coming from Ravi Dayal was not something that could be ignored, as the man knew his work!

We published 12 volumes on Mahabharata by Ramesh Menon—a majestic undertaking

When I was finally able to meet Ramesh in 2003, along with Amrita Kumar, who was working with us as an editor at the time, he offered us his two volumes of *Mahabharata: A Modern Rendering* for publication. Initially, I was reluctant to take it on because of a family superstition—my granduncle would always tell me to never publish Mahabharata, as it would divide

The majestic 12-volume set of The Complete Mahabharata

the family. However, as there had already been a family schism before the manuscript came along, I decided to take the plunge, especially because Ramesh's manuscript was a masterpiece. After these volumes, we published other books by him—*Siva: The Siva Purana Retold, Devi: The Devi Bhagavatam Retold* and *Bhagavata Purana*. Then, we decided to get a little more ambitious and persuaded him to write an extended retelling of Mahabharata in 12 volumes.

DR TERRY O'BRIEN

It was a decade ago that Rupa and I had the good fortune of having Dr Terry O'Brien on board. He is an academician of repute, a motivational trainer, a broadcaster, a political analysts, columnist, a well-known quiz master and a multidimensional person. Born mute, Terry got his speech at the age of seven and then excelled in his speech and communication skills. We reached out to get him to write books on a plethora of subjects. The writer in him brought in a new dimension to our book

Read, record and recall has been Terry's benchmark of his literary life

Rupa has published more than 130 books by Terry O'Brien, including his bestselling 50 Greatest Short Stories

list that empowered and enriched our readers. He demonstrated the art and skill of writing books on literature and English language, general studies, quiz and amazing and fun reading, and much more. He believes in the simplicity of language. Don't impress, express. A pen writes only when it bends low. Within a span of a decade, he has churned out above 130 quality books for us with elan. His fan following is immense as he holds forward the banner of brand Rupa.

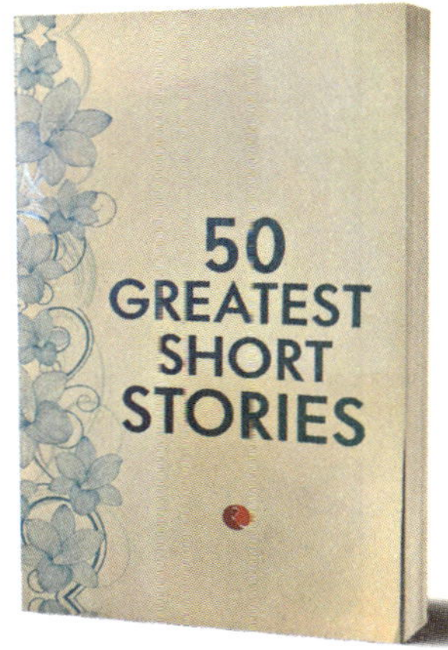

Dilip Salwi used to conduct quiz sessions in schools, which were attended by students in huge numbers.

• Chapter 38 •

NEVER SAY GOODBYE

It is said that you die twice. Once, when you stop breathing and the second time, a bit later, when somebody says your name for the last time. For me, these people who are no longer among us, are still alive, in my memories.

DILIP SALWI

Dilip Salwi used to be a regular customer at the Rupa showroom. He was addicted to books that had to do with science. I first met him when he was in his late 20s. He wanted to review a book that we were distributing for *The Hindustan Times* and spoke to me about it. I was tremendously impressed by his depth of knowledge and enthusiasm for scientific subjects and asked whether he would be willing to do a book for us—an almanac of 1,000 science quiz questions. He was quick to agree and within a month, the manuscript came in. Nirupam da wrote in his brief that he had never seen a manuscript as well organized and written with as much clarity as this one. It hardly needed any editing.

Thereafter, he wrote several quiz books and biographies of scientists for children in our Rupa Charitavali series. Sales of some of these books almost touched six figures.

I remember he was in our office the day after Kalpana Chawla, the American astronaut of Indian origin, died on 1 February 2003. I asked him if he would do a quick biography of her. He said he wouldn't do a quickie but would be open to doing a properly researched biography. He immediately started work—collected material from NASA, interviewed her father and the principal of the school where she had studied. He visited Karnal, Kalpana's hometown several times to thoroughly understand her background. After extensive research and interviews,

Science quiz sessions were attended by Rupa editors too. (From left) S. Sinha, Sugeeta and Atriya.

he wrote a wonderful book. We decided to launch this book at Kalpana's alma mater, Tagore Bal Niketan in Karnal. The principal of the school was more than happy to provide the launch venue for his most famous alumna. Next came the question of who we should invite as the chief guest. An influential politician? Some well-known businessman? I recalled that I had bumped into Wing Commander Rakesh Sharma, the first Indian in space, at Bangalore airport a couple of months ago. Now heading Hindustan Aeronautics Limited in Bangalore, he would be the perfect person to release the book. I phoned him and was delighted when he agreed to do the honours. On the day of the launch, the traffic to Karnal was heavy and there were several traffic jams that we had to negotiate. Rakesh Sharma and the Rupa team managed to get through on time, but there was no sign of the author as he was stuck in traffic. The function was almost over when Dilip Salwi made an entrance to thunderous applause. While talking about the book, he got emotional and expressed how Kalpana's life had touched him and the tragic way it had been cut short.

Not very long after this, late one night, while I was travelling to Dehradun by train, I received a phone call—my caller told me that Dilip had a heart attack and passed away. It is truly what they say, 'Those whom the gods love die young.'

Wing Commander Rakesh Sharma, the first Indian in space, readily agreed to launch Kalpana Chawla's biography. The author is missing from the picture, as he was stuck in a traffic jam!

Remembering Dilip Salwi. We requested Ruskin Bond to present authors recognition award posthumously to Dilip's wife, to which he delightfully agreed.

ANUP KUMAR

Pain and suffering can break the human body. But there are some who do not let their spirit break, come what may, even if they are staring death in the face. One such person was the indomitable Anup Kumar. Ill with cancer, he somehow managed to find things to be positive about through adversity. Even as he was nearing his end, he wrote an extraordinary book: *The Joy of Cancer*.

Anup was married to Amrita Kumar, who did freelance editorial work for us. One day, she told me that she could no longer work for us, as Anup was terminally ill with cancer. I was dumbstruck. It was hard to imagine the brilliant, energetic young man I knew lying ill in a hospital bed.

Amrita continued to be in touch with me while Anup's treatment was going on. One day, she asked me if I would be willing to meet him. I asked her where and when I should visit him. She replied, 'No, Anup will come to our office on his own.'

On the appointed day, to my great joy, Anup walked into the office. A year later, in pain and under the most difficult circumstances, he had written *The Joy of Cancer*. He insisted on the title. We immediately put the entire team to work on this book. Nobody said it out loud but everyone knew how urgently the book needed to be published.

The Joy of Cancer had three launches in Delhi, Bombay and Bangalore. The then CM of Delhi Sheila Dikshit released the book to a huge gathering in Delhi. In Bombay, Sunil Dutt did the honours—Sunilji's wife, the mesmerizing Nargis, had also died of cancer in the '80s. Anup was present at all the launches, and it was only during the last of the launches, in Bangalore, that he looked exhausted. But undeterred, he took his medicines and carried on. The man was a fighter!

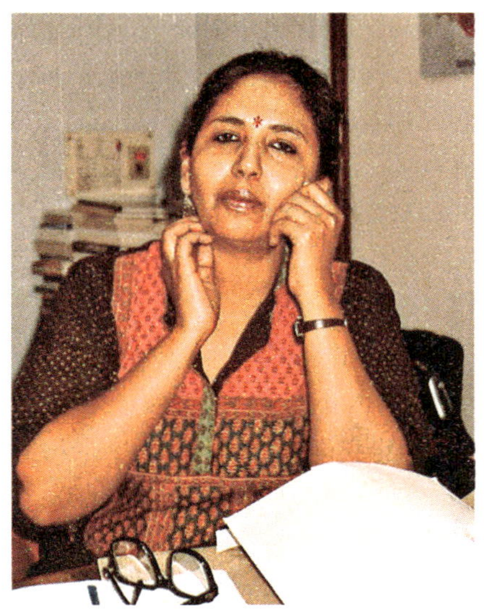

Amrita Kumar, who always stood by her husband Anup Kumar

Death be not proud: that's how Anup dealt with his terminl illness

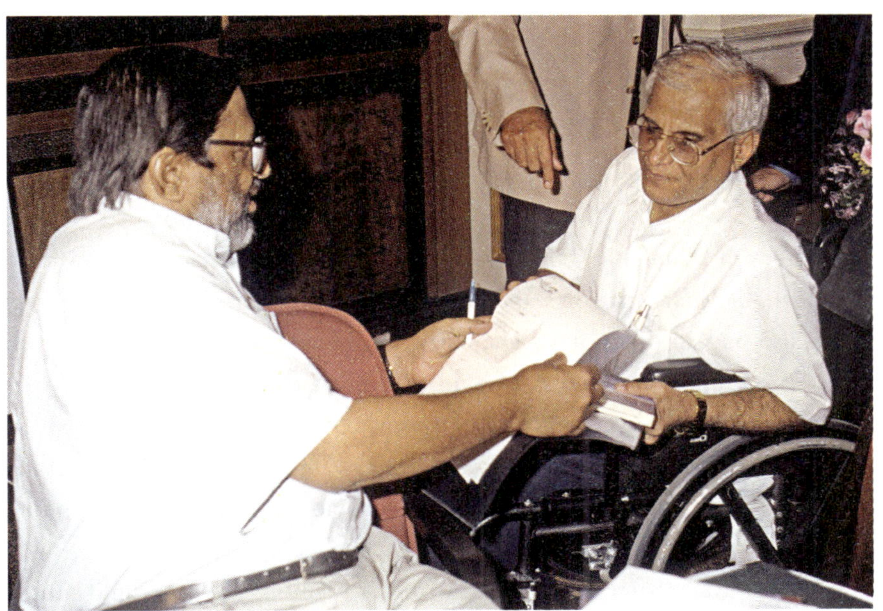

An inspiration for all! Anup Kumar seen here with the wheelchair bound famous oncologist of Jaslok Hospital, Dr Suresh H. Advani, who released his book both in Delhi and in Bombay.

The Joy of Cancer was followed by a second book *Smiles and Tears* in which he describes his experiences of meeting and interacting with various people who were fighting the same disease. One Sunday evening, Amrita called and said that Anup was gone. Both my wife and I rushed to his Safdarjung house to pay our last respects. Anup now lives on in my memory.

Dileep Padgaonkar with Sham Lal

SHAM LAL

In 1974, Rupa's Bombay office was quite literally falling apart. Into these dilapidated premises walked one of the most erudite men I have ever known—Sham Lal who would become one of the most respected editors of *The Times of India.* With him was his then deputy Dileep Padgaonkar who would also go on to edit the newspaper. They were friends with B.P. Patel, the manager of our Bombay branch.

A number of years later, both Sham Lal and Dileep Padgaonkar moved to *The Times of India* office on Bahadur Shah Zafar Marg in Delhi. *The Times of India* also had an office at 10 Daryaganj. Rupa's office was located between their offices, and their staffers, foremost among them, Sham Lal, would visit our office. Sham Lal was not just a customer but a connoisseur of books. It was this gentleman who made our sales team aware of the brilliance (and sales potential) of authors like Tom Morrison, Octavio Paz, Ivan Illich and so on.

I would always be after Sham Lal to write his memoirs and he would simply laugh it away. One day, he finally made a promise to do not one but two books with us—both would be collections of his articles that were published

Abid Hussain releasing Sham Lal's book at IIC. It was Sham Lalji who made our sales team aware of the brilliance (and sales potential) of authors like Tom Morrison, Octavio Paz, Ivan Illich etc.

as *Indian Realities in Bits and Pieces* and *A Hundred Encounters*. These were superb examples of journalistic writing, and I still recommend them to students and working journalists.

Towards the end of his life, Sham Lal's eyes became very weak. Even though his eyesight was fading fast, his love for books never diminished. He would have friends (especially Inder Malhotra) over at home to read out books to him. A week before his final journey in February 2007, he called up our office enquiring about a specific book. Such was his insatiable desire for books till the very end of his life. His memorial service, held at IIC, was jam-packed with journalists, editors, politicians and intellectuals of the city. I was able to manage a seat only to find former PM Inder Kumar Gujral sitting next to me, in the back row.

As we come to an end,
I'm reminded that the
publisher's journey is a
tale still unfolding, filled
with unwritten stories.

·PART THREE·

RENEWAL IN THE NEW MILLENNIUM

OLD AGE

Verily, the well-painted royal chariots decay;
then this body too comes to old age.
But the good dharma does not
come to old age.
Indeed, good people are taught
by good people.

Just as a cowherd drives cows to their
destination with a rod,
old age and death drive living beings.

A quote I read somewhere describing the finality of our existence and which I too believe in

• Chapter 39 •

AN EVENTFUL DECADE

As the twentieth century dissolved into the twenty-first, there was hype, hoopla and celebrations all around. There was fear and excitement about Y2K bugging computer systems across the world and driving everyone into a frenzy (in the end it was all for nothing!); the first crew landing on International Space Station; and Big B reinventing his career with lifelines in *Kaun Banega Crorepati*, the Indian version of *Who Wants to Be a Millionaire*. For me, though, the world was not so rose-tinted. HarperCollins was planning to part ways with Rupa, a move that was made conducive by the then government policy of allowing foreign companies to own 100 per cent equity in India. I was anticipating this, but a partnership was ending after 10 glorious publishing years and I could only celebrate it with poignant lyrics by Sahir Ludhianvi:

वो अफसाना जिसे अंजाम तक लाना न हो मुमकिन,
उसे इक खूबसूरत मोड़ देकर छोड़ना अच्छा ।

Wo afsana jise anjaam tak lana na ho mumkin,
Usey ek khoobsurat mod de kar chorna accha.

The tale that cannot be concluded,
Should be left on a nice note.

Life moves on and mostly for better. Between 2000 and 2010, Rupa books left an indelible imprint on our reader's mind. With J.R.D. Tata, Chetan Bhagat, Arun Shourie, Natwar Singh, Jaswant Singh, L.K. Advani, and many more, it was all upright and sunny. Kapish had also joined the business and was brimming with ideas; the young man was eager to make his mark. I was not pausing for even a bit, and it took a toll on my health. While I was watching an IPL match in 2010 in Jaipur, I experienced a sudden bout of perspiration and found myself fighting for my next breath. The symptoms came and went, but they left me a little bewildered. And then one day at my home in Delhi, the same symptoms resurfaced.

'Is Bitia back from the hospital?' I asked my wife nervously.

'No, not yet. Maybe in a couple of minutes.'

No sooner had my wife finished speaking than Kapish's wife, Asheena, whom I fondly referred to as Bitia, walked in wearing the doctor's coat and carrying a stethoscope in her hand.

I always insist on her not wearing the doctor's coat at home, but that day, strangely, I was rather pleased to see her in her doctor avatar. What was happening to me? Why was the presence of a doctor comforting? Was I seeing Yamraj smirking at me?

'What's wrong?' Asheena asked.

'Nothing.'

Slowly, I could feel myself vanishing. I was fainting. Immediately, I was put into a car and was driven away. My fighting spirit was still intact while my 102-kg body was giving up on me.

Seeing me argue with the driver, both my wife and Asheena heaved a sigh of relief. As long as I was being argumentative, there was still hope. They were now rubbing my chest and back and were trying to comfort me. It had a calming effect on me, even though I was feeling breathless. When we got to Woodpack Nursing Home, I could see that there was no space to park the car.

Just then, I heard the security guard at the gate shouting, '*Gaadi badhao* (Take your car ahead).' However, when he saw me inside the vehicle hunched over and gasping for breath, his tone changed immediately. '*Patient ko yahan utaro, jaldi karo* (Get the patient out here, hurry up),' he yelled at the driver. When the car door opened, I supported myself on the shoulders of Kaminee and Asheena, and slowly walked into the hospital; I refused a wheelchair. Dimly, through my discomfort, I saw a familiar face—Dr Rajesh Grover, the head of the nursing home, swarmed by anxious relatives of patients. Over the years, I had brought many patients to the hospital; it was my turn now.

With a faint smile, I shook hands with Dr Grover saying, 'Doctor, I need help.'

He immediately took charge. 'Don't worry. All will be well,' he said reassuringly. I was quickly taken to the Emergency ward. Nurses took over. My blood pressure was checked, an oxygen mask was placed on my face, various tubes were inserted. The doctors completed their initial checks in the Emergency Room—my blood pressure was 190/120, my pulse rate was high and oxygen was below 90, a rather poor intake. Dr Grover immediately wanted me to be taken to the ICU on the first floor for constant monitoring.

Once I had been settled in the ICU and made comfortable, I was in the mood to chat. When a young doctor came by on his evening rounds and asked me how I was feeling, I replied that I was doing much better but wanted to share a story with him. He took a seat by my bed and I began telling him about a recent visit to Kathmandu.

Whenever I would visit Kathmandu for business, I would make sure to pay my obeisance to Lord Shiva at the Pashupatinath Temple. Apparently, during the reign of King Gyanendra, the temple was given a facelift just before Shivaratri. All the three gates to the south, west and east were closed for renovation and entry to the temple was limited to the north gate. The northern gate opens towards the bank of the Bagmati River, where the last rites of Hindus are performed. The funeral pyres and cremation platforms I had witnessed had been familiar to me—they could be found in the vicinity of temples in India as well. What had been unusual was a stone platform a short distance away surrounded by Aghori babas, smeared in ashes, chanting some mantras. There had been a body on the platform but I had suddenly realized the man was still alive—his family members had left him there to die. This tradition of Moksha Bhavan is also practised in India, where older people retire to die in the holiest of all places, Banaras. Having done my puja, while leaving the temple, I had asked a security guard at the gates whether any of those who had been left to die by their relatives, ever made it back home. He had replied in broken Nepali, 'Sahib, out of 100, 99 go back and their families cry.'

The young doctor was still listening patiently to me: 'So, Doctor, this ICU reminds me of the scene I witnessed in Kathmandu. I imagine myself lying on a stone platform and wondering who, except my immediate family, will shed a tear for me, who will sigh with relief as I burn on the pyre.'

The doctor could not help but laugh, breaking the eerie silence in the ICU. He shook hands with me and then formally introduced himself, 'I am Dr Mohammad Noor… Salaam-Alaikum.'

Yes, I thought, *they are all the same, Mount Kailash or Mount Sinai.* Prayer is most certainly the key that locks the night and opens the day for all. As the great poet Khwaja Mir Dard wrote:

जग में आ कर इधर उधर देखा,
तू ही आया नज़र जिधर देखा ।

Jag mein aa kar idhar-udhar dekha,
Tu hi aaya nazar jidhar dekha.

I looked everywhere once I came into this world,
Wherever I looked, I found you and only you.

اهکـیـد رهدا رهدا رک آںیم گـج
اهکـیـد رهدج رظن ایآ یہ وت

I woke up early the next morning, drugged, uncomfortable, missing my usual morning routine, but, most importantly, still alive. I was restless to get back home. That, of course, was out of the question. I was given a meagre breakfast by the efficient nurses from Kerala, X-rayed and an ECG was conducted. The doctor on duty was reassuring—he said my condition hadn't worsened, and that I could be shifted out of the ICU. Kapish and Asheena were allowed to see me. They had extensive consultations with the doctors. I was allowed to meet other family members as well as anxious friends and well-wishers. I noticed three people sitting very close to each other, so close that not even air could penetrate their proximity. It reminded me of Gandhiji's 'three monkeys'. But as soon as I closed and opened my eyes, I found that there were not three but five of them. The great Indian adjustable muscles were at work! Poor fellows from Kapish's in-laws' place had come all the way from Haryana to wish me a speedy recovery, but they were soon asked by the nurse to leave the room. In no uncertain way, I expressed appreciation for their presence but couldn't even bid them adieu, being tied up from almost all sides. Surprisingly, they all got up together. The 'fevicol' effect was working on them and, like school boys do, all five of them wished me good luck in unison. Before I could say thank you, they vanished from the room. Nurses sternly admonished me to not talk too much, and I was hooked up to a variety of monitors and gadgets.

Shortly after this, Kapish and Asheena told me that they would shift me to Max Hospital, as my breathing was abnormal and I would need to be put on round-the-clock cardiac observation. The doctor on duty said they would need my consent in order to shift me; I gave my consent and was soon transferred to an ambulance that took me to Max Hospital, where I was admitted to ICU.

Several days and many sleepless nights were spent here

Once I was ensconced in my new surroundings and hooked up to the inevitable monitors again, I made the acquaintance of some of those who would be taking care of me here—Dr H.S. Rissam, a Sikh doctor in a light blue turban, and a nurse Kaushalya, in a green dress—the colour of the green gate to Mother Teresa's home in Calcutta that I used to visit in my schooldays.

'How many patients are here?' I asked Kaushalya.

'Houseful—16 beds—all full.'

'Sister, why is my bed number 17?' I enquired.

'We do not have 13!'

'Very good. You want everybody to be lucky,' I quipped.

'Sir, you should sleep now. You are on tranquillizers.'

'I don't feel sleepy,' I complained.

'All right! What do you do for a living?' she asked.

I was surprised by the question at that hour. 'I am a bookseller,' I replied.

'Great. I read a lot.'

'Good,' I said, adding a new customer to my business.

'I recently read about Karna. This character has highly influenced me.'

I nodded.

'I also read fiction,' she continued. 'I recently read *One Night at the Call Centre*.'

'Chetan Bhagat!' I smiled, 'I shall give you all his other books.'

'Really?'

'We publish Chetan Bhagat, he is our bestselling author.'

She seemed pleased at the prospect of reading a new book by Chetan, but by now my eyelids were beginning to feel heavy and I dropped off to sleep. When I awoke the next morning, I hardly felt rested. I'd been hospitalized for two days now and I yearned to get back home.

Kaushalya was replaced by another nurse, Lily.

'Sirji, do not worry. I am Kaushalya's friend. She has updated me,' said Lily. 'I shall give you some tea and biscuits. The dietician will be here soon and advise you on your meal plan.'

But before I could have my next meal, I noticed a crowd of doctors and nurses approaching me, led by Dr Rissam who was going through various notes. After examining my heart and chest, he ordered his panel of doctors to carry out an ENT check, an examination of the heart and full chest, and a variety of other tests.

'It's just chest congestion, Sir,' I exclaimed.

'How do you know? Let us check whatever needs to be checked. Do not panic. We are all here to help you recover fast. We do not want to hold you here unnecessarily, but there are some symptoms that need examination,' Dr Rissam said.

The word 'symptoms' made me worry. I fell silent. Both my parents had died of cancer. My thoughts drifted to Rajesh Khanna playing Babu Moshai and Lalita Pawar as his nurse in the iconic movie *Anand*. It's a movie I have always loved and I began humming the popular song from it, *'Zindagi, kaisi hai paheli haaye, kabhi ye hasaaye, kabhi ye rulaaye…'*

Doctors came and went. Dr Rissam was replaced by the nutritionist, who charted out the meals I was going to eat at the hospital. When I asked her whether she could change a couple of items on the menu, she said firmly, 'You will need to be disciplined. You have had a medical emergency. Moreover, you are obese and can't even breathe properly. You will need to take better care of yourself.'

I realized I had to be submissive and do as I'd been instructed. I found myself becoming a bit philosophical. I had never been ill for years. What was all this about? I needed to reassess and adjust to this situation to survive. Gradually, as I began to feel better and adjusted to my surroundings, I began to take a little more interest in the things around me. I asked the nurses about their work and lives. I started to have some understanding of how hospitals worked, the economics of the medical business, and so on. It was a relief not to be constantly worrying about my medical condition and to have my brain engaged again.

A nurse came into the room with a checklist and marked something on it. I thought she was recording something from a doctor's visit.

I asked her, 'How is it looking?'

'Sir, I am just checking the room items.'

Soon, another nurse came in and helped her. And then, two more nurses arrived. My curiosity was aroused. I asked them what was going on.

'Sir, we have to do periodic system checks. When we tallied all the items in the room, we found a sputum tray missing.'

I was fascinated by the inner workings of the hospital. Hospital management is an art in itself. All this drove my mind away from the pain, annoyance and solitary confinement that I was experiencing.

After a while, I began feeling lonely and decided to do something to take my mind off my situation. I asked a nurse to give me a piece of paper and a pen. She handed me two sheets of tissue paper and her pen. I started scribbling on them and didn't realize that more than an hour and a half had passed. By the time I finished, Dr Rissam was by my bedside.

'What are you writing?' he asked.

'He has been doing it for the last one and a half hour,' said the nurse.

Little did I realize it was almost 7.00 p.m. After all, there was no night or day in the ICU.

I replied, 'Sir, I have made a lot of notes on the hospital. It is worth learning about such things.'

The doctors accompanying Dr Rissam wanted to see what I'd written but I said it was private. As the doctors were leaving, my wife arrived and I handed her one of the sheets of paper. When Kaminee read what I had written, she was in tears for the note contained a list of my assets and who they should be distributed to in the event of my passing—almost a last will and testament! I broke down too, took my wife's hand and we sat quietly for a while. The silence was broken by the cheerful voice of Kaushalya who had arrived for night duty. When she saw me in tears, she said, 'No, Uncleji, I am back. *Kal ki tarah baat kariye* (Talk to me the way you did yesterday).' I told my wife how well Kaushalya was looking after me and asked her to bring me all the Chetan Bhagat novels the next day.

'She has read *One Night at the Call Centre* and I promised to present all other books,' I said.

My wife and Kaushalya smiled. As we were chatting, the team of doctors looking after me made another appearance. They discussed my case. While I understood only a little of what they were talking about, I gathered my case fell in the grey area between a terminal and non-terminal condition. I would have to undergo some more tests. These included the following:

- Bronchoscopy
- Laparoscopy
- Endoscopy
- Heart check-up
- Gastro
- Chest
- ENT, full
- CT scan

Phew! The long list reminded me of a book that I had read way back in the '60s. It was called *Medical Nemesis* by Ivan Illich. Illich inveighed against the rapid industrialization and consumerism that had crept into the medical profession. He concluded that by making a patient undergo many diagnostic tests, doctors actually make him more vulnerable by reducing his immunity. Oblivious to my thoughts, Dr Rissam told his team not to stress me out and spread the tests over the next two days.

If I were to be here for two more days, I would miss my Tuesday visit to the Hanuman temple, a ritual that I hadn't skipped for the past 36 years! I knew the kind of tests that I would have to go through. I prayed 108 times to Baba. I'd already quickly recited the Hanuman Chalisa.

Next morning, Kaminee arrived at around 11.00 a.m. I knew she would have gone to the temple before stepping into the hospital. She walked in, told me she had visited the temple; to my disappointment, I was deprived of my share of the prasad, as I had to do a battery of tests on an empty stomach.

The tests took over two days. The most stressful and lengthy ones, the bronchoscopy and laparoscopy, took place under general anaesthesia. Before I went completely under, I felt a severe pain in the chest as I was only half sedated. 'Breathe, breathe,' the doctor instructed me.

Suddenly, everything stopped. It thought it was all over. When I woke up, I felt dizzy. I saw my wife and family and nobody said anything. The doctors arrived a short while later. 'We have not found any suspected malignancy in the throat or chest Mehraji. You are fine.' My wife broke down.

Days passed. My tests were done, but I was still in the ICU feeling joyless and bored. It had been five days since I'd been admitted to this hospital. When Dr Rissam visited, I asked him when I could be released from this place.

'See Mehraji,' started Dr Rissam, 'We are done with all the necessary examinations. You are absolutely okay. Post our panel discussion, we shall chalk out your medicine plans.'

'Okay,' is all I could get myself to say, hoping I could finally go home.

'Sister, one more CT scan needs to be done today,' said Dr Rissam. 'Make a booking for 4.00 p.m. and just ensure he does not have to wait. Mehraji, 4.00 p.m. it is… It's in the other building.'

'One more! But for what?' I literally shouted.

'See, Mehraji,' began Dr Rissam, 'I never wanted it, but one of the doctors has recommended one more CT in this report. Let's just do it and get it over with just so we are all satisfied…'

'No way,' I protested, stopping my doctor midway.

'Arre, what is wrong today?'

'You will not understand. It's personal,' I replied grimly. In the meantime, my wife walked in. I thought she'd be better able to convince the doctors that yet another CT scan was the last thing I actually needed. But the doctors were adamant. I wept tears of frustration.

'At 3.45 p.m., they will take you to the next building for your scan. But you need not worry. Your file is absolutely clear,' said a familiar voice. It was Kaushalya. I was really taken aback at seeing Kaushalya there because it was still not her duty time.

By now, everybody in the ICU knew Kaushalya had indeed become my confidante. Did the doctors do this on purpose? Did the doctors know the emotional pulse of every patient? Had she been asked to change her duty hours simply, so I would undergo the CT scan without making a fuss? It was indeed a masterstroke!

Eighteen years ago, my father had been in the process of being discharged from a hospital, to be taken home, when one of the doctors had advised a CT scan at a nursing home in Connaught Place. 'Just as a precautionary measure,' he had said. I, of course, had known what was in store. I had taken my father there knowing that his end was near. Then, after a few years, my mother, too, had undergone a CT scan only to find she had cancer. Those painful memories had been a large part of the reason I was reacting so strongly to the suggestion of another CT scan. *Don't worry about the CT scan,* I consoled myself. *History very often doesn't repeat itself.*

I somehow endured the procedure and then, the anxious wait for the results commenced. After hours of waiting, Dr Rissam arrived.

'Mehraji, everything is clear. You were worried, it seemed. Sister told me that you were,' he said. I felt relieved.

'We will keep you here for three consecutive nights. Should you have no more asthma attacks—as you had over the last five days—we shall shift you to a private room by Monday. But remember, three consecutive nights in a row!'

'Hat-trick!' I said and laughed to myself.

I began counting the hours to my release. Another doctor I liked, called Dr Sam, told me a bit more about my condition. 'During endoscopy and bronchoscopy, all we found was heavy lung and chest congestion because of your obesity. Your system was choked and it was dangerous. Anyway, we shall now start with steroids, antibiotics, oxygen support and you should be all clear in two to three phases. Just don't worry. But yes, you have to change your lifestyle,' he said in a matter-of-fact tone.

'Doctor,' I said, 'I know I am the culprit. I used to walk briskly for 2 hours between 12 noon and 1.00 p.m. just before my lunch and then between 6.30 p.m. to 7.30 p.m. every day. In between, I used to do yoga for an hour.'

'Do you have a yoga trainer?' he asked.

'Yes Sir, since five years.'

The doctor was rather surprised. 'You've got to start again, Mehraji,' he said.

'Doctor, the truth is that I have been too busy in the last six to seven months with my business. And clearly, I have allowed my business balance sheet to take precedence over my health.'

I always wanted to be a mota seth. Didn't I? I chided myself.

'You've got to change your food habits, working hours, travel plans,' Dr Sam said before he left.

I resolved to change my lifestyle completely, but first, I had to get out of the ICU.

The next day, when Dr Rissam marched in with his team, I surprised him. I was sitting in the chair next to the bed, not lying down. I rose to greet him. He shook hands with me and laughed.

'So, you had a comfortable night?' asked the doctor.

'Oh yes, and I am past one night. Just two more to go and I'll be out of here!'

'Please sit down. Why are you standing?'

'I prefer this, Doctor.'

'You,' continued Dr Rissam, 'remind me of a novel by Hermann Hesse I read years ago. It was about a father who wanted his son to sit down, but the latter continued to stand. I think the title was *Siddhartha,* which later became a movie too.'

I kept listening patiently till he finally opened the green file.

'Sir, we did publish that book some 50 years ago,' I interrupted.

'Really? Well, in that case, I must say you are not a VIP patient, but an MIP—the most important patient—out here.'

As he gave me an injection, I told him that I had a request. 'See, Doctor, I am locked in this ICU and do not know whether it is night or day. It is just this wall clock that lets me know the time, though I have no idea whether it is 'a.m.' or 'p.m.'. Please allow me to go into the garden area for a while, so that I can feel the fresh air on my face.'

Dr Rissam relented. He jotted in my green file : '10 minutes…garden area…in a wheelchair…with a nurse.'

The moment the doctor left, I asked my nurse, Manu, to wheel me out. And within a few minutes, I was out of the ICU. Just as we were about to exit the building, we were stopped by a security guard.

'*Kahan le ja rahe ho* (Where are you taking him)? He is a patient, na?' he enquired.

'The doctor has advised some sun for this patient,' Manu said firmly.

The 'all clear' was given and finally, I was going to see the sun!

For the first time in a week, I was out in the sun. I slowly stood up and with folded hands, looked straight into the powerful rays of the sun, and did a surya

I went under his scalpel and then published his The Scalpel. *A delighted Dr Rissam seen here with his book*

namaskar. Not a real one but more of a gentle bow, full of gratitude for my gradual recovery. I then sat down again and said my prayers.

'*Thoda aur baithenge* (Would you like to sit a little longer)?' asked Manu.

'Yes,' was all I said. After all, there were no ambulances and stretchers here. This part of the hospital was full of trees and fresh air. Half an hour later, I did a surya namaskar once again and was wheeled back to the ICU.

Back in the ICU, I felt more active and cheerful. I chatted with the doctors, nurses and ward boys. In fact, I started distributing copies of a book written by Richard Gordon on medical humour. This was enough to keep me in the good books of the entire ICU staff.

When Dr Rissam arrived, he sat next to me and outlined what the next days would hold for me, 'Since tomorrow is Sunday, we will next do the check-ups on Monday morning and if all is well, we shall shift you to a private room the same afternoon. Thereafter, you'll be observed for another three days. If all is well, you will be discharged on Thursday. As of now, there is no tumour and no blockage. But we are a little concerned about the chest congestion you have. Until we get that to a manageable level, we cannot discharge you. It could result in choking if not checked properly.'

I nodded in agreement.

On my ninth night in the ICU, I did some late night reading to ensure I had a sound sleep. Sometime during the wee hours, I felt a little uncomfortable. The nurse noticed certain changes in my intake of oxygen and my pulse rate. It appeared I was heading for another attack of breathlessness. I pressed the emergency bell. By now, I was not able to breathe. A dry cough was choking me. Doctors and nurses arrived immediately. Someone began pounding on my back, so I would stop coughing. A nurse put on an oxygen mask, another gave me an injection and in a few minutes, I was very tired. I was mentally exhausted too. I fell into a deep sleep. The next morning, I was up by six and the same routine lay ahead of me—tea, wash, breakfast… But then what really worried me most was Dr Rissam's reaction. Would he allow me to be moved out of the ICU after what had happened last night?

At around 8.00 a.m., I started a slow walk around the ward despite feeling weak. When Dr Rissam arrived, he asked, 'What exactly happened this morning, Mehraji?' I had no answer for him. To my great relief, after briefing me thoroughly on the precautions needed to avoid such an episode, Dr Rissam authorized my move to a private room. When I was wheeled into the room, I was overjoyed to see it had natural light. Beside my bed, there was another bed.

'That's for the attendant,' my wife told me. 'No. That's rubbish, I can manage alone. No one needs to stay here,' I argued. Kaminee chose to ignore me. Just then, a doctor arrived and in a rather friendly manner asked my wife, 'Aunty, is everything okay?' I wondered who she was. Later, my wife told me that she was my daughter-in-law's friend.

Just then, I began to feel breathless again. The only word I managed to get out was 'oxygen'. Unlike in the ICU, it took the emergency team a while to get to me. I was getting to know how big hospitals operated. The team of doctors and nurses finally arrived and made me comfortable. As the day passed, I was immensely relieved by how much more relaxed everything was outside the ICU.

When life knocks you down, get back up. My friend and cartoonist Irfan made and gifted me this caricature.

• Chapter 40 •

RECOVERY AND RETURN

The morning before the day of my discharge from the hospital was rather peaceful. I got up late only to realize my wife was still asleep in the bed next to mine. She looked so at peace that I decided not to wake her up. As I kept looking at her, Sudama, our long-time family retainer, walked into the room. It was a deeply emotional moment for us both, and we had tears in our eyes. I introduced Sudama to the wardboy and he was delighted to find that he also hailed from Orissa. When my breakfast arrived, I persuaded him to share it with me.

'No salt,' Sudama exclaimed.

'No salt for the last 11 days, Sudama,' I sighed.

My wife had woken up by then, and we awaited the arrival of the dietician who briefed us thoroughly on the sort of diet I would need to follow at home.

'By the way,' the dietician added, 'the soup we served had some medicine in it. That's to help you with your motion considering you have been taking a lot of antibiotics and steroids.' I was horrified. Poor Sudama had eaten the soup. God knows, what he was in for during the next couple of hours! When Dr Kissam arrived, he signed the discharge slip but not before giving me a long lecture on all the precautions I would need to take. As the good doctor was talking, I must confess that my mind began to wander. I recalled these lines by Ghalib:

> आए है बेकसी-ए-इश्क़ पे रोना 'गालिब',
> किस के घर जाएगा सैलाब-ए-बला मेरे बाद ।

Aaye hain bekasi-e-ishq pe rona Ghalib,
Kis ke ghar jayega sailab-e-bala mere baad.

The ruins of love make me cry, Ghalib
Whose home will now be flooded with tribulations when I am gone?

آئے ہے بیکسی عشق پہ رونا غالبؔ
کس کے گھر جائے گا سیلاب بلا میرے بعد

The night before my discharge, there was a bit of a crisis. I had another attack of breathlessness. Gasping for breath and in a state of agitation and desperation, I emptied a glass of water on my wife to wake her up! Poor woman, one moment she was sleeping peacefully, and the next she was drenched in water looking for the emergency bell. The next few minutes saw the arrival of doctors and nurses, nebulizers and oxygen tanks, injections and medicines. It was all very unsettling.

On the morning of 6 May 2010, I was up early. After the usual chores of freshening up and medicines, my wife and I had our last cup of tea in that hospital. Despite everything I could do to reassure her, she kept talking about how guilty she felt about sleeping through my emergency. Luckily, her attention was diverted by the stream of nurses, ward boys, surgeons and others who were moving in and out of the room. 'It's your last day today. Just a few more hours to go,' each of them would say.

Finally, Dr Rissam walked in and promised to discharge me from the hospital despite the attack the previous night. After I'd taken another round of tests and he'd declared himself satisfied by the results, he gave me another long lecture on the precautions I should be taking once I was back home.

At around 1.00 p.m., Asheena, Kapish and his friend, Ankit, reached my room to take me home. What a moment of joy that was. I changed from my

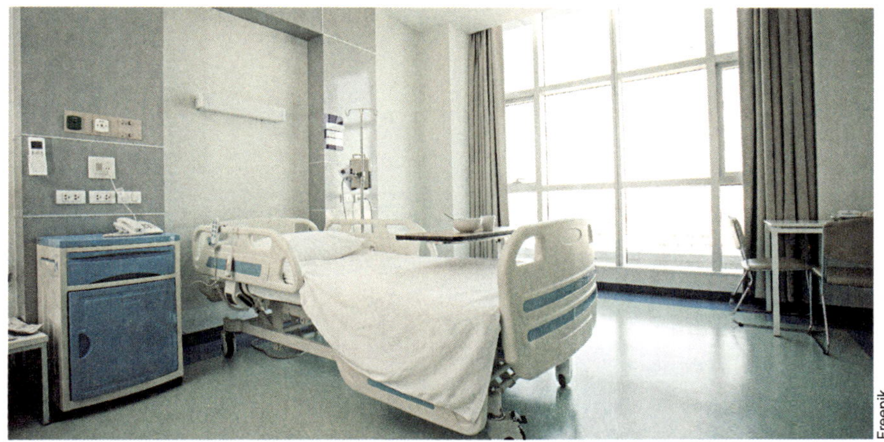

The sight I never wish to see again, the hospital bed

hospital pyjamas and shirt into my usual attire and immediately felt my spirits lift. Sanjay and Rahul, our long-time drivers, were teary eyed when they saw me walking back from hospital.

As we were driving home and I saw familiar sights—the Golf Course, Qutub Minar, AIIMS and, finally, India Gate, my spirits soared. What a joy it was to see the blue sky, to feel the fresh air on my face and watch people and life around me!

Back home, Sudama and Madhav, the housekeepers, had decorated the house with balloons for my homecoming. I was overcome with joy. And then, all at once I was exhausted. I got into bed and fell asleep in no time.

We published Pranab Mukherjee's autobiography in four volumes and he was gracious enough to invite our entire Delhi staff at the Rashtrapati Bhavan.

• Chapter 41 •

THE JOURNEY CONTINUES

'I don't think anyone should write their autobiography until after they're dead,' Samuel Goldwyn, the legendary Polish–American film producer once said. There's a lot of truth to that saying because no one can truthfully recall every bit of one's own life. All we can do is write a version of our life, and that's what this book is. It began as a diary entry, then a series of random notes, journal entries about my time in hospital, and finally a full-length memoir.

On 17 August 2010, Rupa turned 75, a longevity driven by continuity through successive generations. And like autumn, when old leaves give way to new ones and the tree makes itself young again to brace rains and storms, Rupa too was headed for a change. The special logo marking our seventy-fifth year was designed by Rachita Rakyan, the daughter of a dear friend from Jaipur, Ajay Chopra. A function was organized on the first floor of Park Hotel on Parliament Street in Delhi. Political heavyweights, legal luminaries, literary giants and anyone who had ever had any contact with Rupa attended the event. On the dais were L.K. Advani, Jaswant Singh, Veerappa Moily, Gulzar, Mark Tully, Chetan Bhagat and Ruskin Bond. It was a full house and Deepak Chopra, special secretary to Advaniji, remarked smilingly, '*Mehra sahib, Rupa ke 75 saal ke liye hall bahut chota hai* (Mehra sahib, this hall is very small to celebrate Rupa's seventy-fifth year).' A great compliment indeed! All celebrations have that one moment, that crescendo which is etched in one's memory forever. After finishing my introductory speech, I handed over the mic to Kapish who took over the proceedings from there. A seamless transfer of power, new leaves emerging, making the old tree stronger. Autumn strengthens longevity.

A year later, I found myself in the same hospital I was discharged from on 6 May 2010; anxious, nervous and a little excited. Kapish and Asheena were soon going to become parents. And all that I, the nervous grandfather, could do was pace up and down the corridor outside the maternity ward. I must have at least walked a couple of kilometres in the corridor when the news arrived that Rupa's fifth generation had arrived. I noted the date. It was 17 May 2011. Forty-one years ago, on the same date, Rupa's Delhi office had been born, starting a journey for me that had been full of ups and downs, excitement and achievements. And now, I had become a grandfather. It appeared that the two events had been scripted by destiny! A fortuitous coincidence.

Akshaj's arrival into the world was the capstone of a wonderful year for us at Rupa. After I'd been discharged from hospital, I read in the newspapers that the legendary publisher David Davidar was thinking of getting involved in a new venture and was exploring his options. Kapish and I had also been feeling

The birth of Aleph. (From left) The legendary David Davidar with Kapish.

The stage set for unveiling of the logo marking 75 years of Rupa

Authors, booksellers, distributors and well-wishers, all of them came to celebrate the event

the need to infuse new publishing ideas into our business, so we began talking. Several meetings later, Aleph Book Company was born on 14 May 2011 with David as its managing director and publisher and Rupa as Aleph's parent. We were all overjoyed, especially Kapish. Three days later, my grandson was born and our family's joy was bottomless.

As the days passed, the time I spent with manuscripts and balance sheets contracted to be replaced by hours spent with my grandson, talking gibberish, crawling alongside him, rocking him to sleep, watching over him as he slept.

One day, Kapish and Asheena informed me that the little one had been admitted to a playschool. 'But the child is only 22 months old!' I cried in dismay. I was eventually persuaded by the parents that what they were contemplating for their child was the right course of action. So, of course, I had to record this special milestone in the little boy's life. I took out an old diary and wrote: '5 April 2013: Akshaj goes to school.' And then to my amazement I found another entry on the same page in faded ink. 'Kapish went to school. 6 April 1988.' Only the characters change, the drama of life goes on.

Once Akshaj started going to school, our routines changed once again. Dadi amma would take charge of him as soon as he returned from school, and my time with him was restricted to IPL matches, which we would watch together whenever he could take time off from homework and playdates.

As the years pass, our routines continue to change. Kapish largely runs the business, Asheena is busy at her clinic, and I devote myself to special projects and advising Kapish whenever required. Kaminee and I are able to spend a lot more time together now, poring over old photo albums, reliving special moments in our life and reminiscing about life's highs and lows.

And whenever Akshaj is home, he is, of course, the centre of our attention. He is old enough to surprise his Dadu by 'Swiggying' dishes online. He is smarter than my smart phone and generously offers me technology tips. Wait, is there a book idea here? *365 Smart Technology Tips for Dumb Granddads!* Well, I'll leave it to Akshaj to decide when his time comes. Just the other day, when I was finalizing photographs for this book and rummaging through my old albums, I found an old photo of a young Kapish trying to look more mature than his years.

'When was this taken, Dadu?' Akshaj enquired.

'When your Papa was ready to join our business. I will title it "The Journey Begins" in my book.'

'No, Dadu. "The Journey Continues",' said Akshaj with a smile.

'Yes,' I smiled back. The journey continues.

75 YEARS AND COUNTING

Honouring the Past, Writing the Future

A milestone: when Rupa turned 75

All gathered in full attendance at this unforgettable event

Jaswant Singh and Gulzar

With Kamlaji and L.K. Advani

Murli Manohar Joshi graced the occasion with his presence

(From left) Nivedita Joshi (daughter of Murli Manohar Joshi), Tarla Joshi (his wife), Kamlaji, Aarti Mehra, Deepak Chopra, Aniruddha Bahal, Raju Barman and Kaminee

Happy moments! Vishal Bhardwaj (left) with Arif Mohammad Khan (right)

Vijay Sharma (left), our sales manager, with P. Khurrana, father of Ayushmann Khurrana

Uniting the political rivals: L.K. Advani with Veerappa Moily

Speaking at the launch of the logo marking 75 years of Rupa

75 Years logo unveiled

Political meets the poetic! Advaniji and Gulzar greeting each other.

When the two stalwarts met: L.K. Advani with Ruskin Bond

(From left) Rachita Rakyan, Asheena and L.K. Advani. Rachita had designed our 75 Years celebration logo.

(From left) With T.S.R. Subramanian, former cabinet secretary, and Aarti Mehra, former mayor of Delhi

Chetan Bhagat and Advaita Kala

Mohanji in his element, teaching Rupa people the power of yoga

Krishna Makhija (left) with his father Mohan Makhija and Sunny Mallick of East West Publications (centre)

(From left) Nutan Pandit (author) Ritu Topa (who was once Rupa's designer) and Sunita Dwivedi (author)

Arif Mohammad Khan and myself. Arif's book Text and Context *is a bold commentary on issues of Islam.*

Being congratulated by Keki N. Daruwalla, a former IPS officer who served as chairman of Joint Intelligence Committee (R&AW). A poet by heart, he published his book with us. On the extreme right is Aarti Mehra, former mayor of Delhi.

Dear friend Sudha (standing in red sari) with the family members of freedom fighter P.D. Tandon from Allahabad

The well wishers of Rupa have been our biggest support and strength.

(From left) G.C. Jain of BPB Publications and J.P. Jain of Motilal Banarasidas

With senior journalist Pankaj Vohra

Kapish with Purvish of Student Agency, Bombay

Chetan Bhagat with Ruskin Bond

(From left) Pradeep Arora of Universal Book Traders, with his father M.G. Arora and Mini Kapur of Select Book Services

(From left) With Amarnath of Star Publications and Hindi Book Centre, and his brother

(From left) With Narendra Kumar of Vikas Publishing and B.S. Uppal, a famous bookseller of Delhi

20/10/21

Dear Dadu,

You are turning only 74,
Besides you, we are only 4.

You are seventy and we are the ~~balance~~
four, Without you, everything is a bore. balance

We both, have so much fun together,
After all, we only make each other better.

I wish you a very happy birthday,
Because you are my hero, today and everyday!

The best birthday gift any grandfather can receive; my grandson Akshaj's poem for me—priceless!

EPILOGUE

14 November is celebrated as Children's Day marking the birth anniversary of the country's first PM, whose heart warmed for children. One day, as I dropped Akshaj to his school (a routine I never miss), I missed out on something. Akshaj complained that his Dadu didn't wish him on Children's Day the young one demanded an answer. The smart mind of an ageing grandfather could only say that every day is children's day. He seemed satisfied. It assuaged my conscience too.

Jogging my memory, I recalled another Children's Day years ago, when Kapish was five years old. The school had a fancy dress competition and this future publisher's father dressed his son as a book with the following doggerel plastered all over him:

> I am a book,
> Any old book.
> You will find a friend,
> When you look.

Received with adulations and claps, this human book was an instant bestseller. I have led a life in books and my son has only continued the journey turning over some new pages.

The pages of my own life were never meant to be a memoir. They were random notes, etched from memory, scribbled from time to time, to be read by me in moments of loneliness and reflection. But then, life throws lemons at you and sometimes you do make lemonade out of it. I was admitted to Max Hospital in April–May 2010 and was on the brink of death. I survived, returned home and was advised to rest completely before undergoing an angioplasty. Mine was a complicated case, as during that period of rest, I had several bouts of asthmatic attack, a condition not conducive for angioplasty*. During this period of lull, I immersed myself in music, books and writing random notes on my life (I avoid watching TV now). Friends enquiring about my health were subjected to listening to my notes. Who else but friends would listen to the rantings of an old man? Encouragement from my dear listeners ensured that I continued writing. By the time I was at my office desk, I had 30,000 words of material with me—including notes from my childhood days and hospital diary. It kept lying on my table till one day, an oldie editor looked at it and requested me to finish what I had started. I was never interested as, in a celebrity-obsessed society, I was nobody. Why would anyone read me? We hardly read life stories of doctors, engineers or teachers. We have voyeuristic curiosity about the lives of politicians, movie stars and sports icons, and I am lowest in the food chain of anyone's curiosity. But I kept writing, and scribbles and jottings from 2010 became a memoir by 2023!

'We prosper and suffer with you' has been Rupa's lodestar. I am reminded of lines by Lao Tzu, which defines our journey.

> I have three treasures,
> Guard them and keep them safe.
> The first is love,
> The second is, never too much.
> The third is, never to be the first in the world.

Being modest and meaningful, sharing our triumphs with our readers and accepting our trials has been a constant of our personality. R. Venkataraman never wanted to write his memoir. He was also not the first president who would have penned his life. But he did and the book was a success. On the other

*Angioplasty was performed three months after being discharged.

hand, George Fernandes, former PM Chandra Shekhar, Lala Amarnath, Vijay Merchant, Vinoo Mankad never wrote their autobiographies for us in spite of continuous persuasion.* On meeting Arun Nehru, the famous backroom boy in Rajiv Gandhi's government, and asking him to write his life story, he remarked that he may not be able to speak the truth. The matter ended there. In 2013, we received Natwar Singh's autobiography and it kept me busy for 10 months.

I had resumed travelling by this time. Kaminee and I took a trip to Cambodia, which was planned secretly by Kapish and Asheena. The place has several old Hindu temples where the statues of Shiva and Vishnu, said to be a thousand years old, are commonly seen. Angkor Wat, the largest and oldest Hindu temple of the world, is situated near the Siem Reap river in Cambodia, about 965 kilometres away from Laos. It has the biggest statue of Lord Vishnu in the world. Rajiv Gandhi, during his prime ministership, visited Cambodia and contributed a generous amount for the upliftment of the place. This part of the world is known for the clash of civilizations between Hindu and Buddhist cultures over 2,000 years ago. The carvings on the walls and temples around speak for themselves.

Two years later, we went to Bali in Indonesia and the same Hindu culture greeted us. In our hotel, the attendant would burn incense sticks every day and offer prayers. Witnessing a Hindu prayer in the most populous Muslim country in the world felt surreal. In fact, the ten ASEAN countries—Indonesia, Vietnam, Cambodia, Laos, Phillippines, Thailand, Myanmar, Singapore, Malaysia and Brunei—all have seen India's cultural influence on their own cultural landscapes. Be it architecture or food, mythology or festivals, India's presence in their cultural ecosystem is unmissable. As part of our foreign policy, we have started to 'look east' and 'act east' but these countries have, since time immemorial, looked at India as the land of gold, cardamoms and coconuts. Merchants have traded their goods; money has been exchanged and with it, monks and travellers have enriched each other's cultures. India's folk stories from

*Lala Amarnath's son Rajender Amarnath wrote the former's biography *Lala Amarnath: Life and Times: The Making of a Legend,* which was published by Rupa in 2004.

The mesmerizing statues in Cambodia

God emerging from the stone. One of the many facets of Hinduism in Cambodia.

Angkor Wat, the largest and oldest Hindu temple in the world

the Ramayana and Mahabharata have been carried to these lands, where they are still regarded as the finest literary works. Reamker in Cambodia, Kakawin Ramayana in Indonesia, Phra Lak Phra Ram in Laos, Hikayat Seri Rama in Malaysia, Yama Zatdaw in Myanmar, Maharadia Lawana in the Philippines and Ramakien in Thailand—these are all versions of the Ramayana told and retold in these countries; the story of the prince of Ayodhya mesmerizing people in a faraway land. But I found that the libraries from the countries I visited lacked books on India's history and culture, a fact that our missions abroad should take note of. On my return from Cambodia, I immediately gifted books on culture, commentaries on the Ramayana, the Mahabharata, Vedas and Upanishads to some libraries. I had the same sentiment in Maldives too, and after speaking with Taj Bombay, we gave 100 books on various themes on India to Maldives.

India is a land of stories. It is a land of faith, hope and spirituality and we must strive to export and showcase it to the global audience in our own individual capacities. And for that, we have to believe that we too are part of the nation-building.

An incident comes to my mind here. Some 30 to 40 good Samaritans from my colony in Model Town gathered together and took the initiative of renovating

18th December 2018

Shri. Nripendra Misra
Principal Secretary to the
Hon'ble Prime Minister
Prime Minister's Office
South Block
New Delhi 110 011

Sir,

Following the Prime Minister's address to the nation on 15th August 2014 and subsequent launching of "Swacch Bharat Abhiyan" on 2nd October, we the senior residents of Model Town (Ward No.77), North Delhi Municipal Corporation have been greatly inspired and subsequently on our own we devoted ourselves to a small cause of our nation to develop a totally dilapidated park named Bashesher Nath Gotewale Smriti Udyan (Shalimar Park) on our own with labour, materials, finance etc., without any outside support.

We are enclosing herewith a photo album of park of 2014 and 2019 to have a look at it.

We are sure that the Hon'ble Prime Minister will take notice of the efforts made by the senior citizens of the area and felt sure that his appeal was not in vain.

Many congratulations.

With best wishes and regards, & Best wishes for 2019.

Always
9

R K Mehra & Others
F-1/11 Model Town
Delhi 110 009
Mob: 9811206492

Encl: as above

प्रधान मंत्री

Prime Minister

New Delhi
31 December, 2018

Dear Shri R. K. Mehra Ji,

I am delighted to receive your letter. At the very outset, I congratulate you and the senior citizens of the area who pooled in all their resources to rejuvenate a park in Model Town area of Delhi. The pictures sent by you fully reflect the hard work undertaken by the senior citizens in contributing to 'Swachh Bharat Abhiyan'.

It is on the basis of the strength of such individual and collective initiatives that I have often talked about India assuming the world leadership on the issue of environment protection at national and international fora.

I have always firmly believed that community-led initiatives are the solutions to all the ills and can supplement government efforts in any field. I am sure that you will continue to make sustained efforts to make your surroundings and the city clean and green.

My best wishes are with you, the senior citizens and members of the civil society for future endeavours in keeping our surroundings clean.

Warm regards,

Sincerely,

(Narendra Modi)

Shri R. K. Mehra
F-1/11, Model Town
Delhi - 110009

The park in Model Town that was renovated by citizens efforts and for which we received the letter of appreciation from PM Narendra Modi himself

our park in the neighbourhood. Owing to the local administration's apathy, the park there had turned into a safe haven for chain snatchers, drunkards, drug users and nuisance makers. The idea was to make it safe for our children and women while creating a space for recreation. We took it upon ourselves, invested our time and money and within a few months, the result were for all to see. Drug peddlers were replaced by a library. A yoga centre came up in a place where chain snatchers had distributed their exploits. Our park was breathing again. We sent a picture of our initiative to the PMO and pat came an appreciative response from none other than PM Modi himself! In the letter, he even directed the municipal commissioner to visit the place and support our efforts. The concerned bureaucrat came, saw, went back and did nothing. No local leader from any political party came forward to support us in maintaining the park. One Ranjan Mukherjee, who was a retired air commodore and a secretary in the lieutenant governor's office at the time, was our constant support, but the administration's apathy and the politicians' lack of interest was distressing. If you want to tell the world how great your country is, make your neighbourhood a better place first.

While all this was happening, an unexpected guest came knocking on our doors: Covid-19. People died. Friends went away forever without saying goodbye. Relatives were cremated while we locked ourselves inside, masked and sanitized. I lost a lot of friends and relatives. P.S. Bawa, Pyarelal Gupta, one of my cousins and his wife in Calcutta—the list is endless. I sat down one day to remove their names from my contact list. Perhaps deleting their numbers gave me a sense of closure. The battle against Covid-19 had no established blueprint to follow, we had no template or protocol to emulate; this disease was unprecedented. PM Narendra Modi's government still managed to save the country by minimizing the losses. India's Covid-19 vaccination programme was a mammoth logistical exercise, given our population density, and we surely left our imprint on the world. When life was returning to normal, Russian President Vladimir Putin had some other plans. Another conflict ensued in Ukraine. Lives were lost, friends were gone, relatives snatched away by bombs and bullets. Martin Luther King Jr said, 'We must accept finite disappointment, but never lose infinite hope.' Not wishing my grandson on Children's Day had been a disappointment for both of us; wishing that we create a better world for our children is infinite hope. Till then, we strive to create our story which is never out of print. As Sahir Ludhianvi said:

मैं ज़िंदगी का साथ निभाता चला गया,
हर फ़िक्र को धुँए में उड़ाता चला गया ।

Main zindagi ka saath nibhata chala gaya,
Har fiqr ko dhuein mein udata chala gaya.

CELEBRATING LOYALTY AND LOVE
A Legacy of Long-Lasting Bonds

(From left) C.K.M. with a cousin, my mother, and his wife Geeta

Rupa Delhi staff in the '70s

Namma Bengaluru! Our Bangalore staff

Vanakam! Rupa Chennai staff

Rupa Hyderabad staff

Our team spirit kept us going! With our Bombay staff during the Covid-19 havoc in 2021

(From left) Harish Shenoy with Sriram of Crossword and Rajan Das

Catch them young! Junior Kapish and junior Krishna Kumar Mehra

(From left) A.K. Singh, T.C. Alexander and J.C. Bose back in the day

(From left) A.K. Singh, Anil Sharma, Rakesh Arora and S. Karmakar

(From left) S.K. Mehra, A.K. Singh, Sona Mehra (daughter of S.K.M.), Gulzar and Meena Mehra (wife of S.K.M.). A young K.K. Mehra (son of S.K.M.) can be seen standing in the front

C.K.M.'s daughter Mona Mehra

Rupa Barman, daughter of Raju Barman, works at Rupa's Calcutta office. Seen here with Shashi Tharoor

Raju Barman's wife Sarita works at Rupa's Calcutta office

POSTSCRIPT

This book was not supposed to end like this, but my brother C.K. Mehra, the elder son of Daudayal Mehra, had other plans. C.K. Mehra breathed his last on 10 August 2023, in a city he lived and loved—Calcutta.

Rest in peace, C.K.M. Your story will live on forever.

ज़िन्दगी के सफ़र में गुज़र जाते हैं जो मकाम
वो फिर नहीं आते, वो फिर नहीं आते।

ACKNOWLEDGEMENTS

Thanks to…

Terry O'Brien, without whom this book would still be some random diary entry.

David Davidar, for meticulously going through the draft, connecting the dots and highlighting the gaps.

Rudra Narayan Sharma, this book belongs to him. Months of sitting together spent in exchanging notes, of sharing good food and great conversations, of forging a friendship.

Yamini and Aienla for their valuable suggestions on the draft.

Bena Sareen for creating a visually delightful cover.

Kaminee, for silently witnessing everything and being by my side.

Asheena, for constantly motivating me to pen down my memoirs.

Akshaj, who has been excited from day one to read his Dadu's book. At least I have an assured reader in him.

Raju Barman, for providing old photographs.

A.K. Singh, Rosy and other members of the Rupa family, this has been a collective journey together.

And finally to Kapish, my publisher, who agreed to publish this book!

I am grateful to all of my friends, fans and well-wishers who encouraged me in this quest. Unfortunately, due to time limits, some acknowledgments may have been missed or concerns may have gone unresolved. I seek understanding and pardon for these errors. Any flaws or lapses in presentation are entirely my fault, and I hope our readers understand.

INDEX